CARVING OUT THE WILD WEST WITH TOM WOLFE

The Saloon

Text written with Douglas Congdon-Martin

Schiffer Publishing Ltd

1469 Morstein Road, West Chester, Pennsylvania 19380

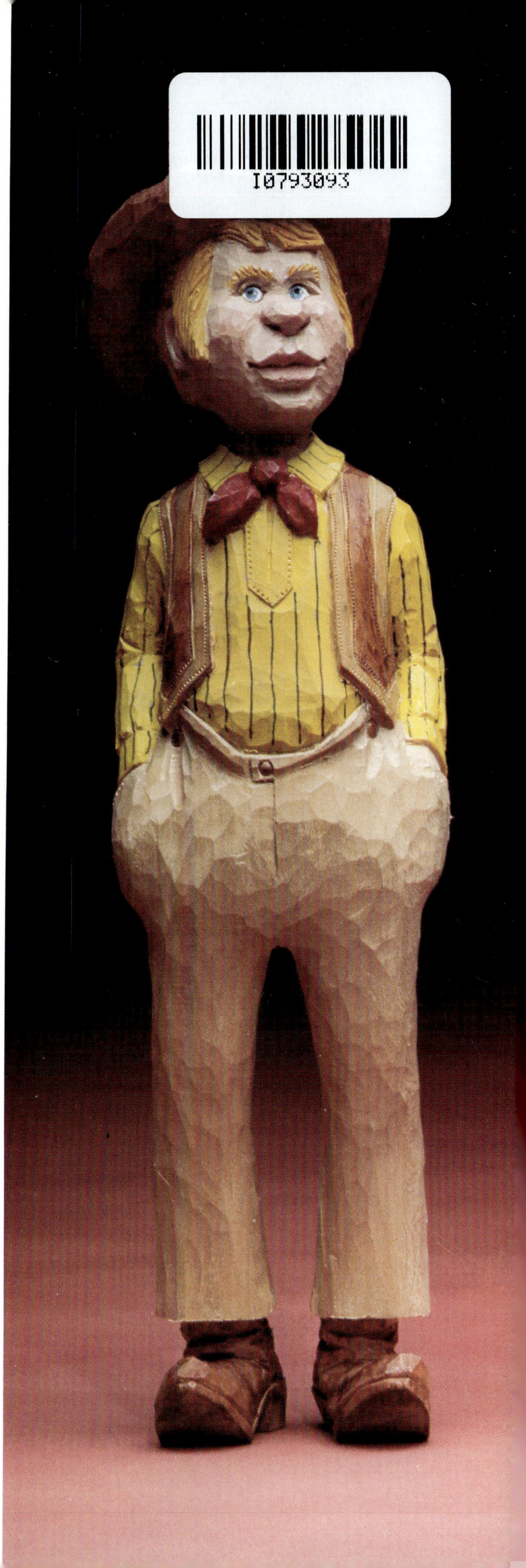

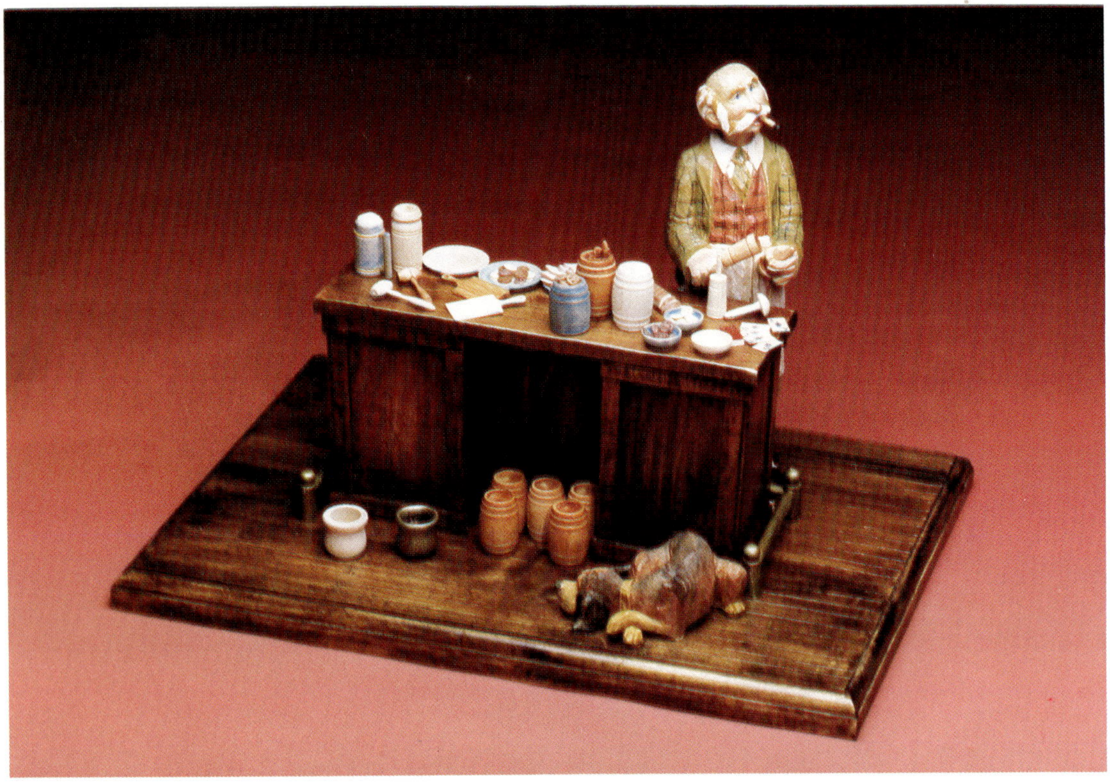

Many wooden forms available at craft stores can be transformed into props for the bar. The barrels come ready-made, as do dishes and bowls. With a little carving, milk cans become bar steins with a foamy froth and a butter churn becomes a mallet. Other objects have been sculpted.

Published by Schiffer Publishing, Ltd.
1469 Morstein Road
West Chester, Pennsylvania 19380
Please write for a free catalog.
This book may be purchased from the publisher.
Please include $2.00 postage.
Try your bookstore first.

We are interested in hearing from authors
with book ideas on related subjects.

Library of Congress Catalog Number: 91-61155.

Printed in the United States of America.
ISBN: 0-88740-368-9

Contents

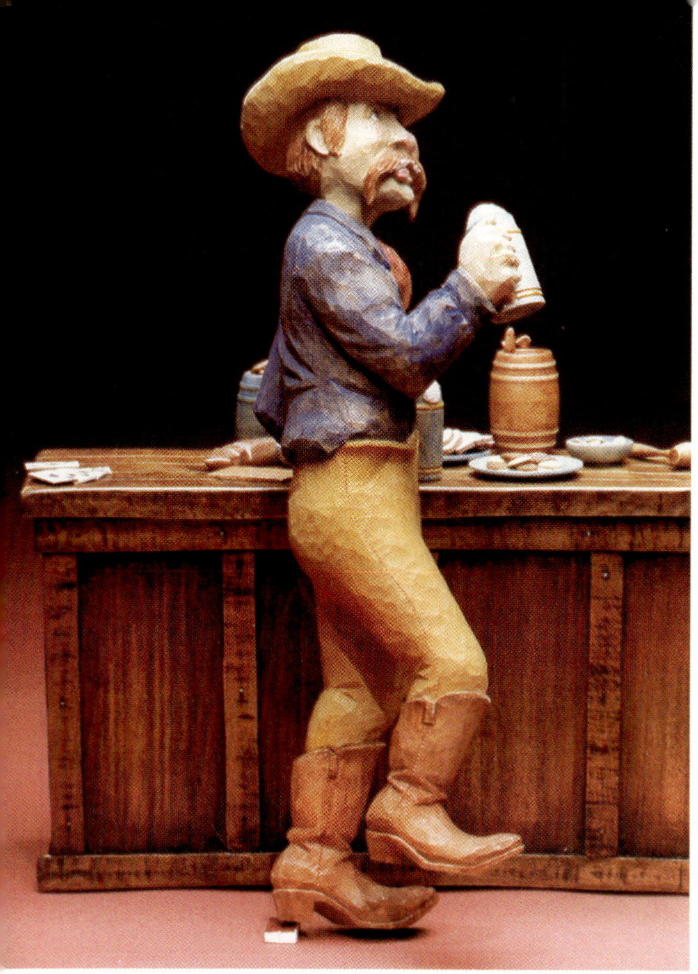

Introduction

The saloon was at the center of the Old West town. In these sparsely populated territories, it was the place where people gathered for company, food, and entertainment. And, if the old movies have it right, they often were the site of frontier justice, in a courtroom or a shoot out. After months on the range, the cowboy would bring his pay to town looking for a little relaxation. His first stop was usually the saloon.

That's where we find "The Kid" in our scene. Still a little wet behind the ears, he tries to make up for his youth by donning his finest, most macho duds. He hopes to catch the eye of Susie the Soiled Dove.

No saloon was complete without its compliment of ladies. They played a great part in the settlement of the West. They served drinks and whatever else the lonely cowboys needed. Aside from their beloved horses, the soiled doves, like Susie, provided the only touch of beauty the cowboys had in their hard lives.

What money the cowboys had leftover after satisfying their various "thirsts" was fair game for the gambler. The saloon was "Ace" Checkalock's office and poker was his stock in trade. He stayed honest enough not to get shot, and moved on to the next town before he overstayed his welcome or his luck.

The sheriff kept watch over all of this. Keeping peace in these western towns was never easy, but it was especially hard when the cowboys brought there pay and their pent-up desires to town. Of course sheriff "Sip" Elbowbender never minded the saloon detail too much.

The Bartender was the master of ceremonies, the father confessor, hosteler, and friend for everyone at the bar. The role does not change much with time or place, and you are as likely to find a Patty MacShort at the corner pub as you are at the Saloon.

The bar dog was usually lying on the floor. It's not clear why he was there. He certainly isn't much of a watch dog. One day a drunk walked in and saw a dog lying in the sun that was streaming through the window. "Does your dog bite," he asked the Bartender.

"Nope, my dog doesn't bite."

The drunk smiles and stoops down to pet the dog. All of the sudden the dog snaps, bites off his thumb.

"Hey, I thought you said your dog doesn't bite!" the drunk cried.

"Mine don't. But that ain't mine."

Of course there are a lot of stories about the saloon. Some of them are even true. There is a story about a place where I used to hang out when I was young. You could usually find two of the locals there. One of them was old Doc. He remembered the "saloon days," the days before prohibition.

The other was called R.C. He used to clean up the bar in exchange for a little beer. He only drank beer, nothing else. If Doc was there when R.C. came in the bar didn't get very clean. He bought him his first beer in the morning and they would drink together for the rest of the day.

One day R.C. came in looking sad. Doc waved to him and said, "Come over and have a beer."

"Can't," said R.C. "I just came from the doctor and he said I can't have no more beer as long as I live."

"No beer?!" Doc was shocked. "How about ale?"

"Aye God," exclaimed R.C., "The doctor didn't say nothing about ale. Give me a bottle of ale."

I hope you enjoy the projects in this book. They require only a few simple tools, and are perfect for the advanced beginner and intermediate carver. They should also be challenging for the advanced carver. I have carved the cowboy so you can see how it is done step-by-step. The other human figures carve in a similar way. The dog is carved from a single piece, and should not be too difficult. Good luck and good fun!

The Patterns

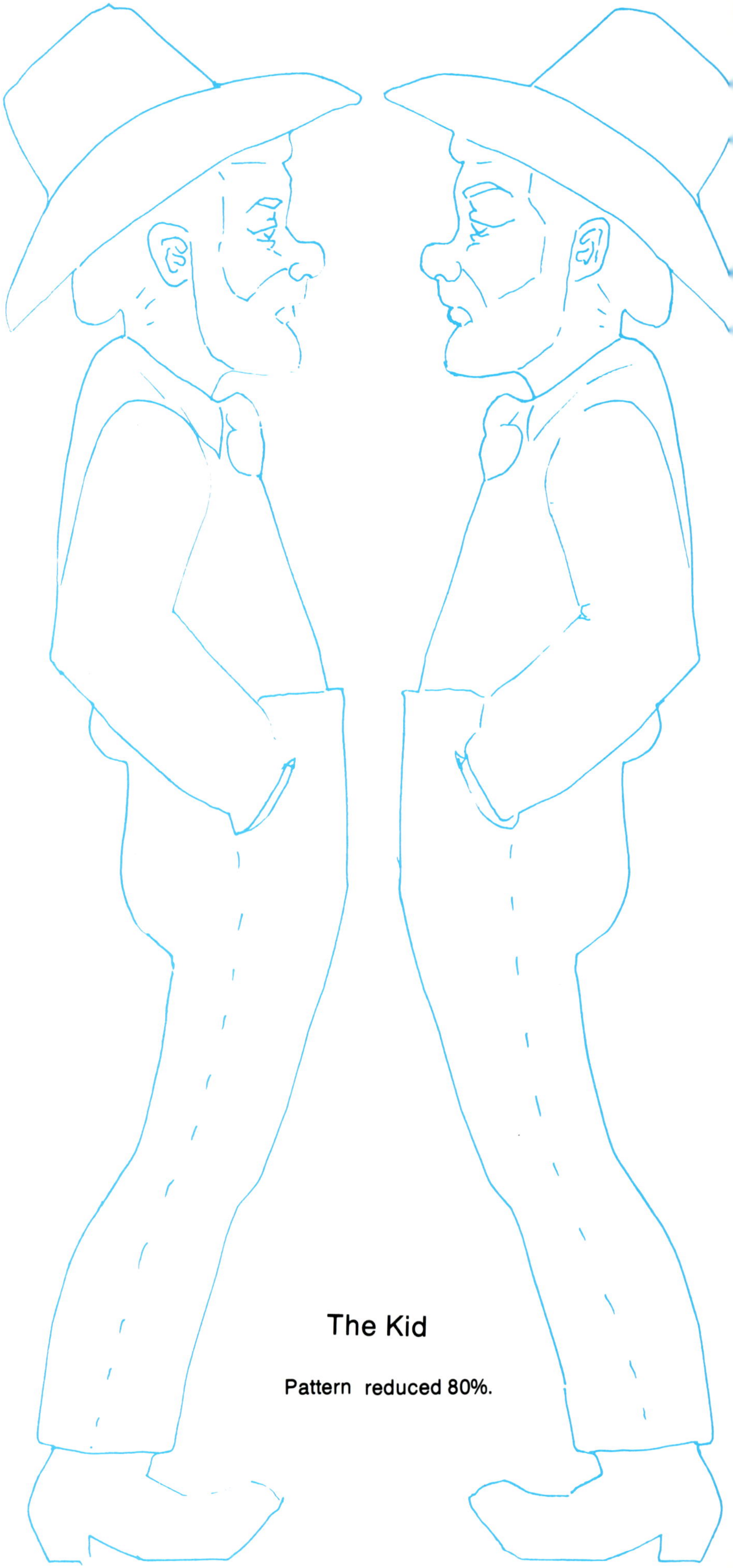

The Kid

Pattern reduced 80%.

The Tools and Patterns

The tools needed for this project include a simple set of palm gouges, a turned-down blade and a turned-up blade, and some eye punches or nail sets for the eyes and buttons. The wood I use is bass, and it is probably the best for these figures. It carves well and takes the paint nicely.

The patterns as reproduced here are 80% of their actual size. You may use them as they appear or enlarge or reduce them on a photocopying machine. While you are at the machine, print several copies so you can cut them apart as needed to help in drawing various parts.

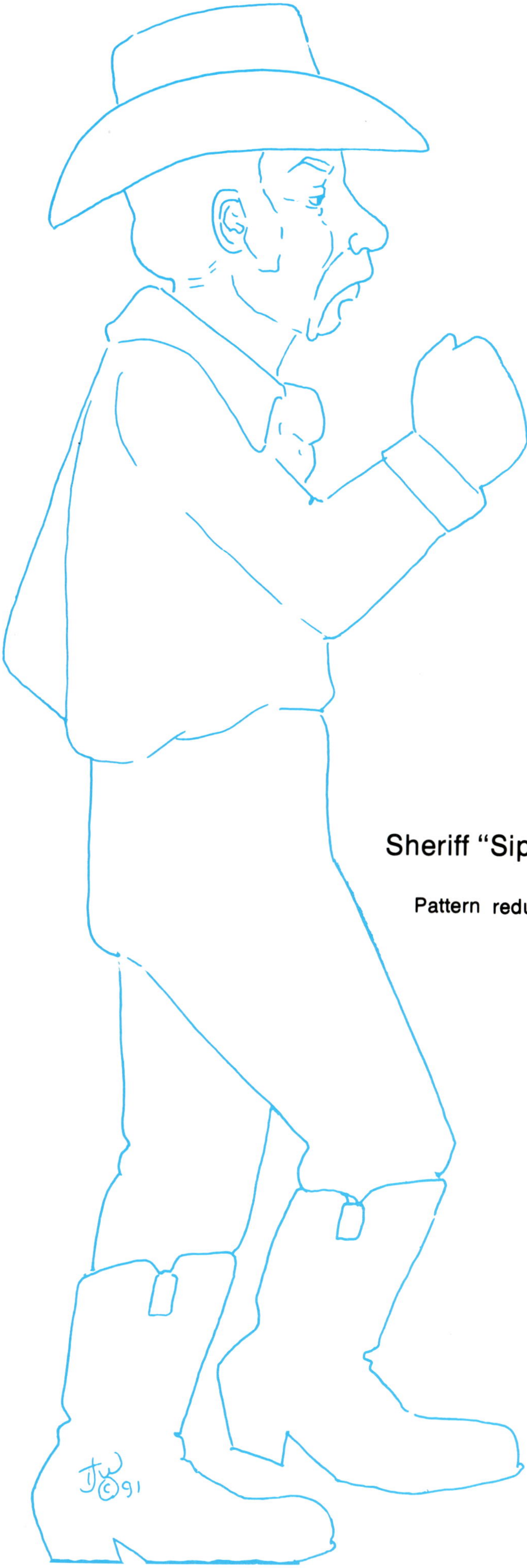

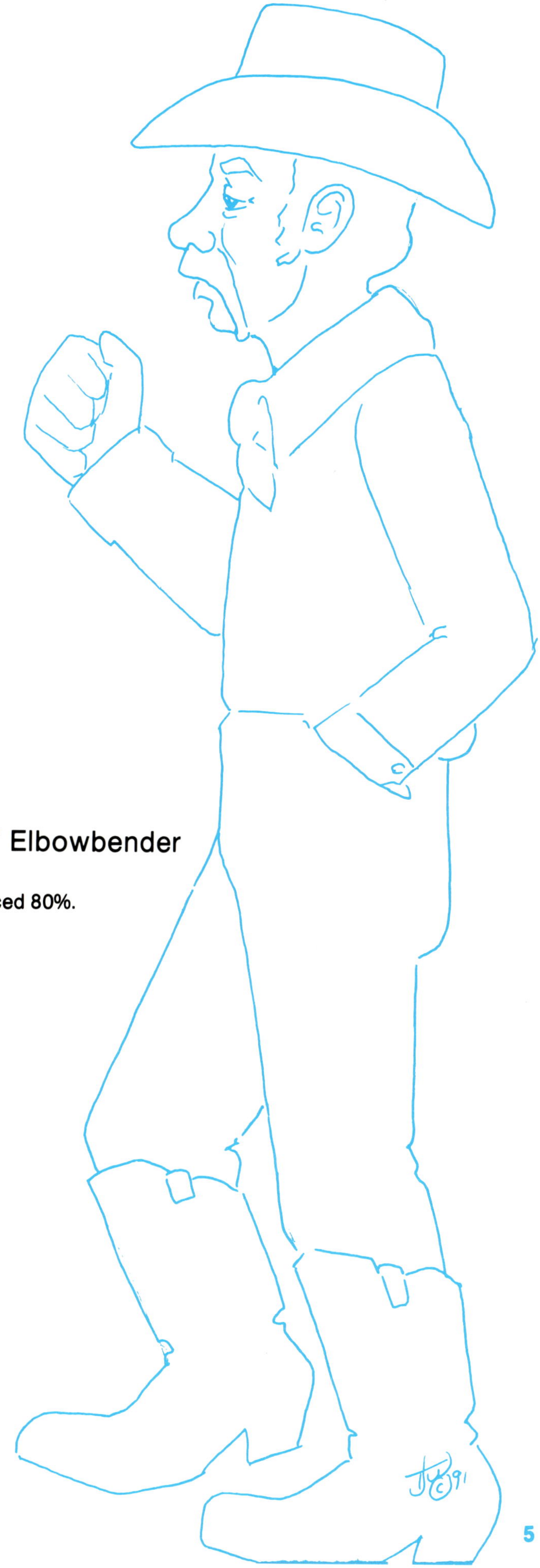

Sheriff "Sip" Elbowbender

Pattern reduced 80%.

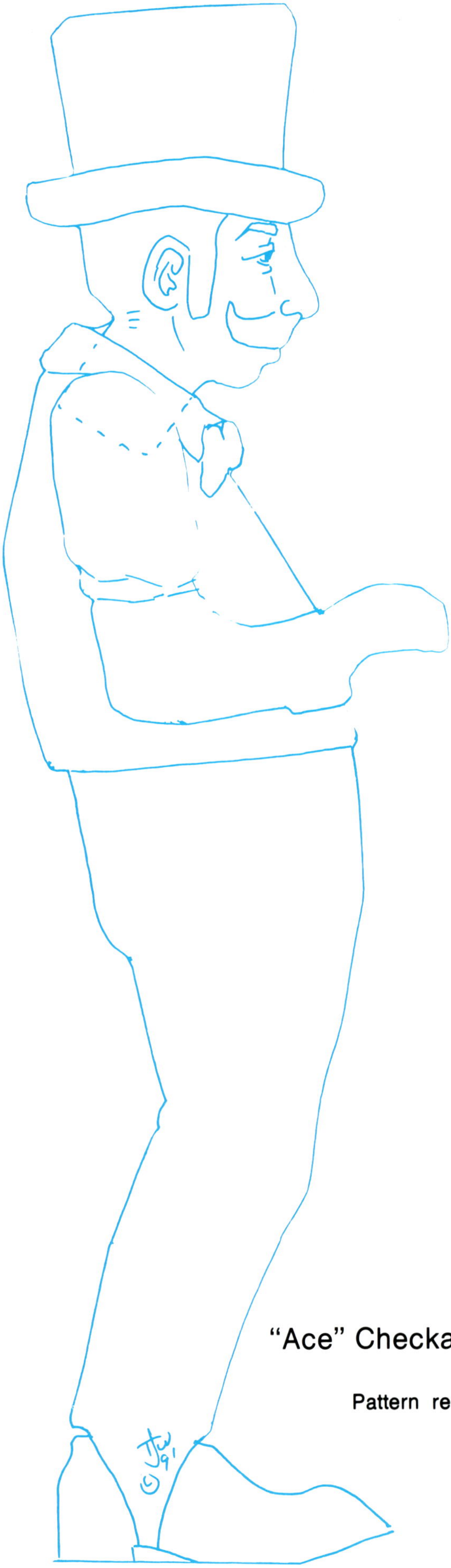

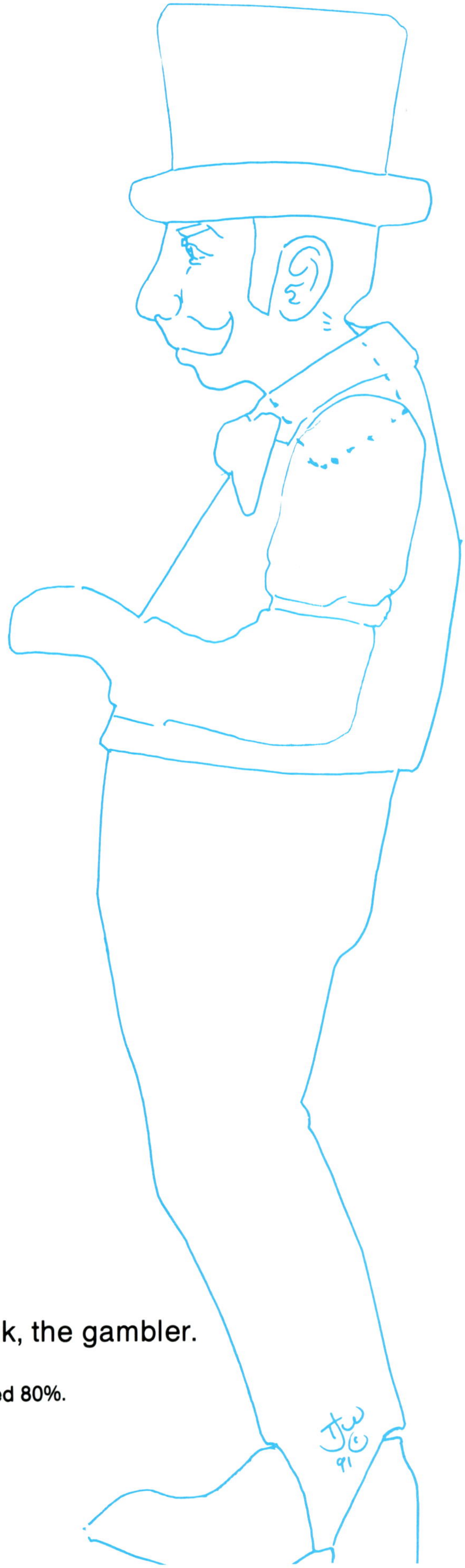

"Ace" Checkalock, the gambler.

Pattern reduced 80%.

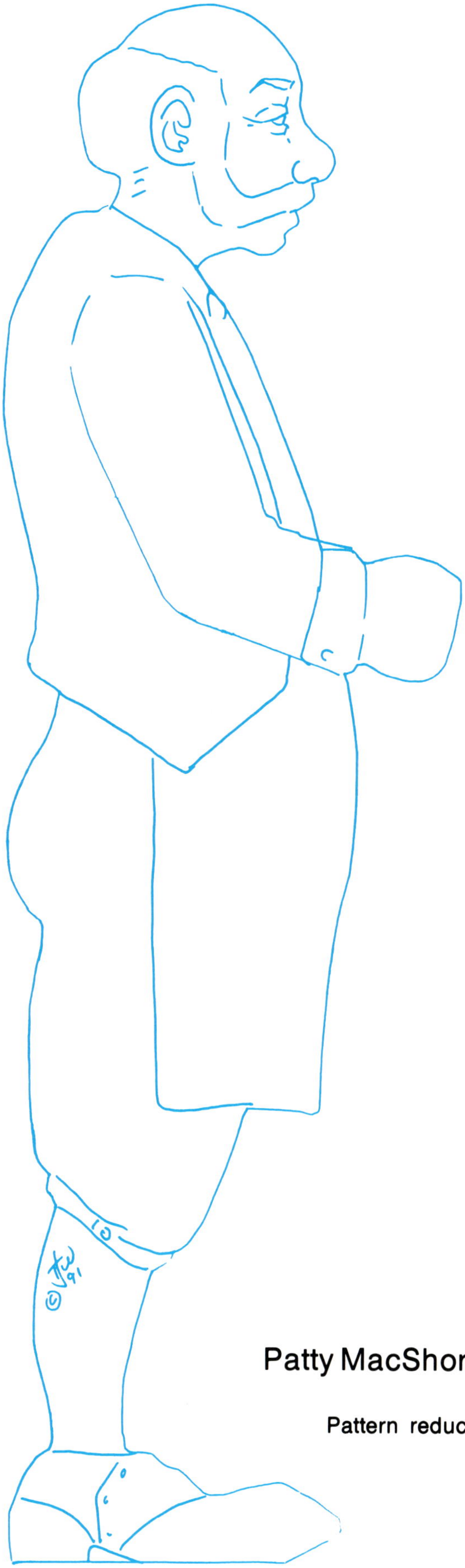

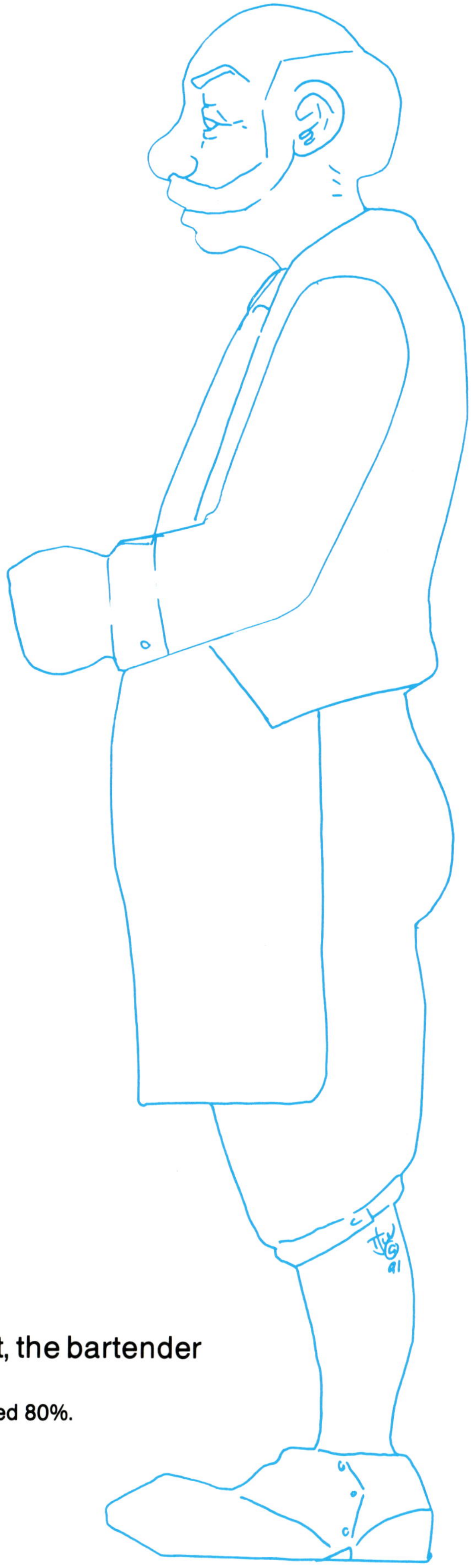

Patty MacShort, the bartender

Pattern reduced 80%.

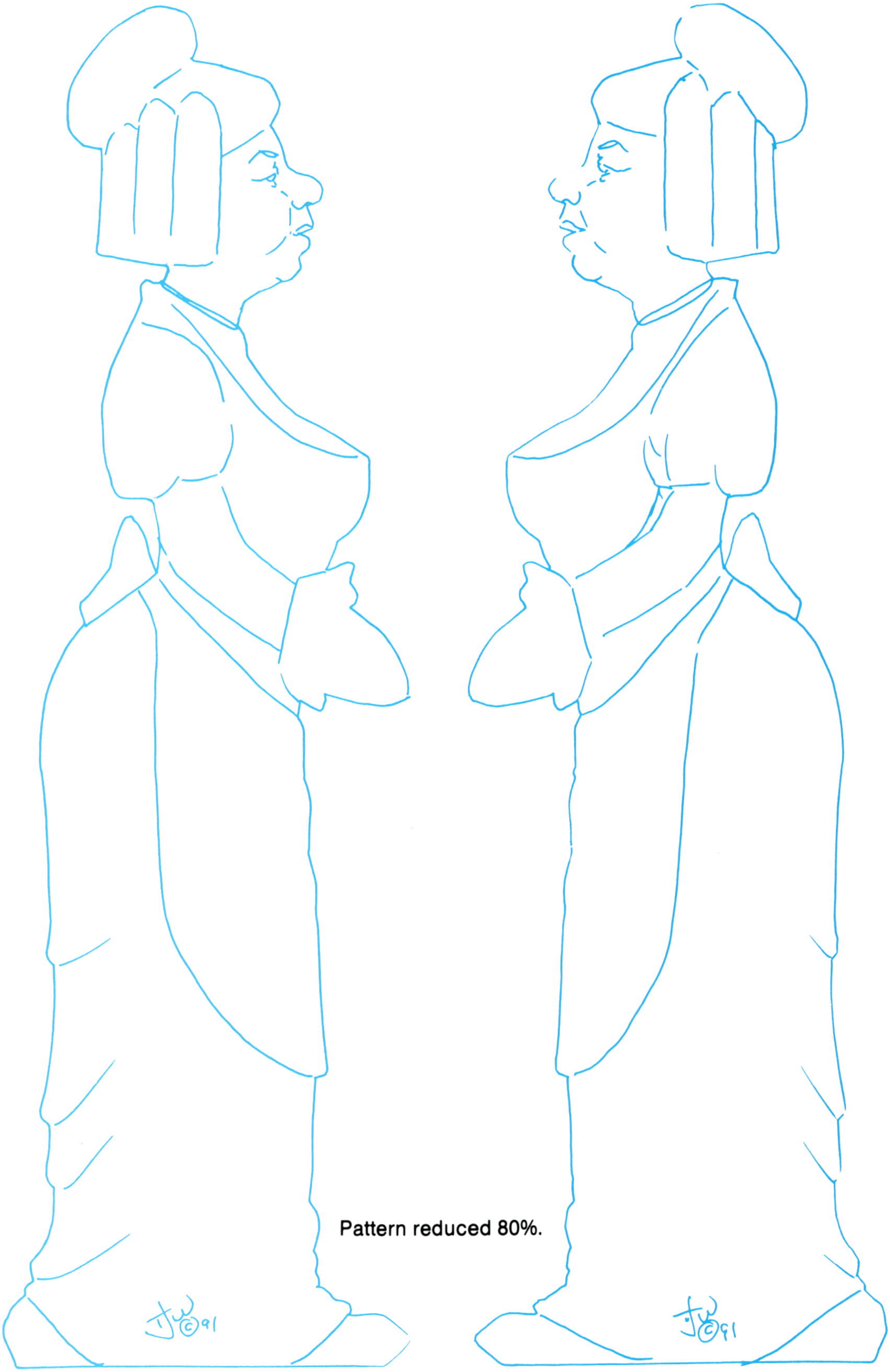

Susie the Soiled Dove

Carving the Cowboy

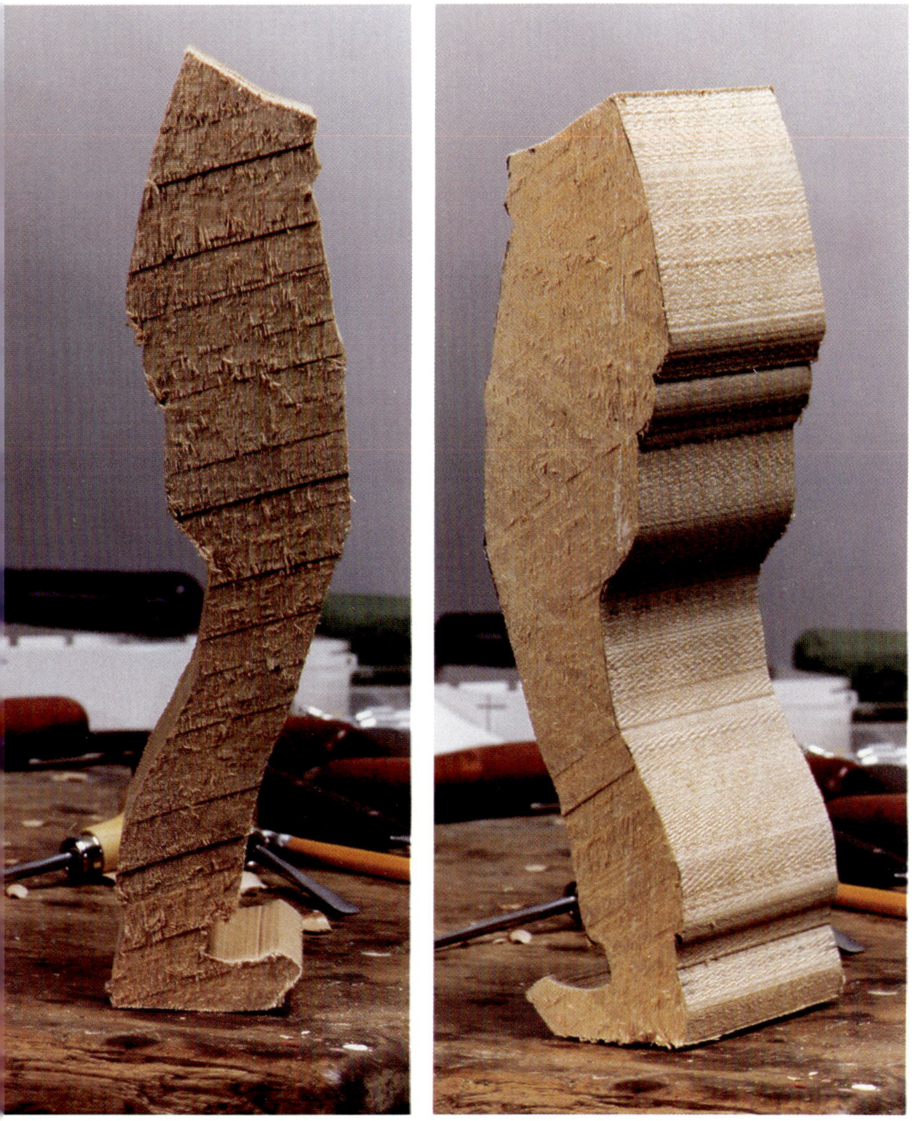

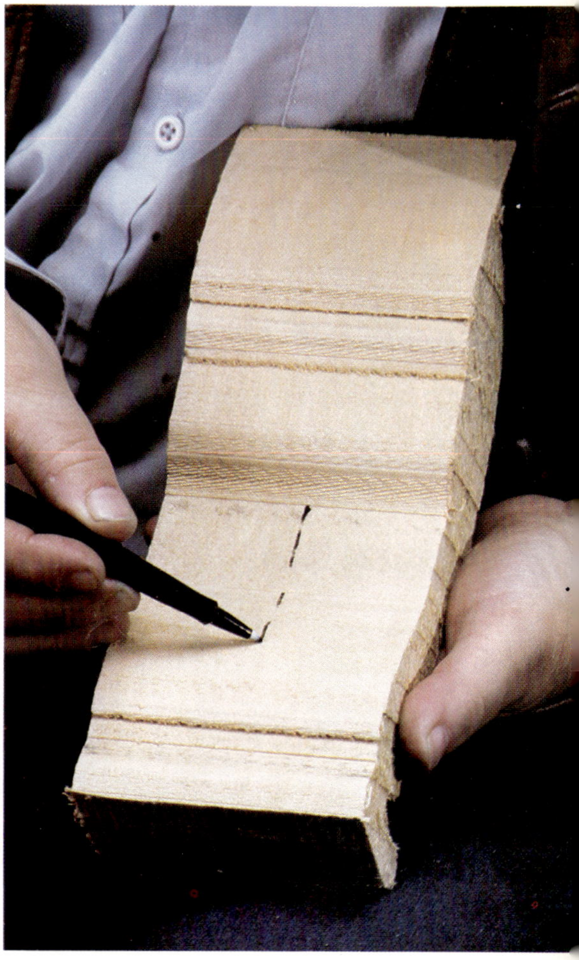

Mark the blank beginning with a mark down the center of the legs.

The blank is cut out with a bandsaw. I pick the most complicated silhouette of the blank to cut out on the bandsaw. This gives the basic shape. Then I mark the other dimension of the silhouetted piece for a few other bandsaw cuts that save work but are simple. I avoid laying down a pattern or cutting a complete silhouette in both dimensions because it almost always leads to mistakes.

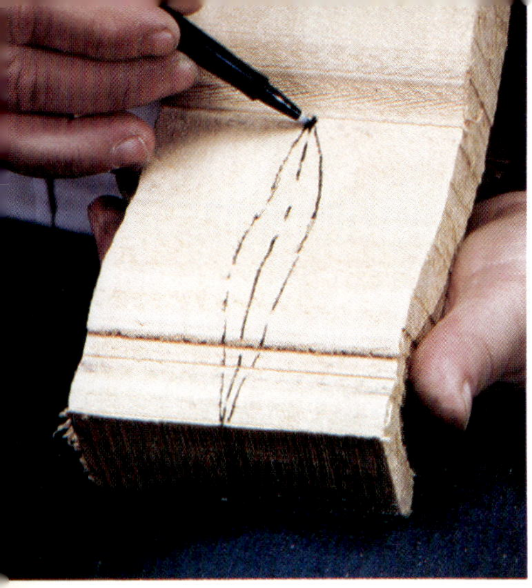

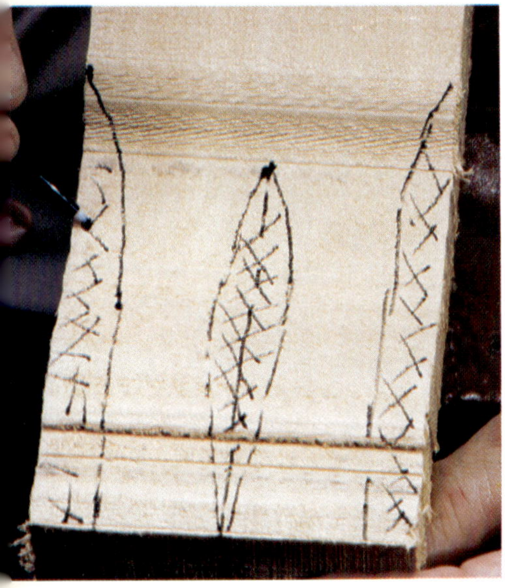

Mark the sides of the legs and darken the areas to be removed.

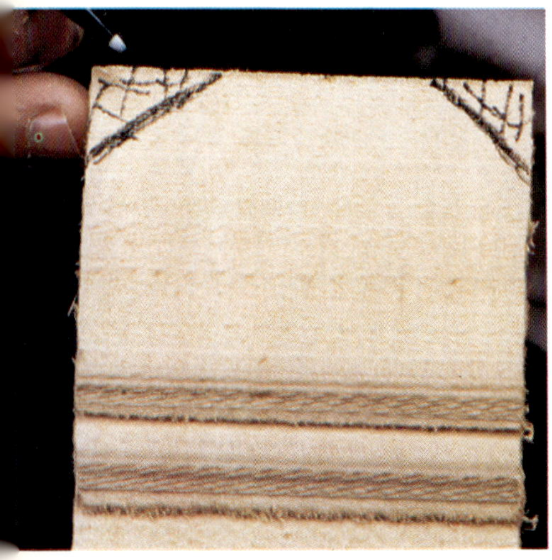

Mark the slope of the shoulders. By cutting the shoulders with the bandsaw you avoid the temptation to have them shrug, and get a nice natural line.

Mark the inside of the legs. They will be bowed out from the center line...our cowboy has spent many hours on his horse.

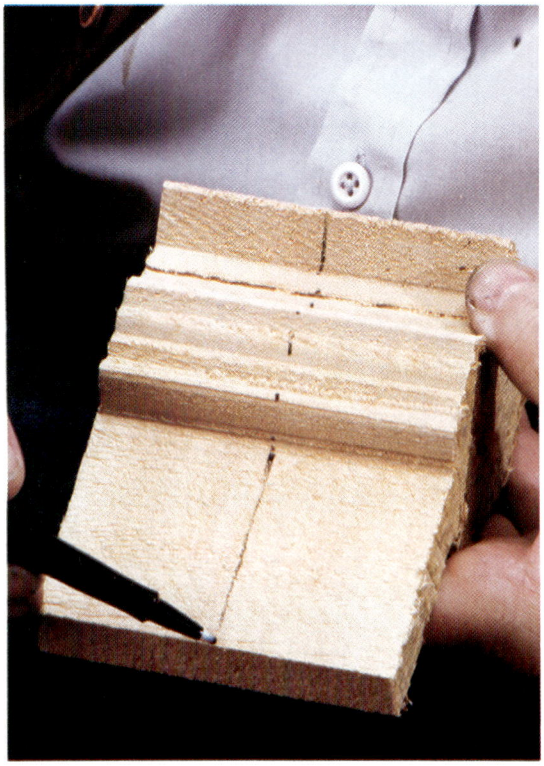

Find the center line of the head.

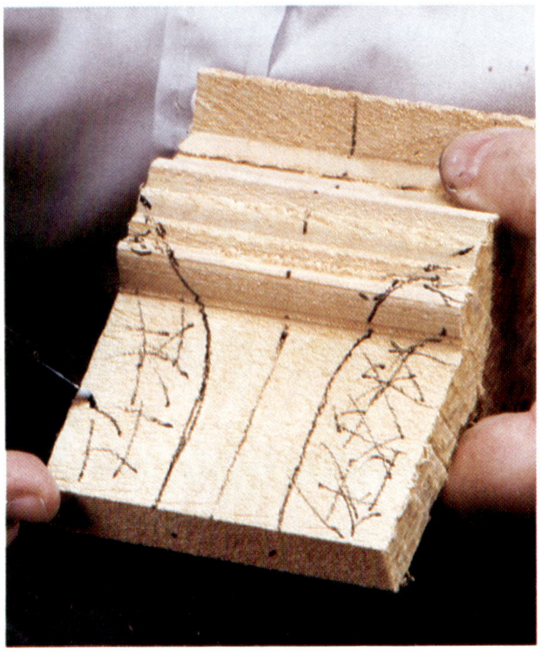

Mark the neck wider than it will be, and darken the areas to be removed.

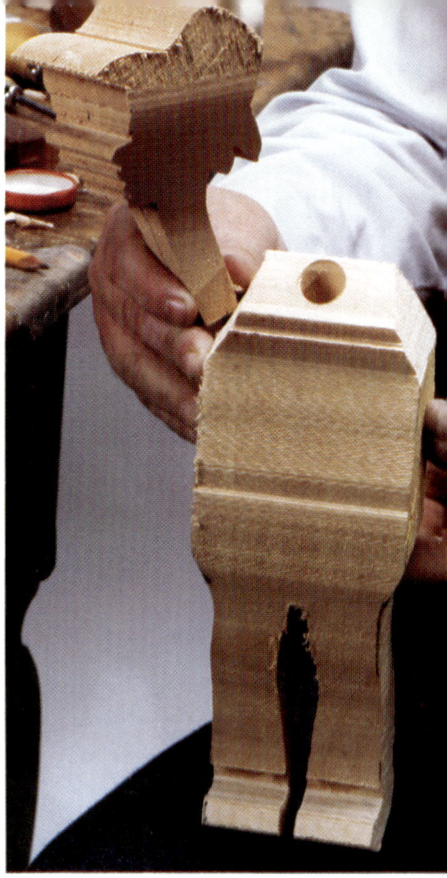

This is the result of the second round of bandsawing. While I was in the shop I used the drill press to make a hole for the neck. This is made to fit the neck and rilled straight into the body. You can give the figure a different character by drilling this neck hole a little off center or at a slight angle.

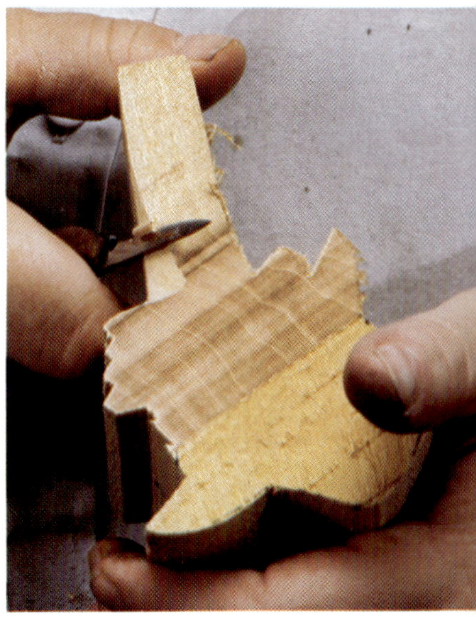

Start the carving by fitting the neck. Remove the darkened sides of the blank down to the base.

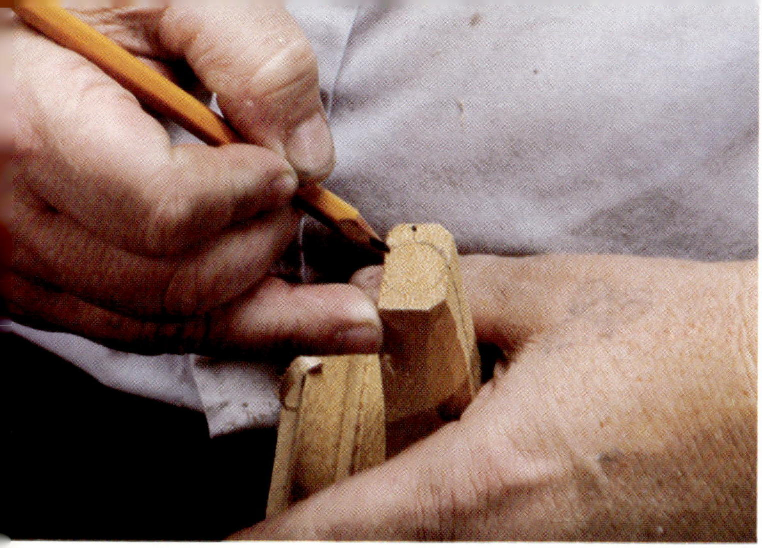

The goal is a round neck. Draw this in the base.

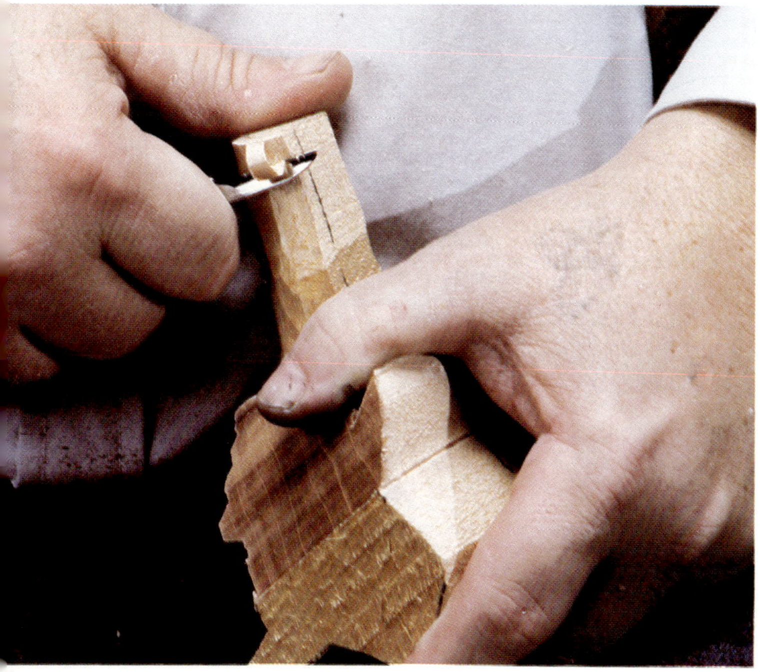

Trim the neck down to size.

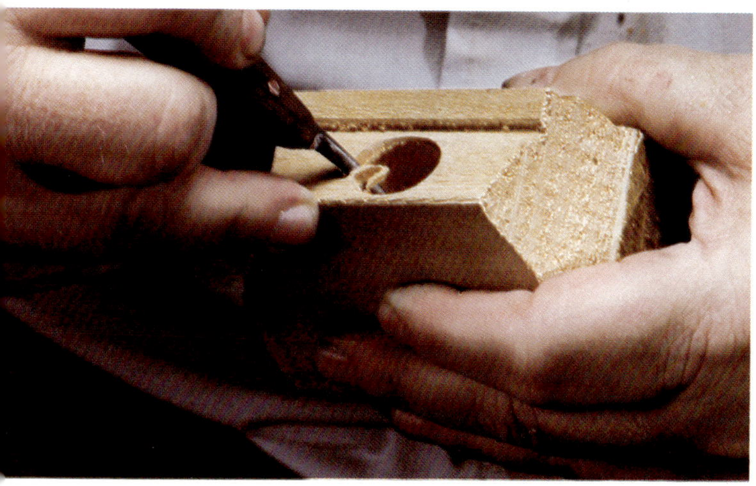

On the body put a slight chamfer around the inside of the neck.

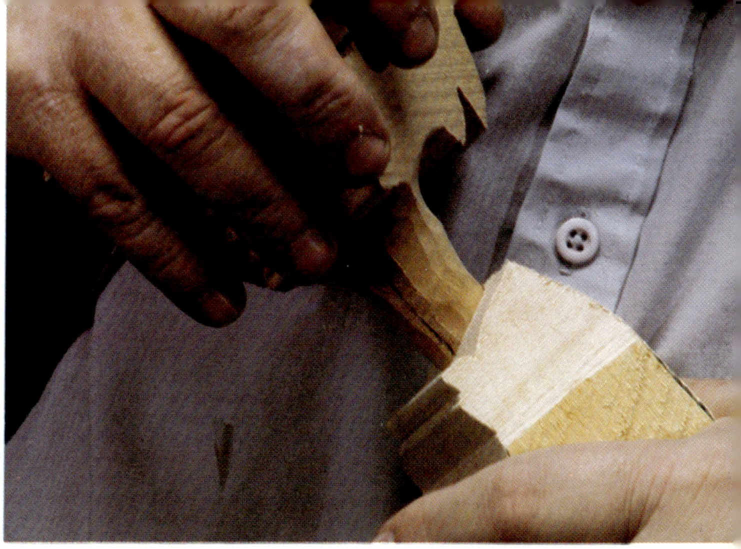

Put the head in the hole, push fairly hard and twist the head back and forth.

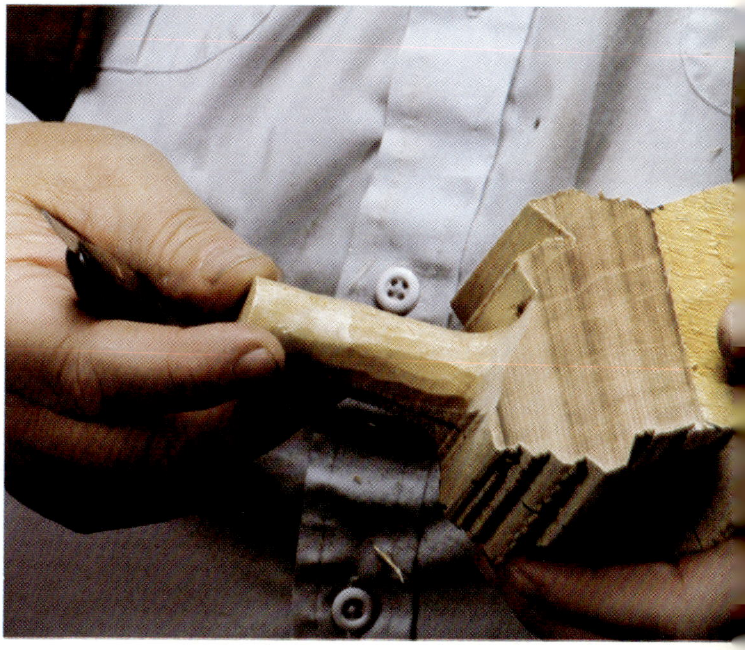

When you take the head out you'll find that the high points of the neck are made shiny by the rubbing.

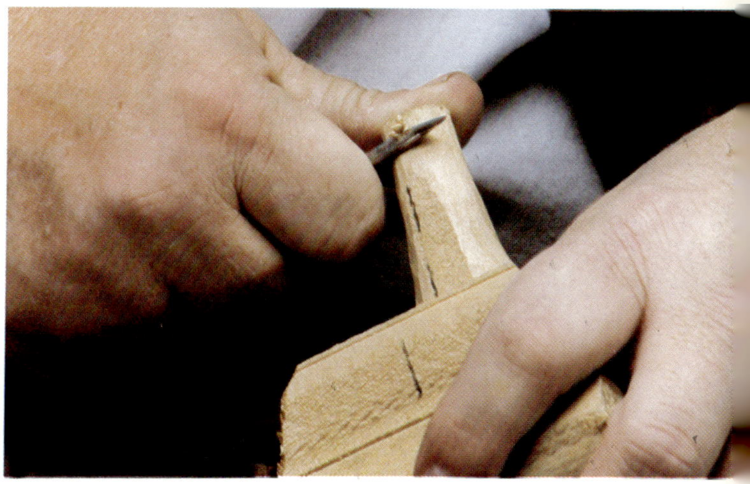

Shave off these shiny spots and repeat the process.

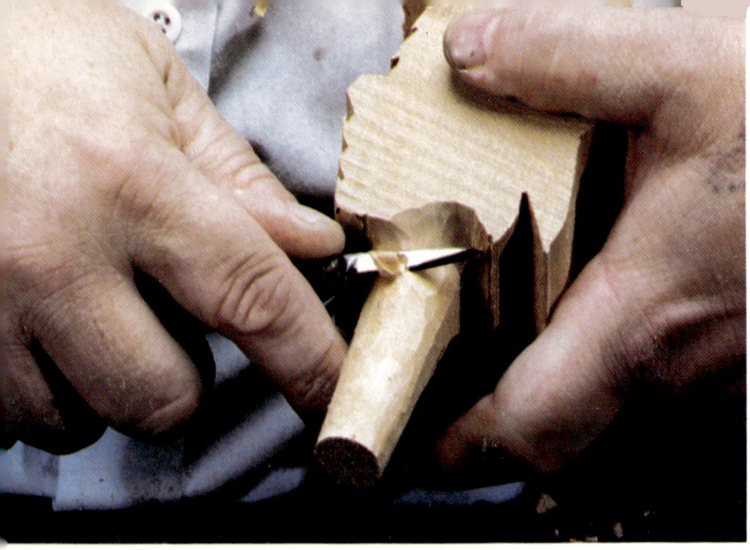

When the base of the neck is round and fitted, trim the rest of the neck down to it.

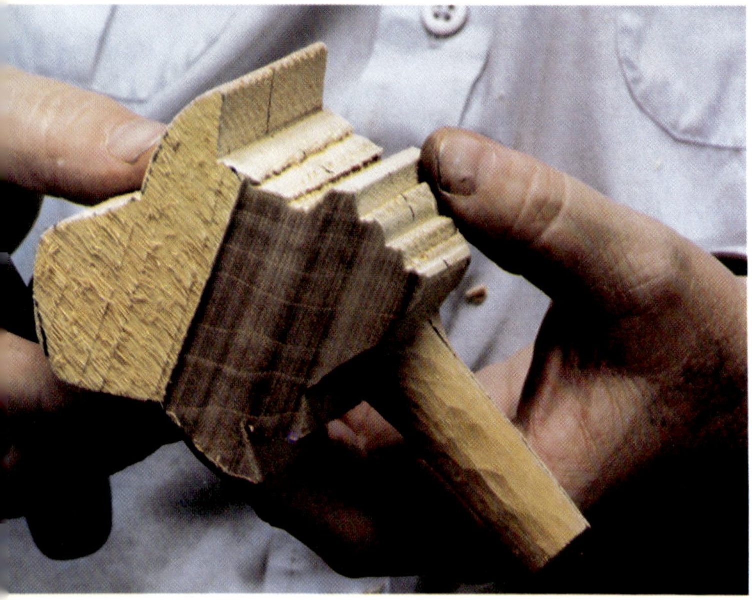

The neck so far. It is a little long and will remain so for now.

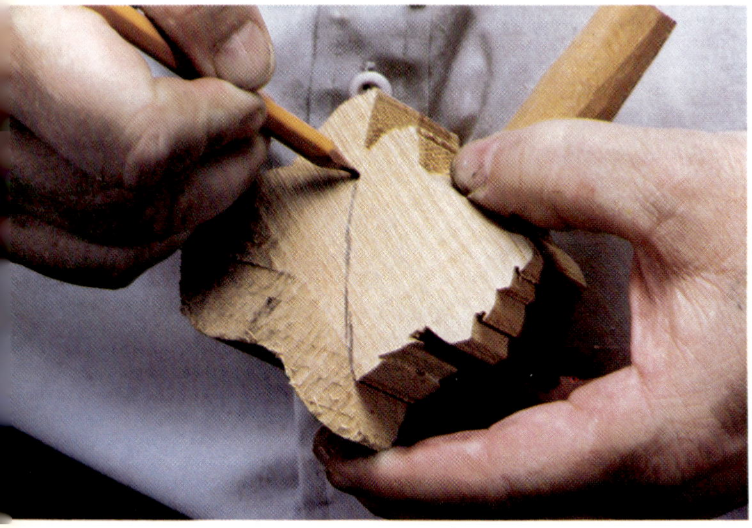

Mark the bottom of the hat brim.

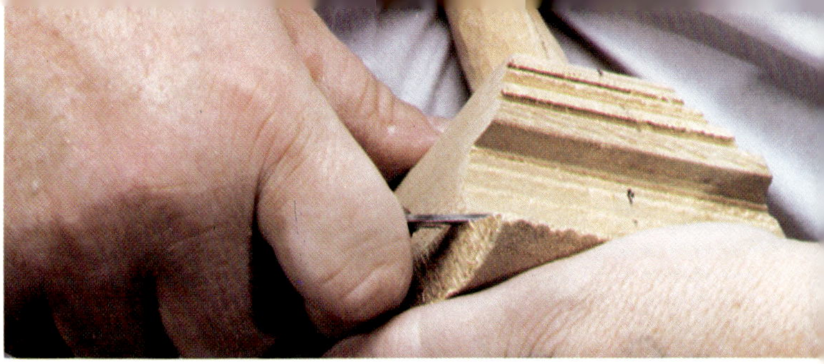

Make a stop on each corner of the head below the hat brim.

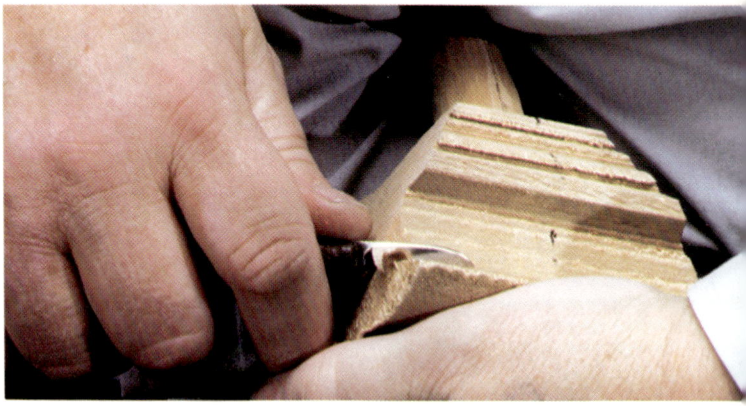

Cut back to the stops from the head.

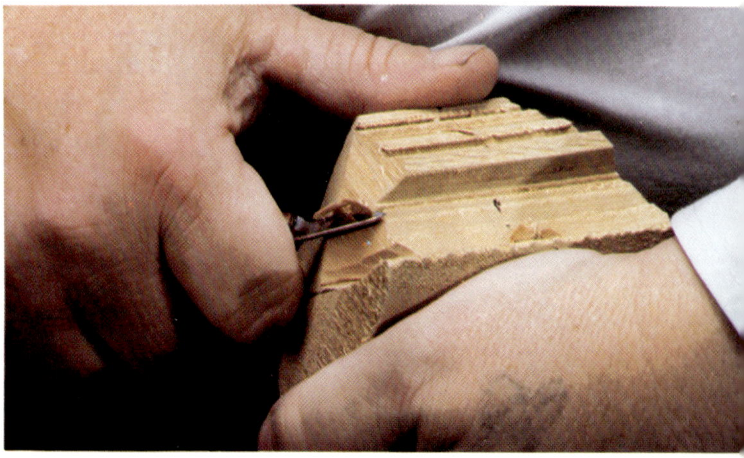

Trim the corners of the head beneath the hat.

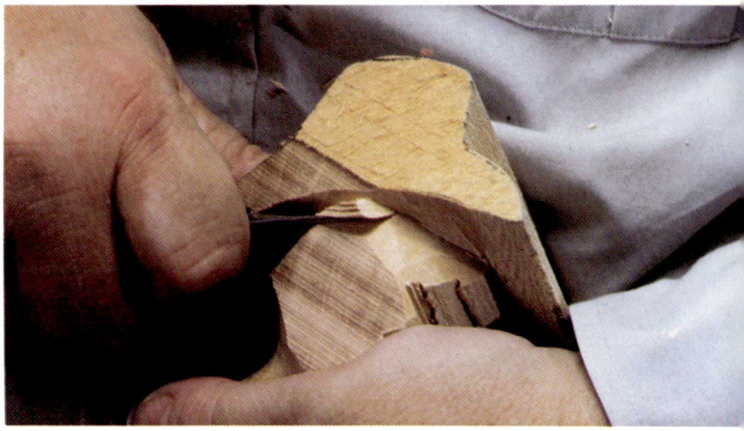

This brings out the brim.

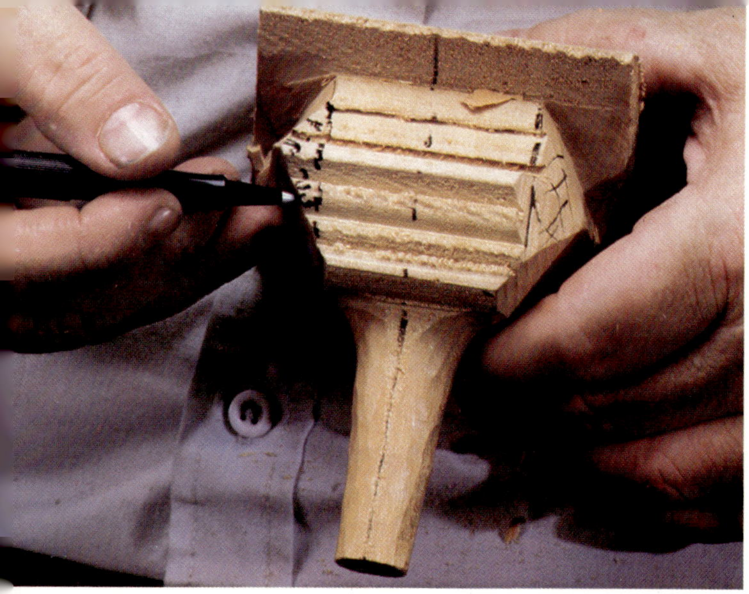

The head now has to be narrowed considerably. With a cowboy figure and his wide brimmed hat, there is a tendency to make the head too wide, so keep it thin.

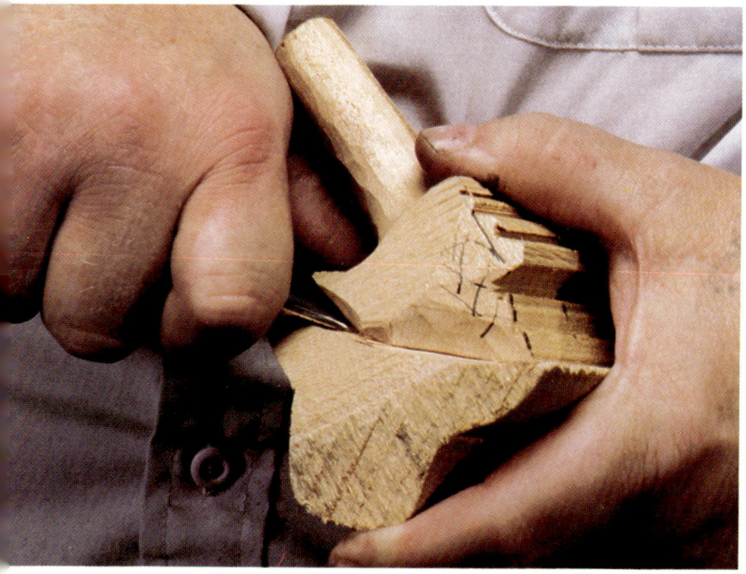

Cut a safety into the head beneath the hat...

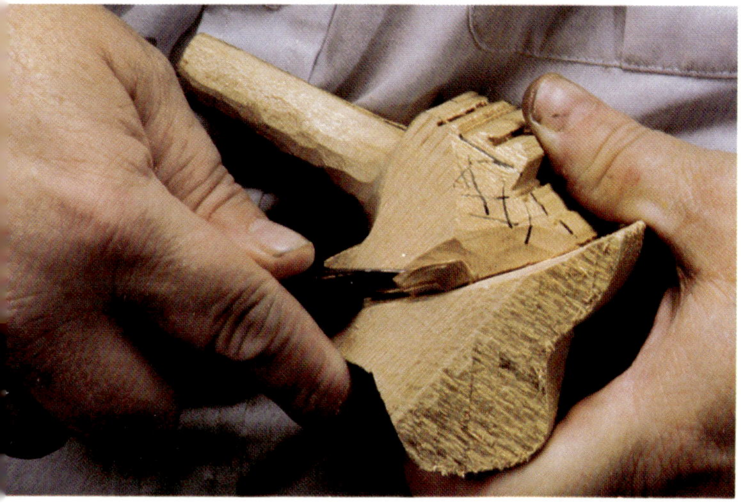

and cut back to it.

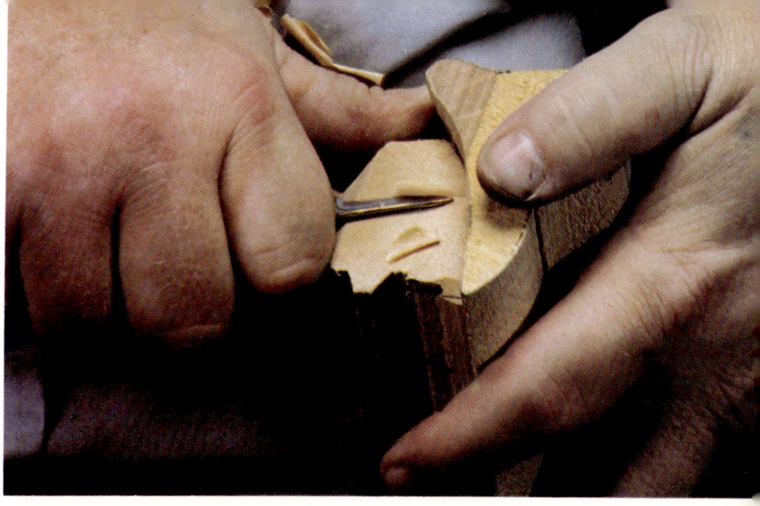

Smooth and flatten the side of the head. Keep things square until you get the proportions right.

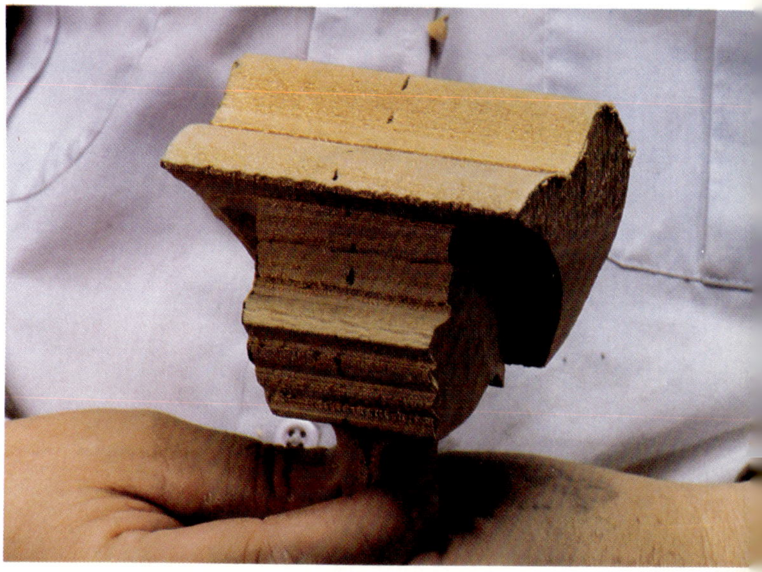

With the head trimmed to proportion, we are ready to proceed with the hat.

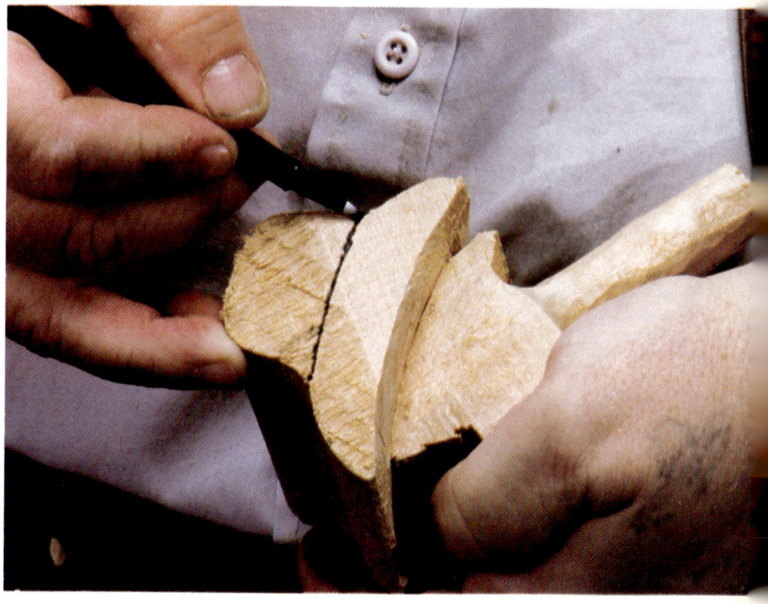

Draw in the top of the hat's brim.

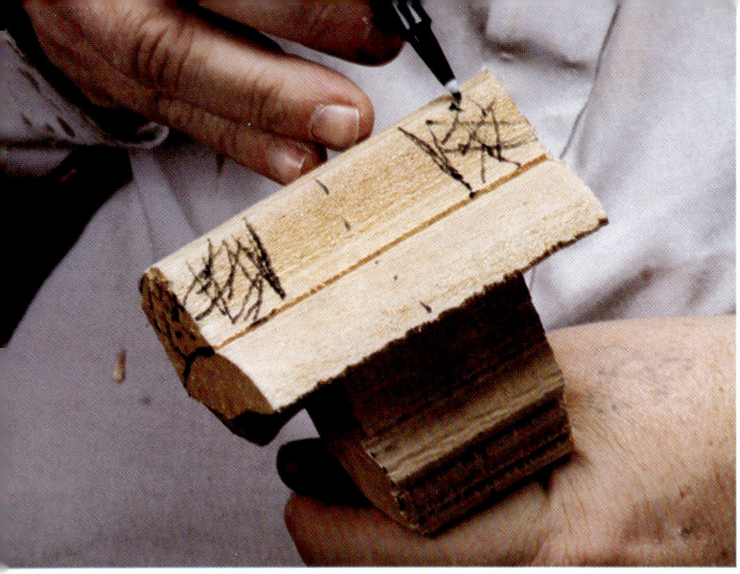

Mark out the sides of the crown to be removed.

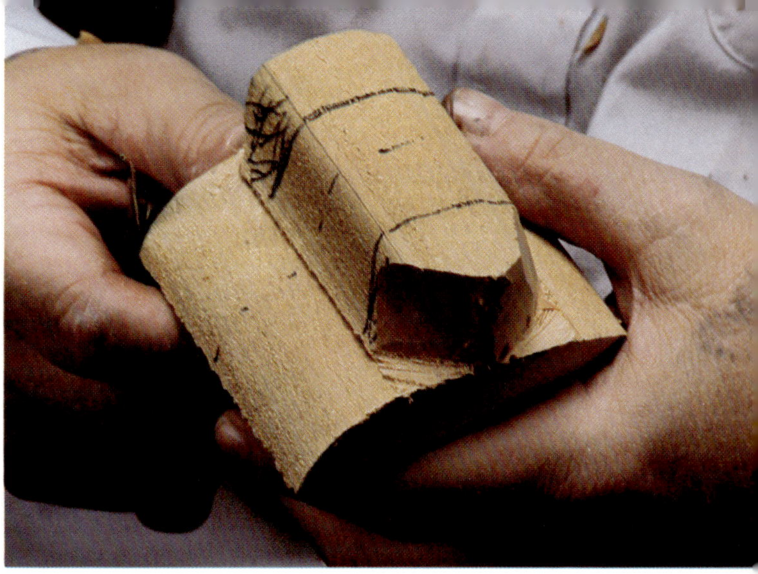

Continue removing the corners back to the crown lines.

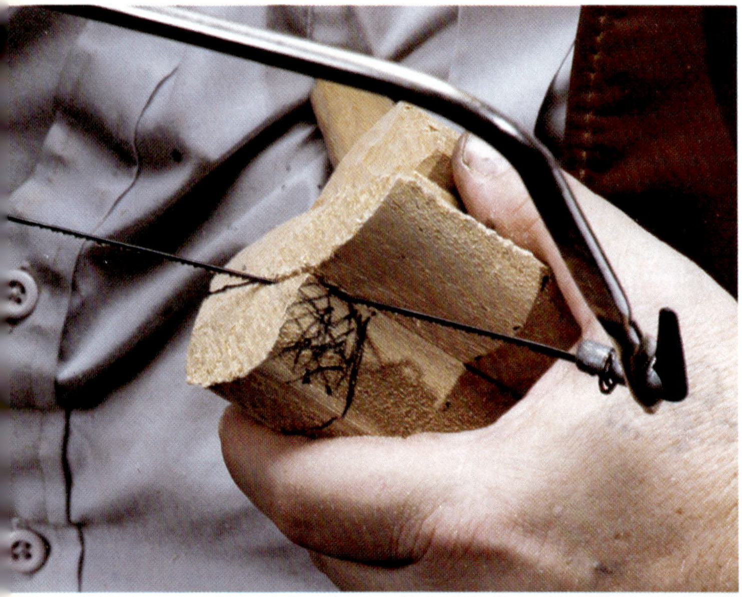

Cut the corners with a coping saw. This will save a lot of work. I put the coping saw blade in backwards, so that it cuts on the pulling stroke. I find this gives me much more control.

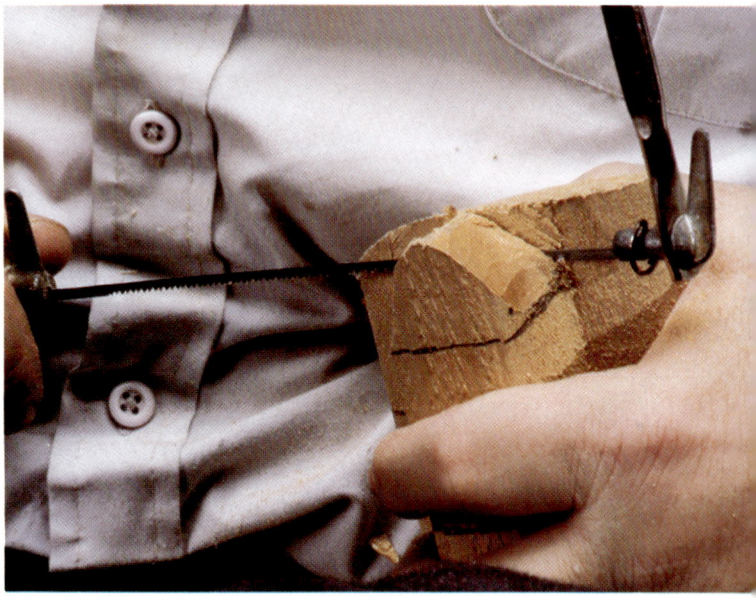

When the corners are trimmed, use the coping saw again to cut into the sides above the brim. You might find it easier to put the piece in a vise or holding clamp when using the coping saw.

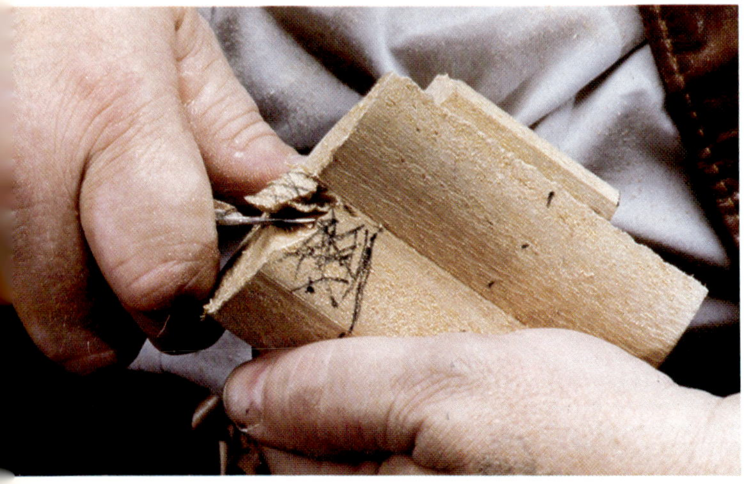

Knock off the corners with a knife.

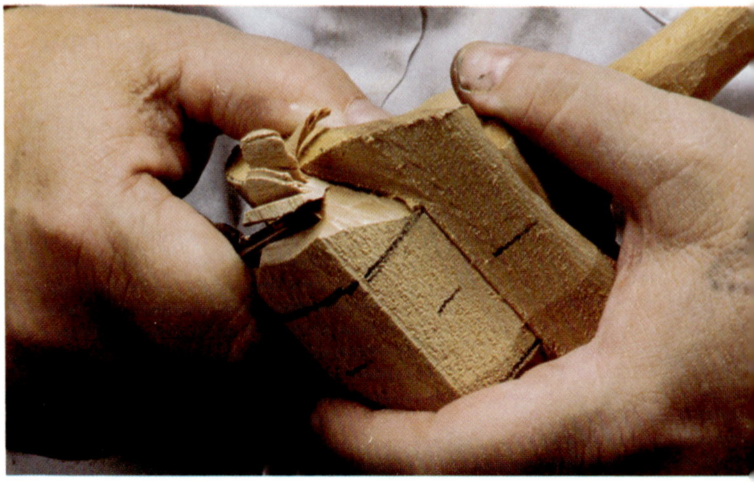

Pop off the excess wood.

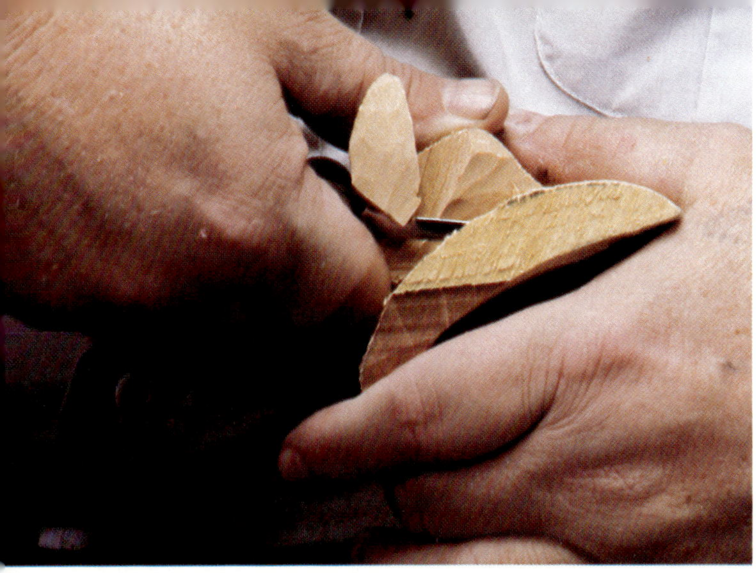

After trimming back along the brim, the sides of the crown should pop off rather easily.

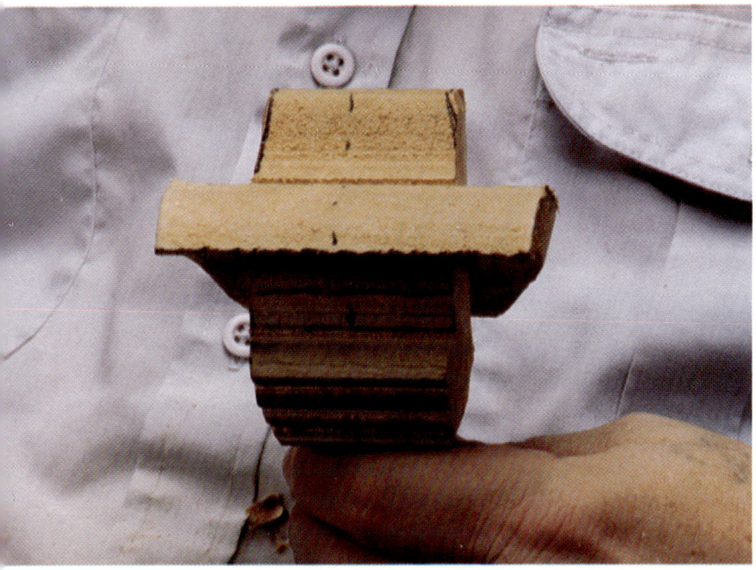

Clean, and square up the crown. It should be at least as wide as the head or it will look impossibly small. It is better for the hat to look a little bit big than a little bit small.

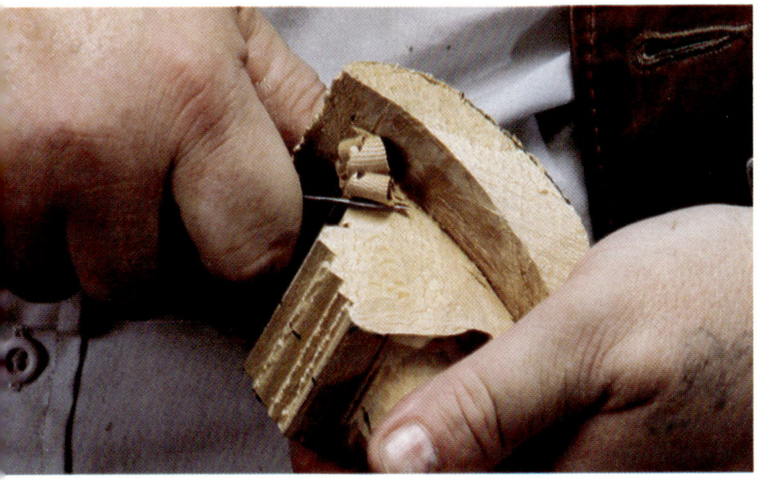

Trim the corners of the face beneath the hat, knocking off a 45 degree edge.

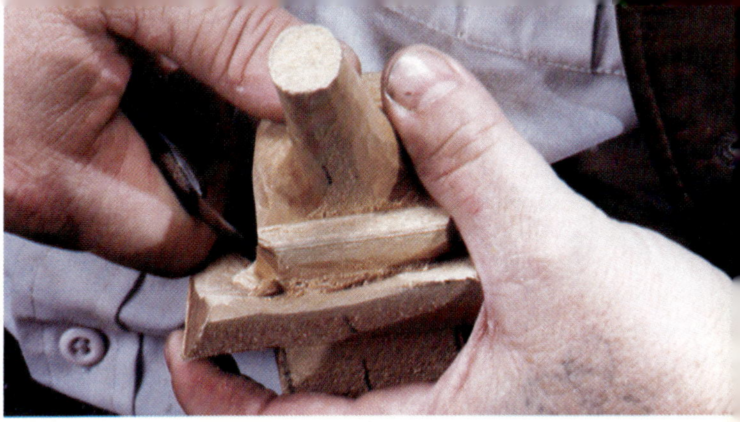

Because of the grain at the back of the head the going is tough. Take smaller bites at first.

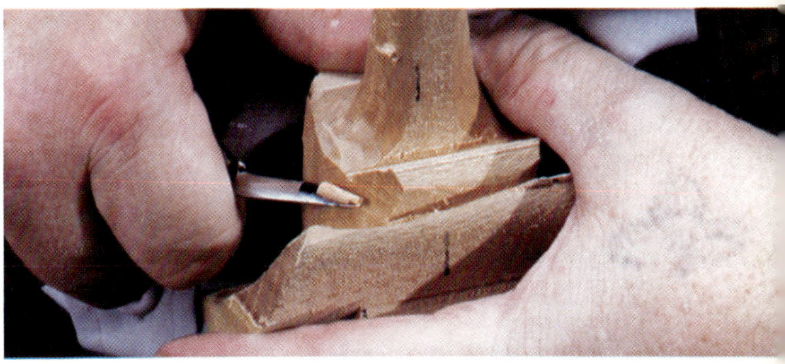

As the area opens up it gets easier.

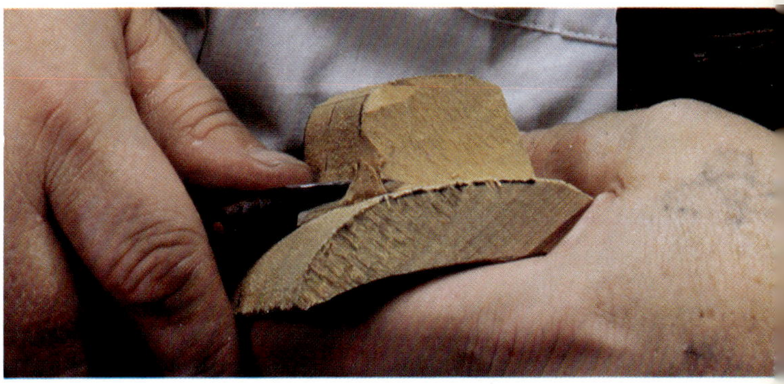

Knock off the corners of the crown of the hat in a similar way.

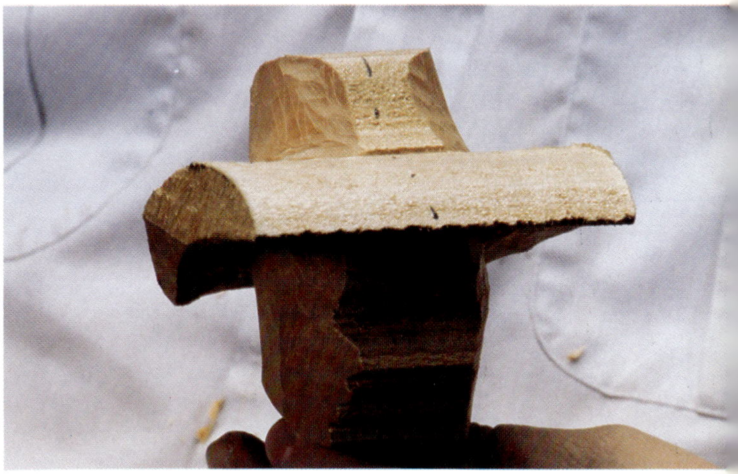

Round and shape the sides a bit to get to this stage.

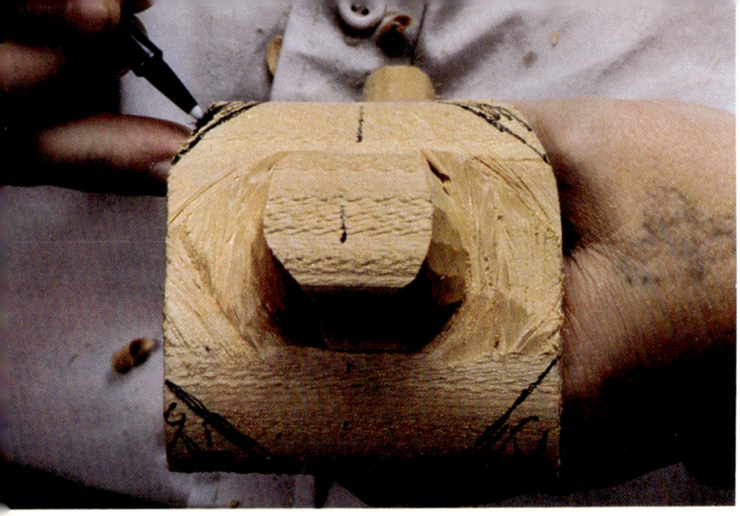

Mark the four corners of the brim. For now make the brim the same width all around.

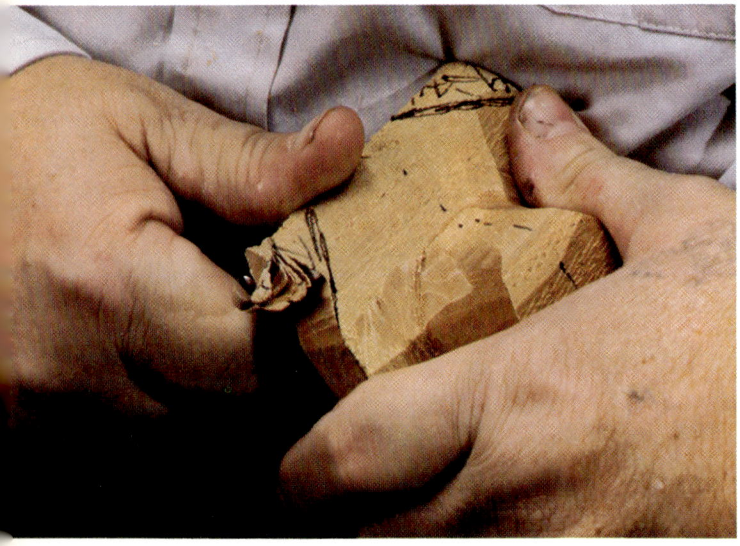

Pop off the corners.

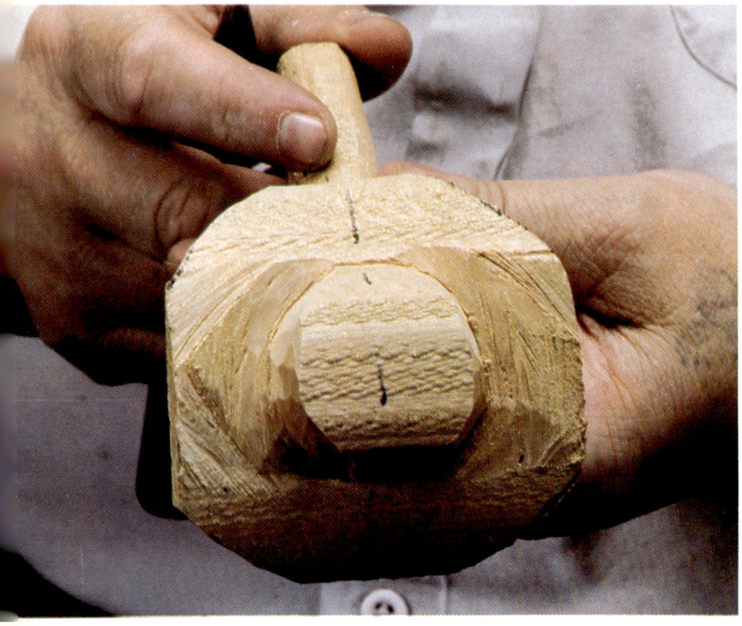

This takes you to this point.

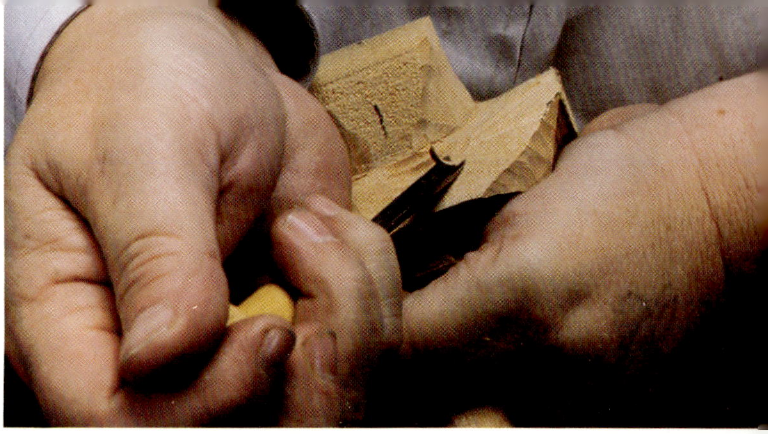

Gouge the top of the brim to give it the rolled up shape it should have. Start out slow...

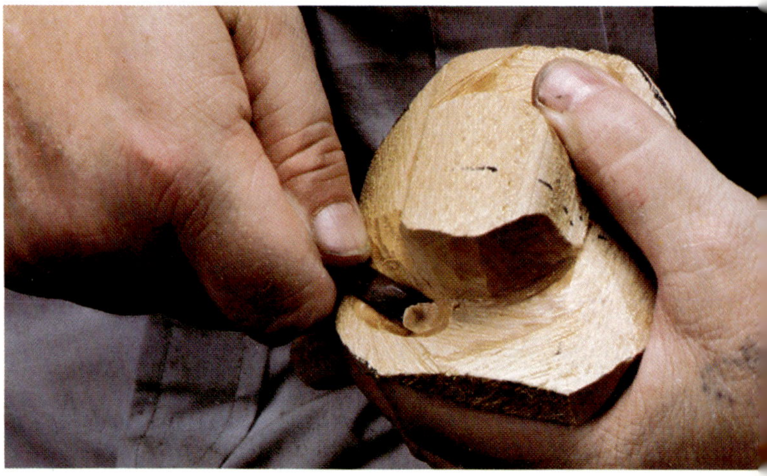

and get deeper. I like to have the hat sitting on the head in a way that the grain does not go straight. Because it is sitting back a bit, I am not cutting at right angles to the grain when I'm gouging the brim.

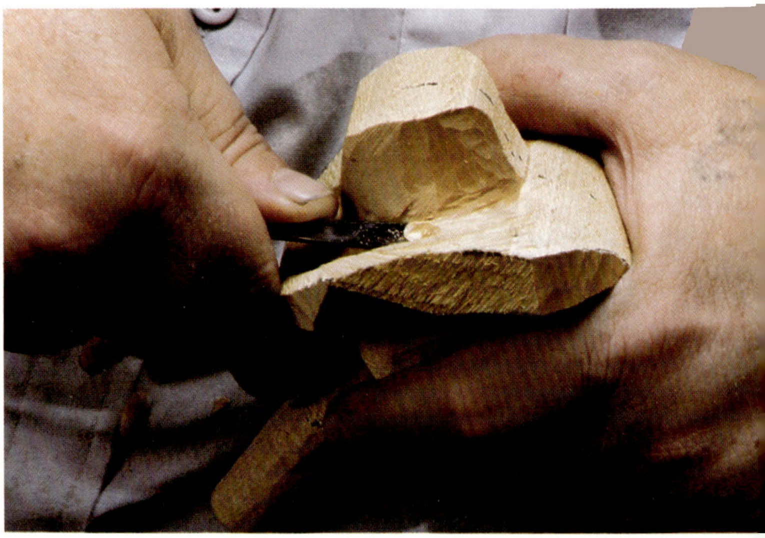

Leave the outside edge of the brim intact. This gives it added strength so it will not break when you are using the gouge. It will be trimmed and shaped later. Notice the finger position of the hand with the tool. It acts as a depth gauge and keeps you from going too far. The safest way, of course, is to put the piece in a vise or hold-down.

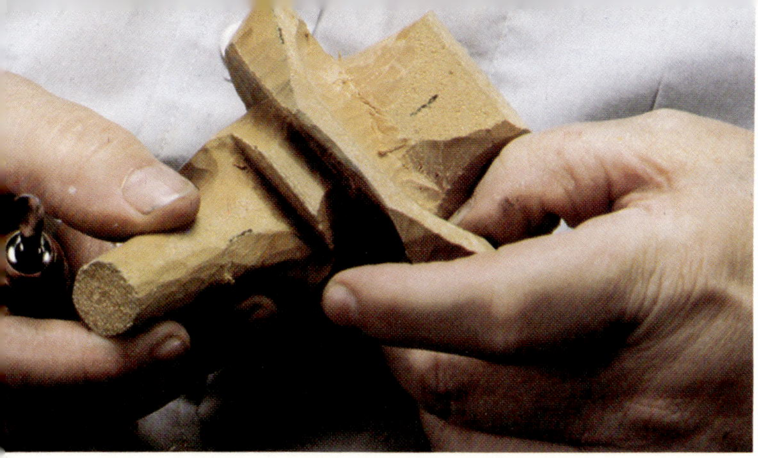

Gauge the thickness of the brim with your fingers. You don't want to make it too thin or it will become very fragile.

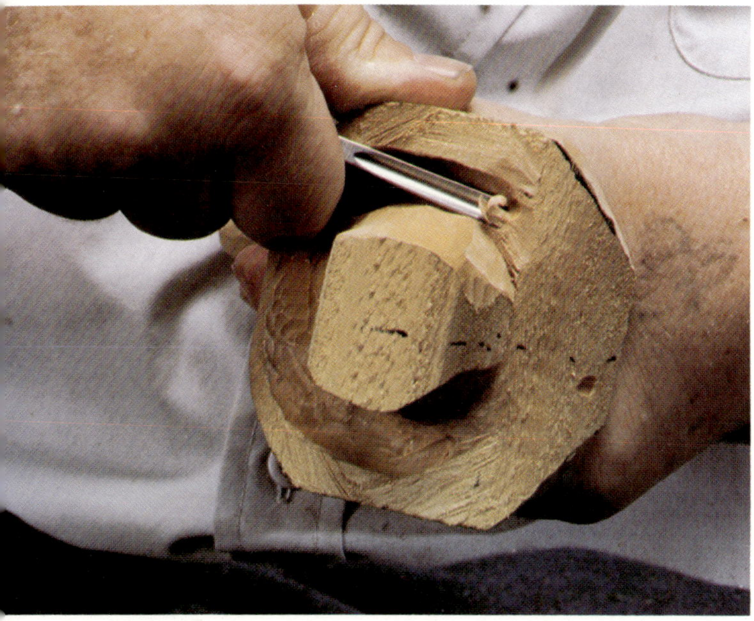

Your goal is to take this groove around the back and sides of the brim.

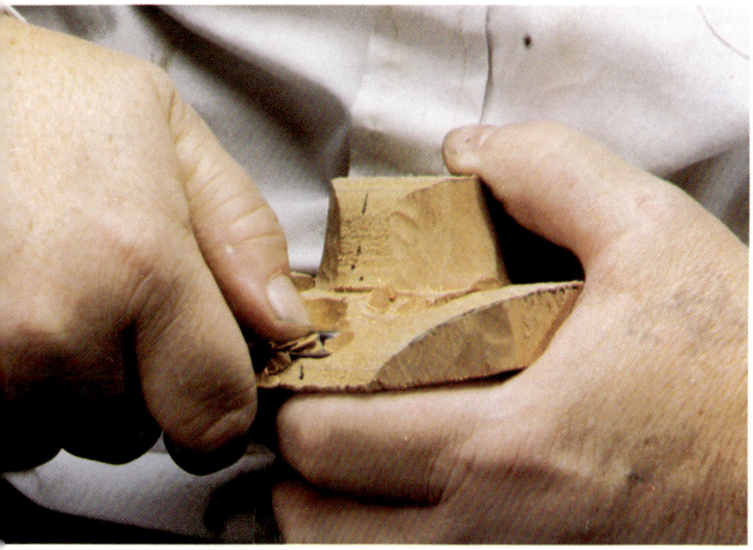

On the front brim we have the problem of going against the grain. The only thing that will work at all is a sharp, sharp tool. A flatter gouge does fairly well.

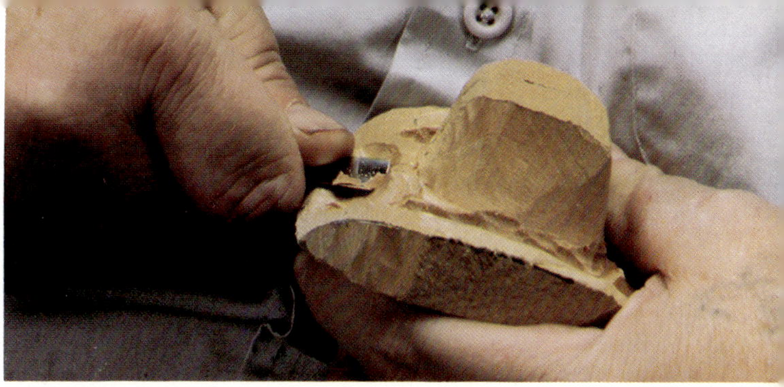

You can try other tools, and by the time you've tried them all you should be just about finished! When using the gouge, a rocking motion seems to work a little better, but it is a bad thing to do to your tools. It also increases the danger of slippage and injury, so be careful.

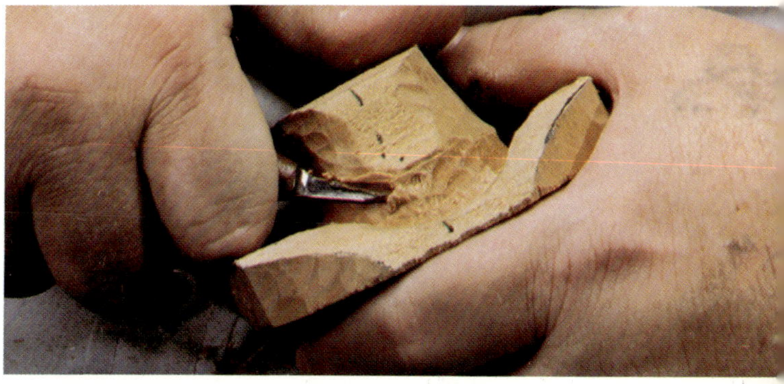

Clean things up with a knife and chisels, as needed.

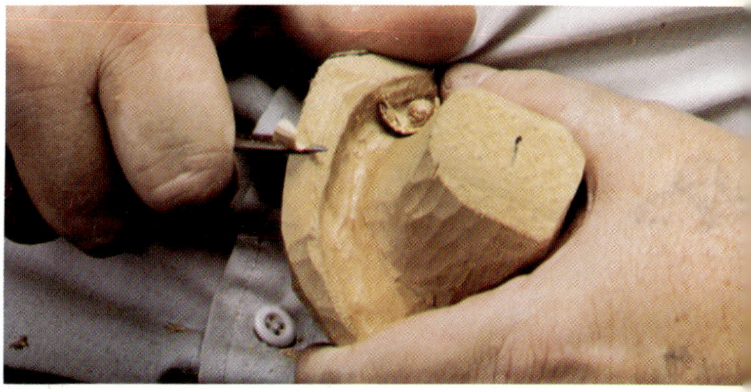

Round the outside top edge of the brim to meet the inside edge.

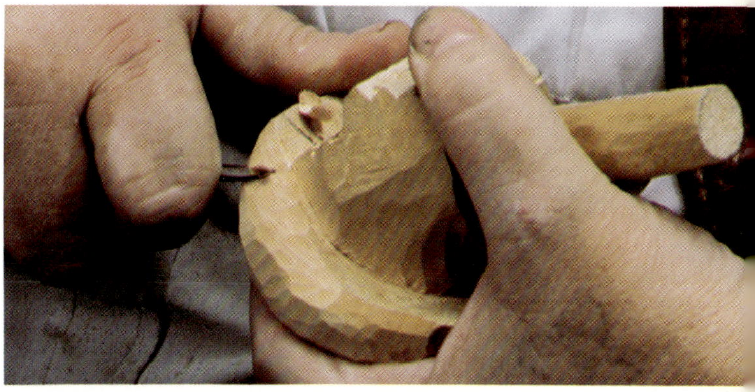

Round the underside of the brim to give it the rolled-over look.

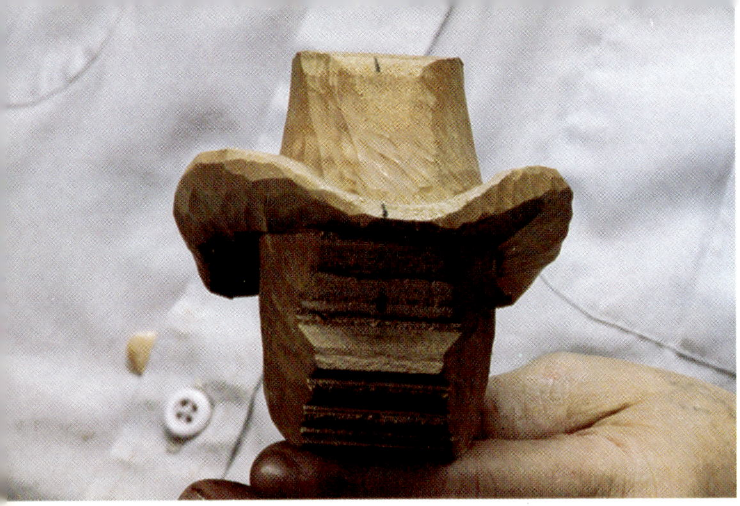

This is the rough shape of the front of the hat.

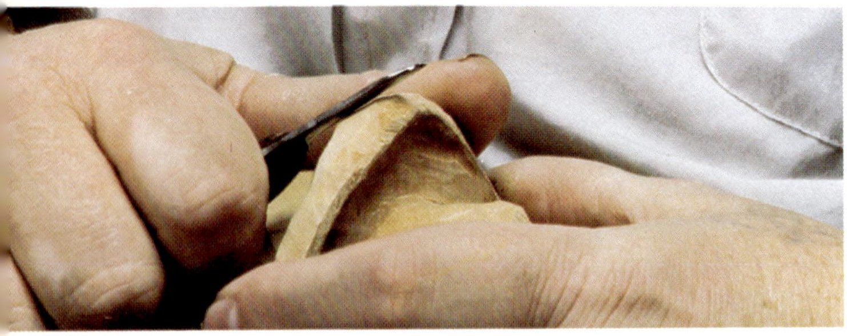

Go over the hat and clean up bad spots and places that look unnatural or unbelievable.

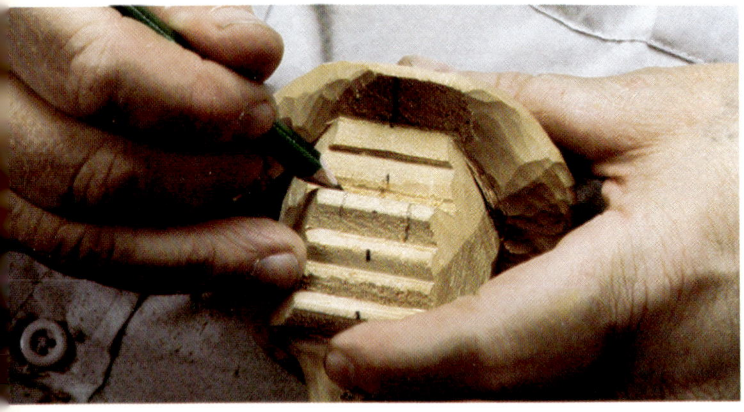

Moving to the face, mark in the nose, making it a lot wider than the finished look will be.

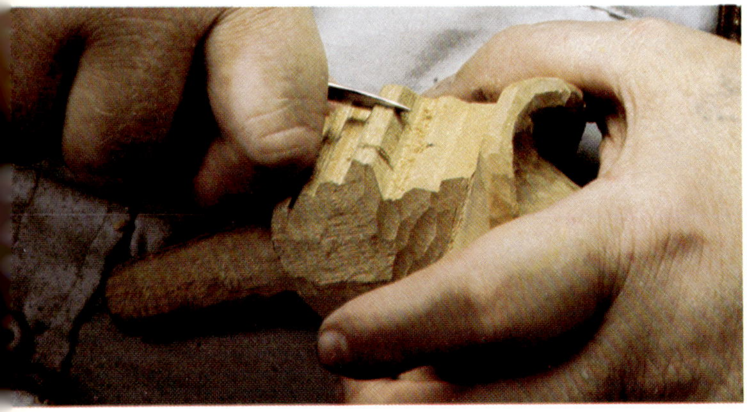

Cut a stop in each nose line...

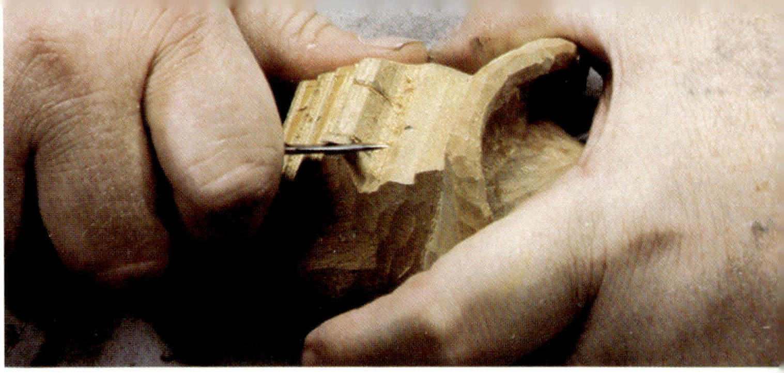

and trim back to it.

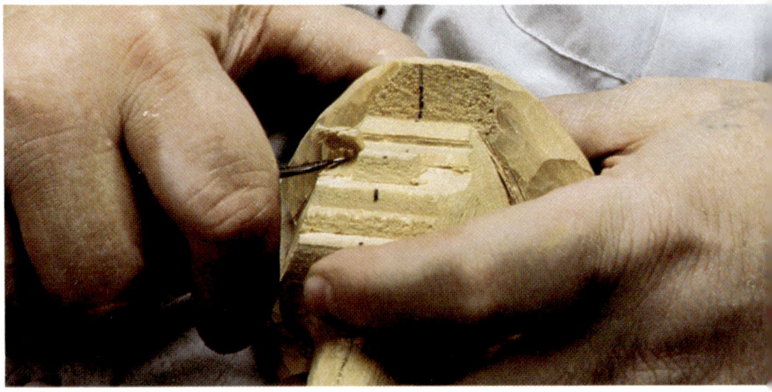

With the grain direction, it may be possible to pop off the piece beside the nose.

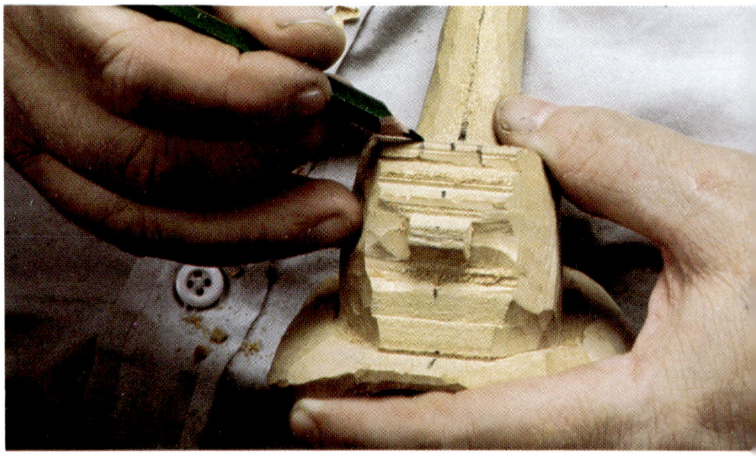

Mark the width of the chin, making it about the same as the nose.

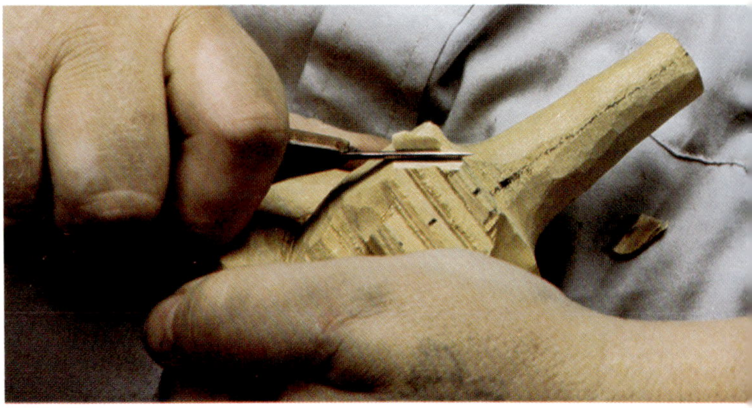

Trim the jaw line down to the chin.

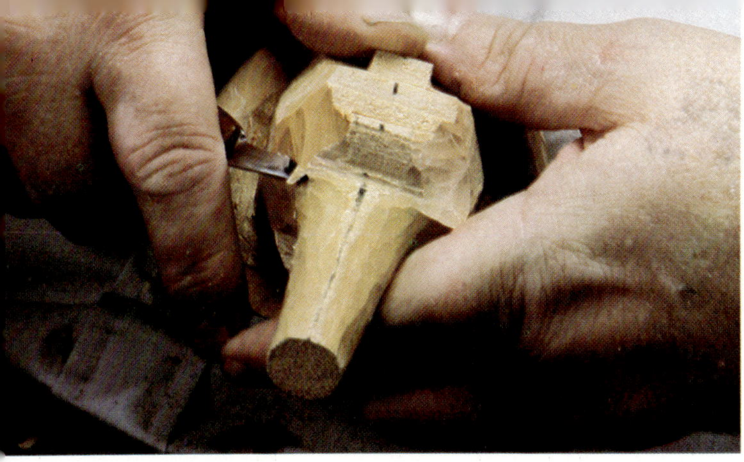

Continue to shape the jawline.

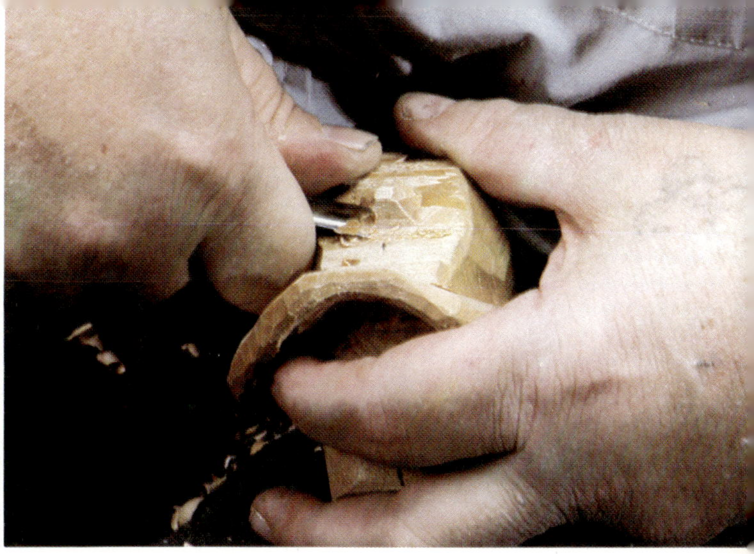

Use a gouge to come into the nose from the side of the face, forming the eye socket and the bridge of the nose.

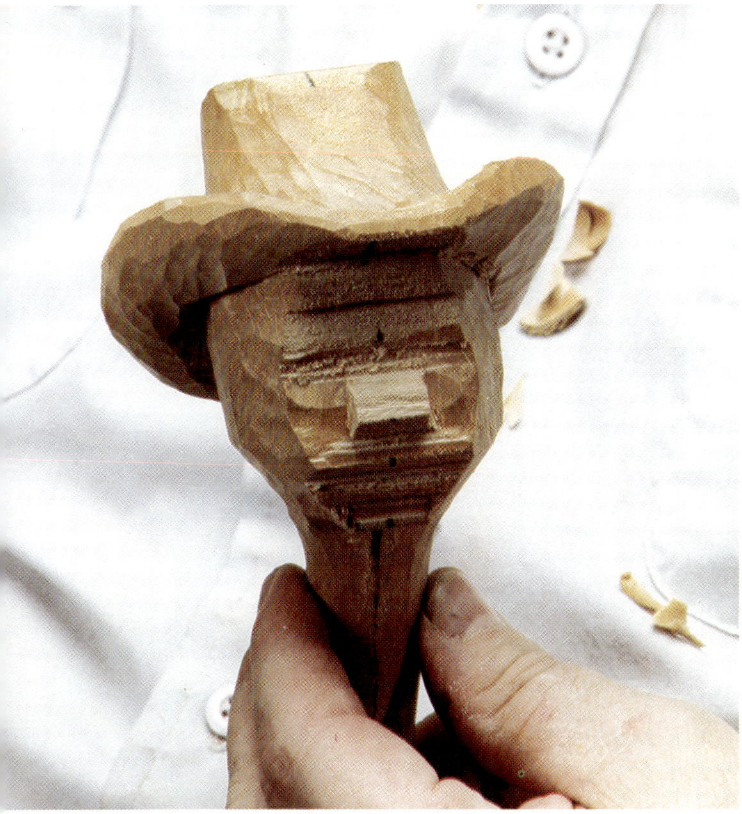

The face so far.

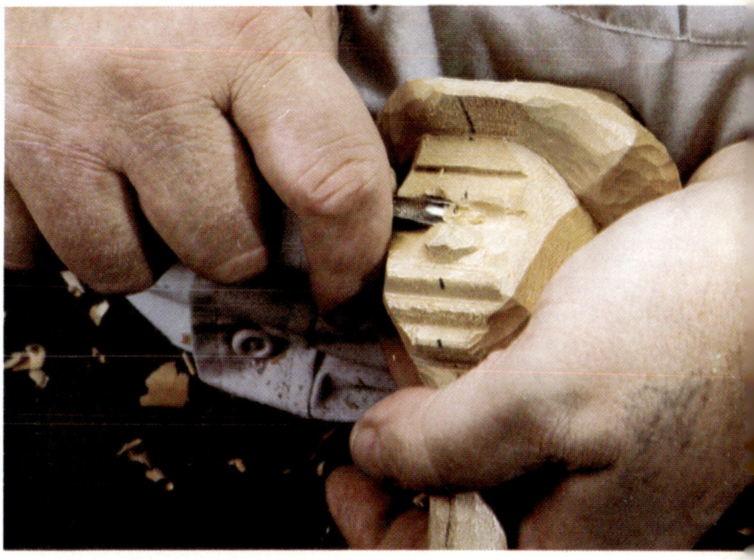

This does two jobs at once.

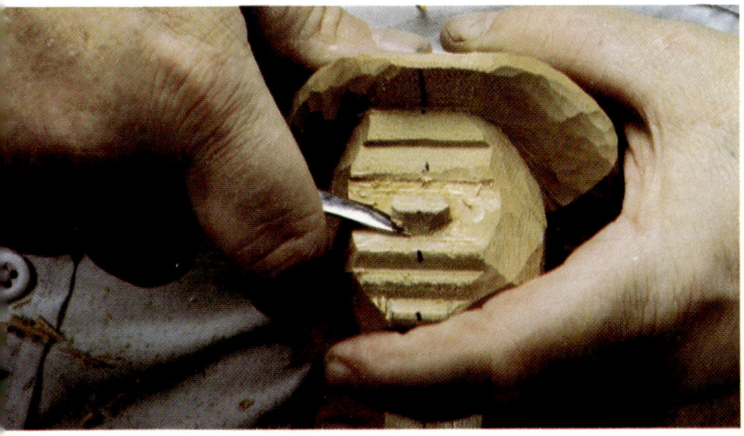

Make angled cuts at the bottom corners of the nose to form the nostril area.

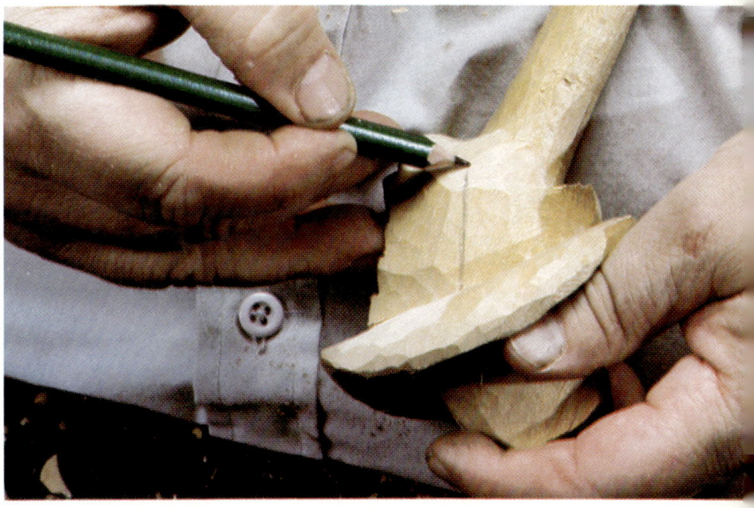

Draw in the ears beginning with a center line down the side of the head. The front edge of the ear is pretty much aligned with this center line, coming down to the back of the jaw.

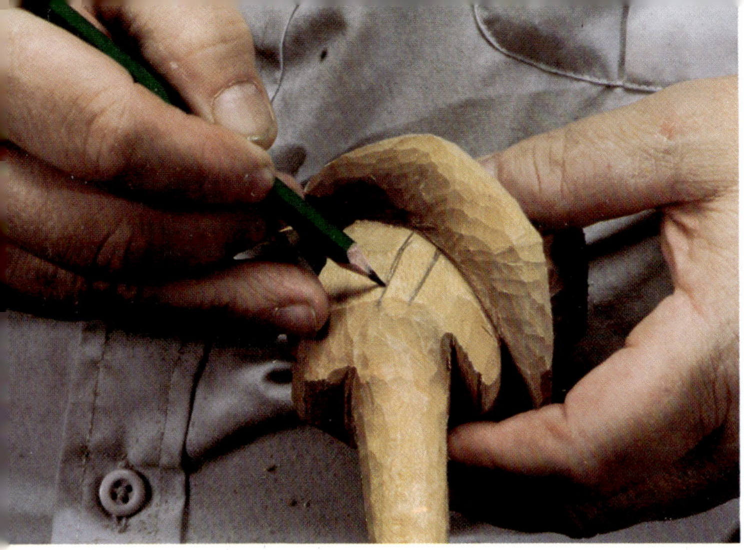

The line of the back of the ear is drawn next.

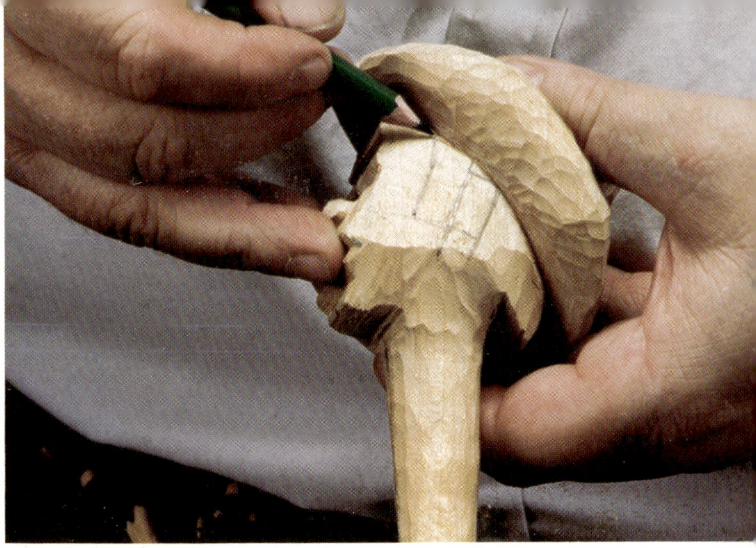

I usually make the sideburns pretty heavy, from the ear about halfway to the eye.

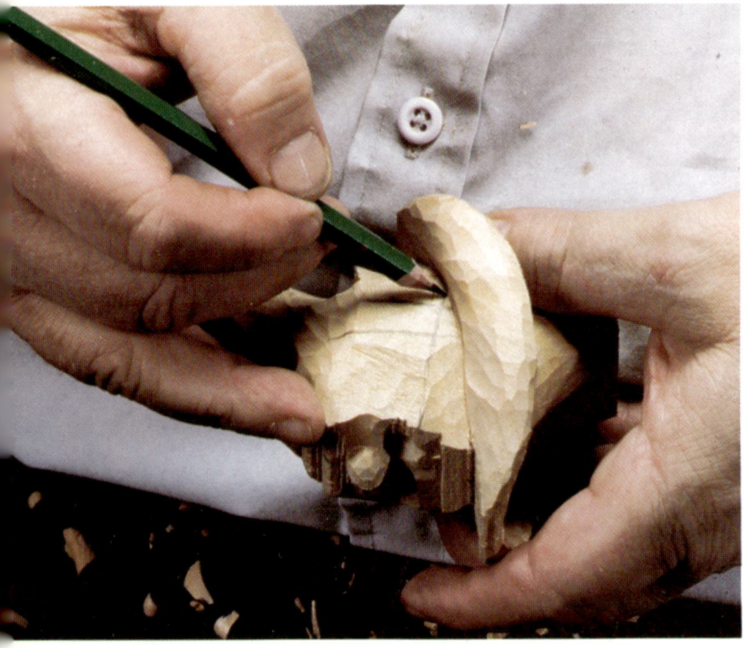

The top of the ear is aligned with the eyebrow. Draw the line.

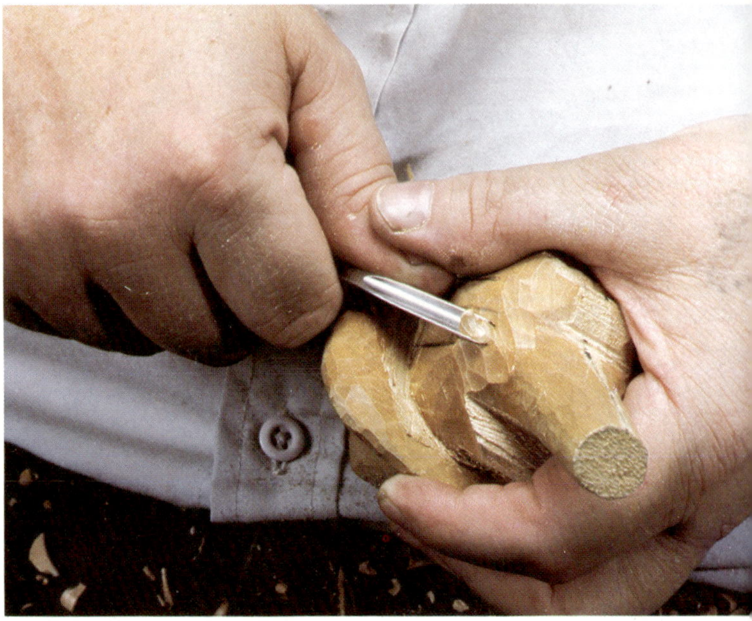

Begin to define the ear with a gouge, cutting from the bottom of the ear down into the neck.

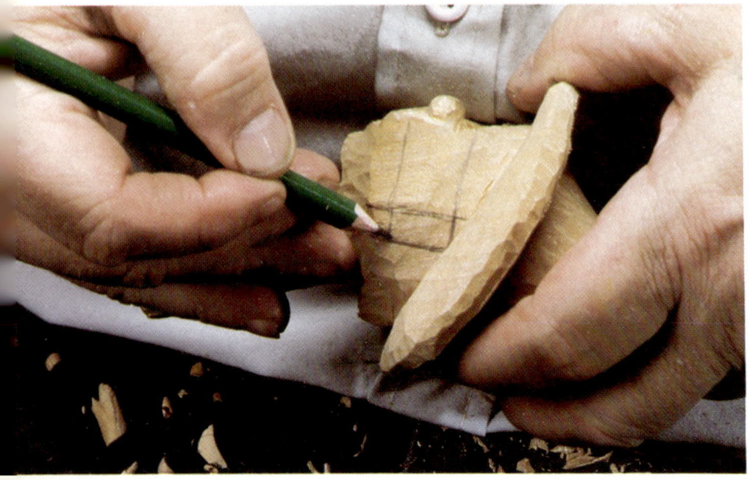

The bottom of the ear is aligned with the bottom of the nose. Draw the line.

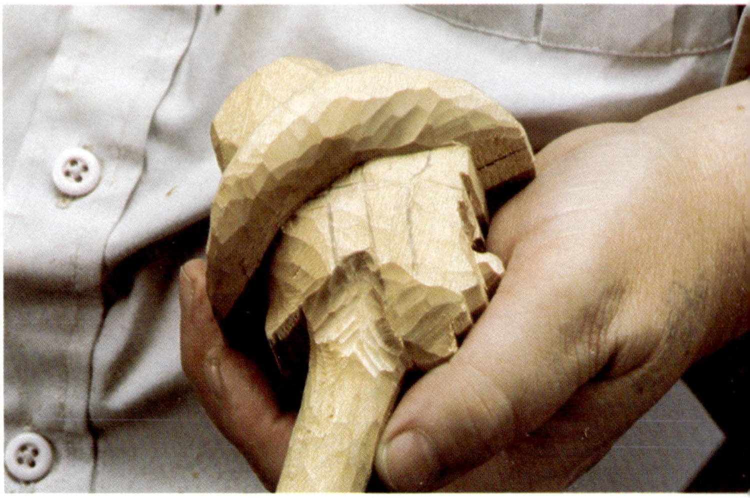

This also defines the jawline.

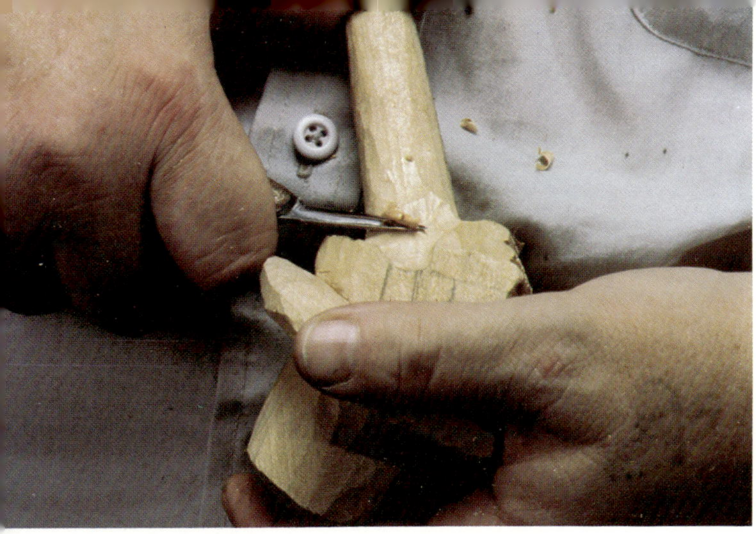

Clean up the gouge marks with a knife.

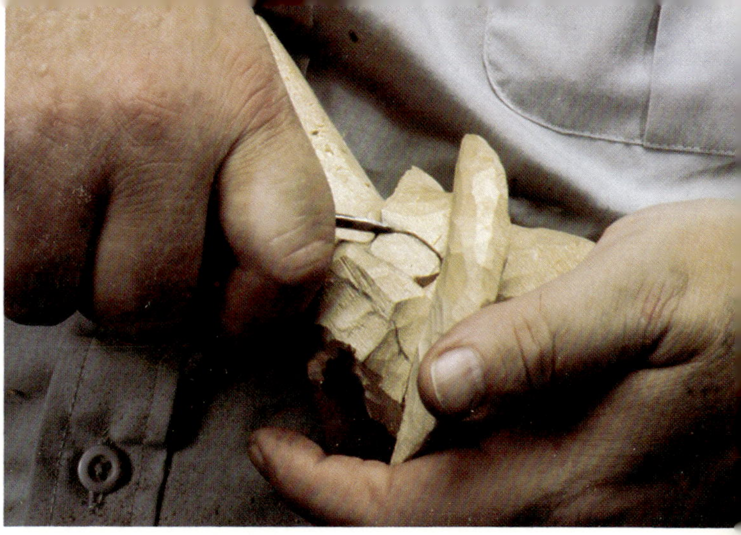

Cut a stop around the outside of the ear...

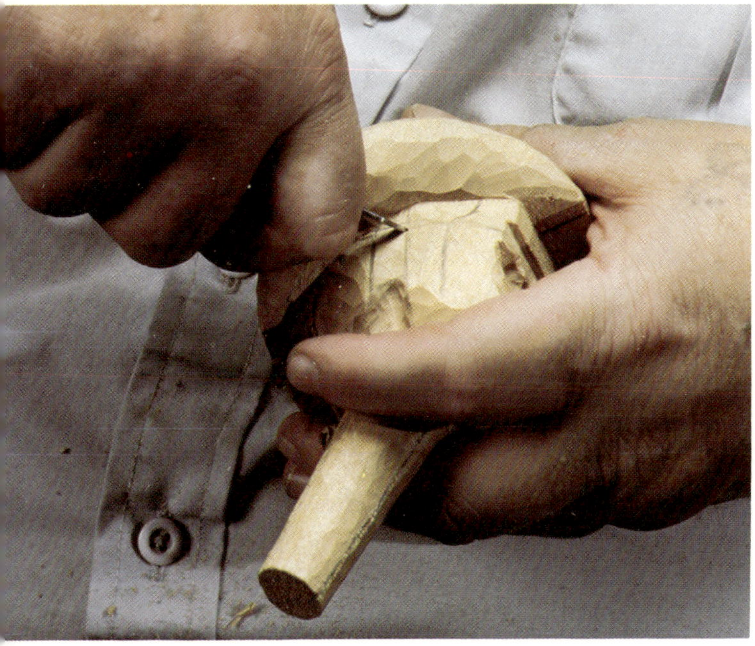

Notch the upper front corners of the ears with...

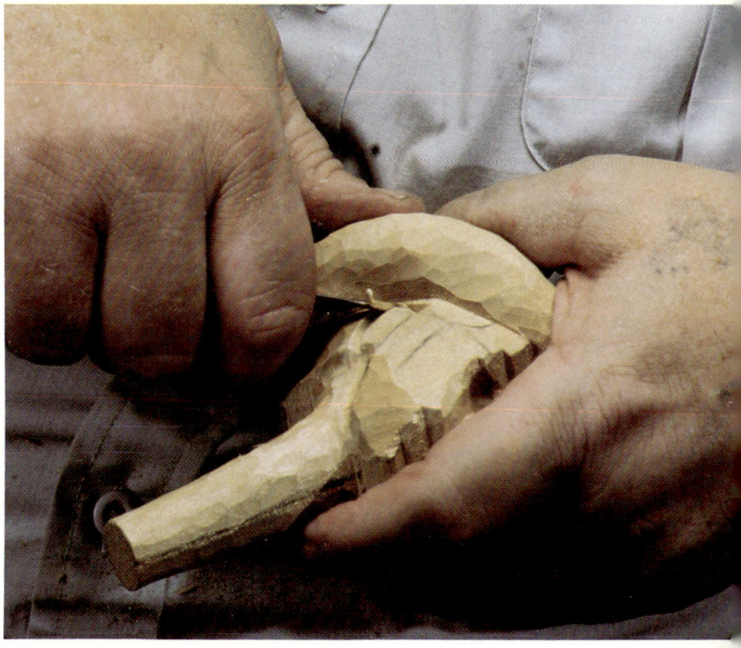

and trim back around it.

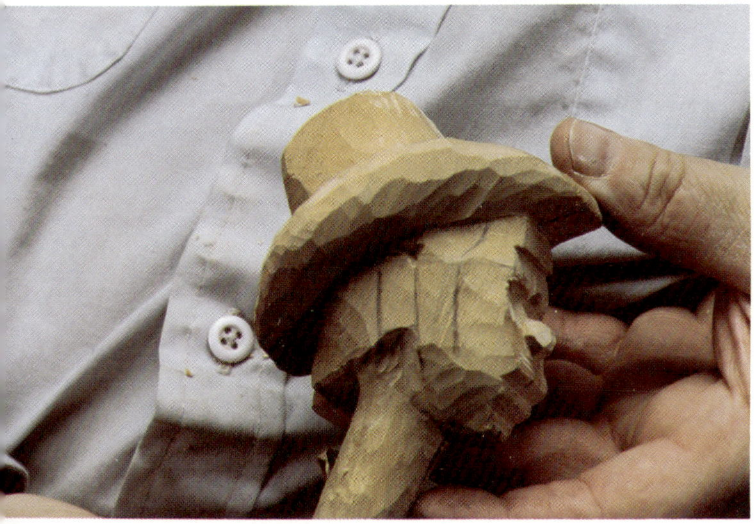

a little incised triangle.

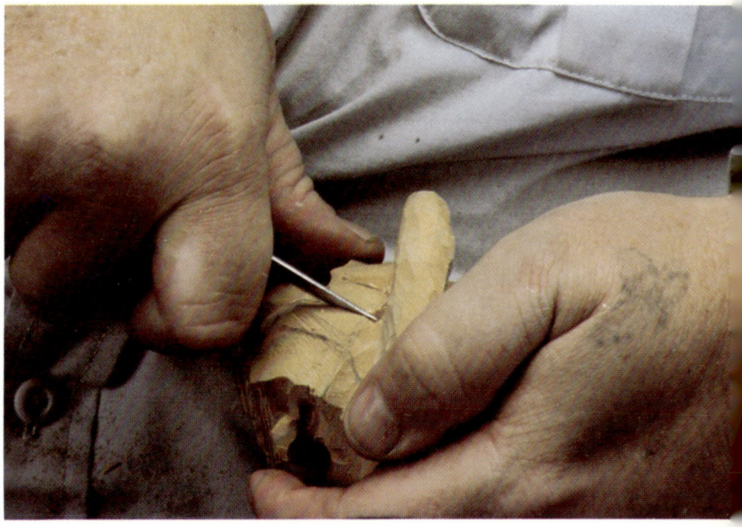

Cut a straight stop cut on the back edge of the sideburns.

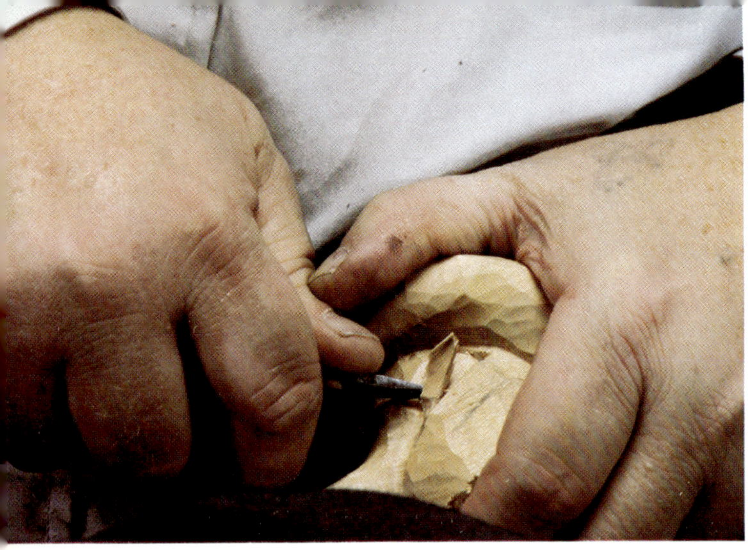

Come back to this stop with a slice of a knife, forming the angled surface of the ear.

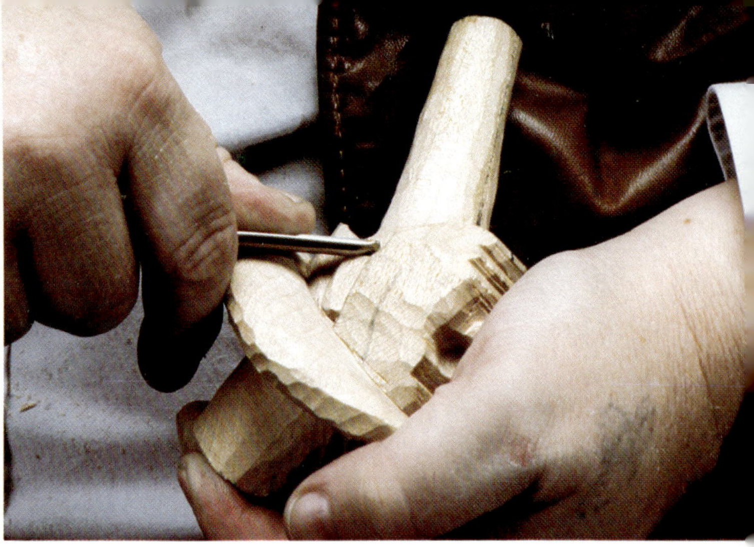

I could see that his left ear was a little lower, so I just clip it off.

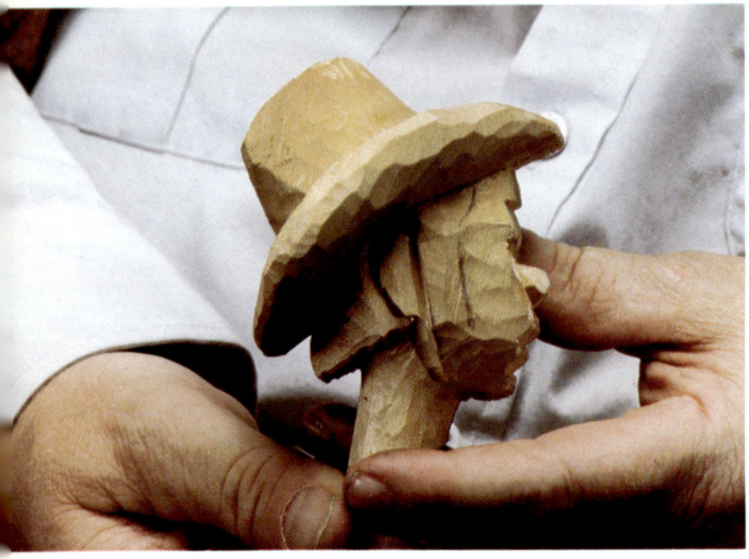

The overall shape of the ear is defined.

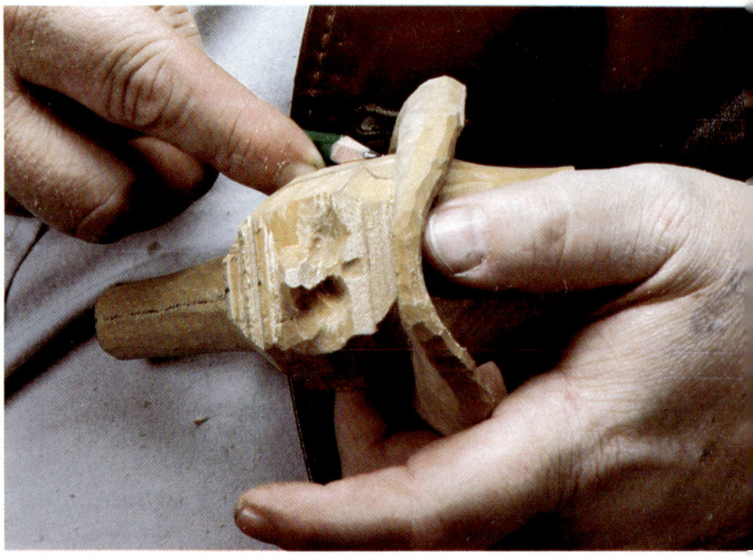

To gauge the length of the ears use a pencil. His right ear is a little long on top...

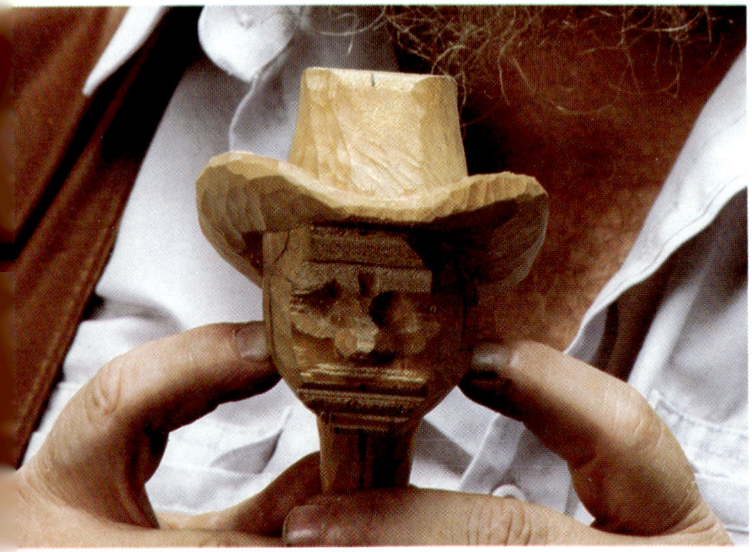

It is hard to see both ears at the same time, so a trick I use is to put my fingernails just below the ears and look at it straight on. This helps the visual alignment of the ears.

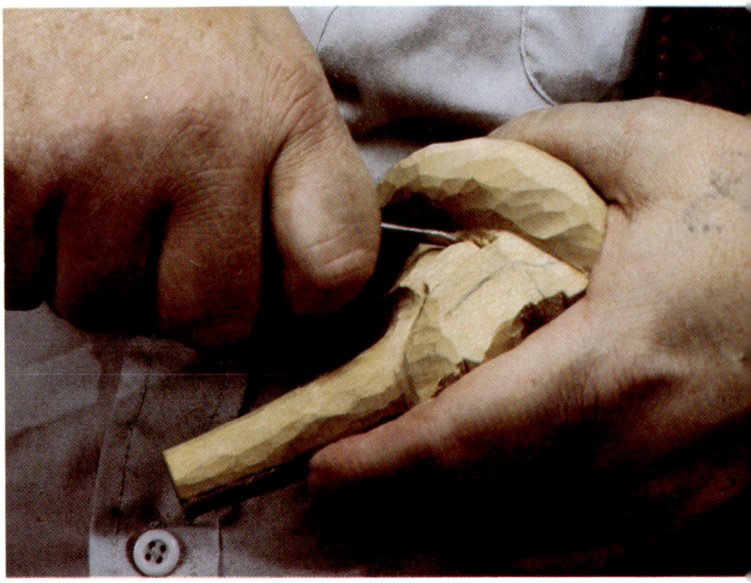

so I'll trim it down.

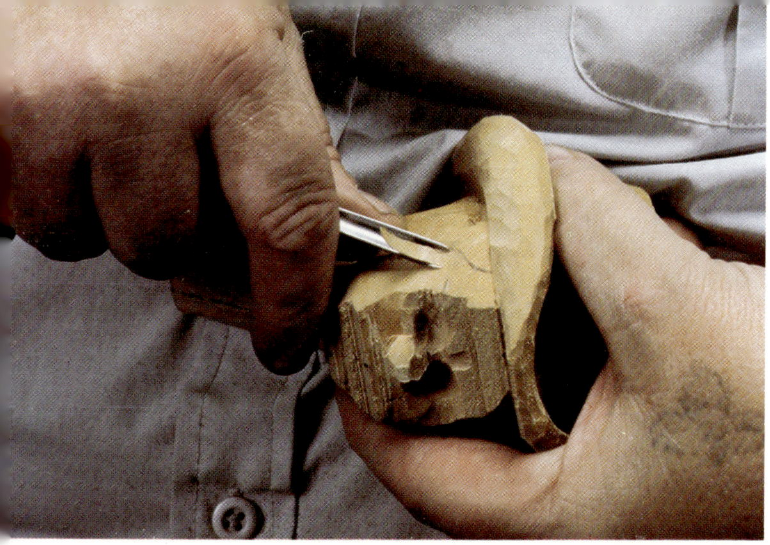

When the ears are balanced, follow the front edge of the sideburn with a gouge. Don't cut a stop first, because you don't want a strong edge.

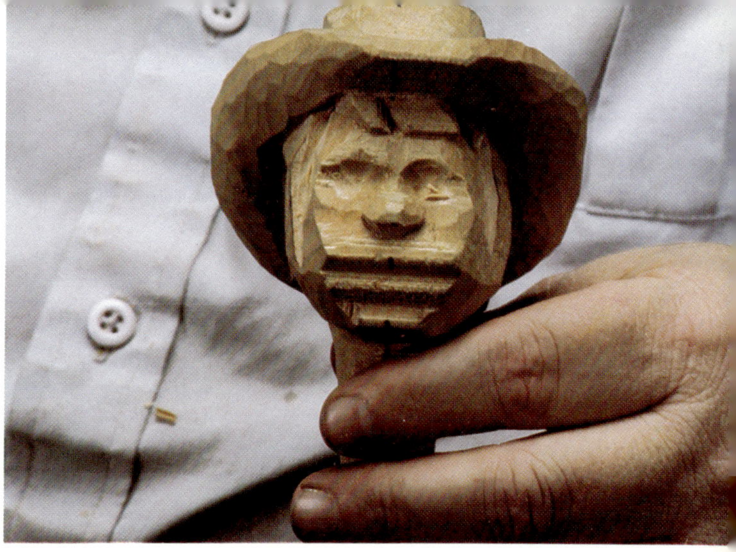

Progress so far.

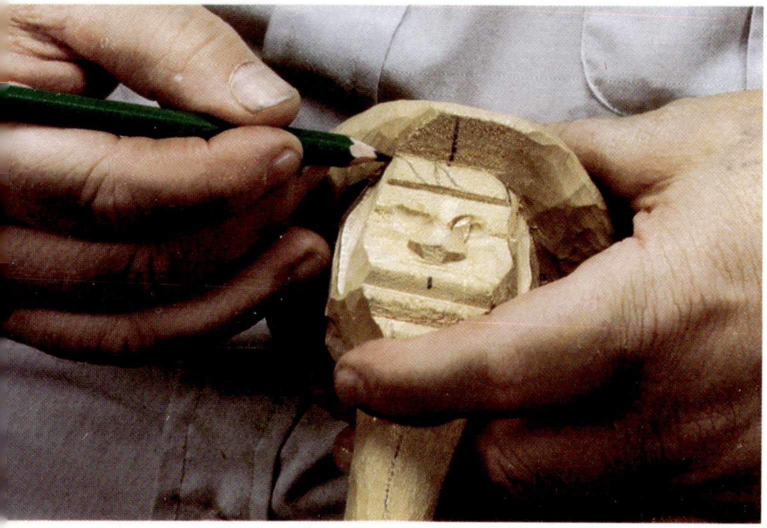

Mark the bangs hanging from under the front of the hat. I think I'll get the effect I want with a couple of swigs of hair hanging out.

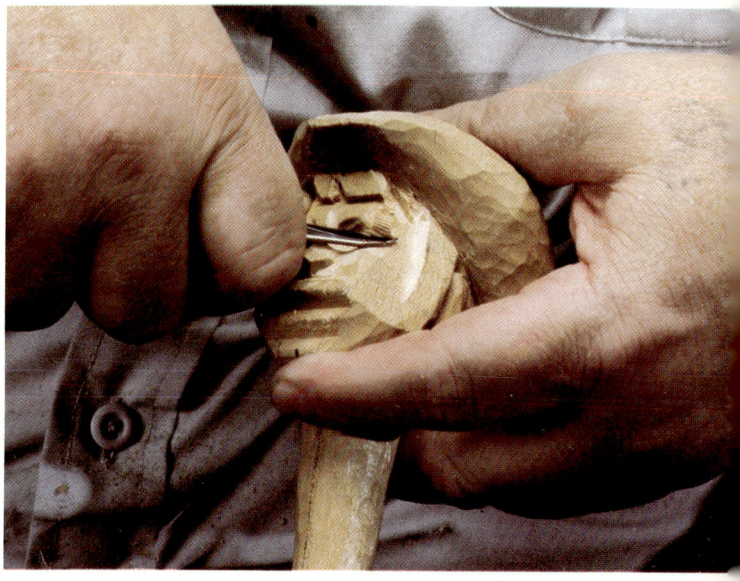

Shape the brow and cheek areas.

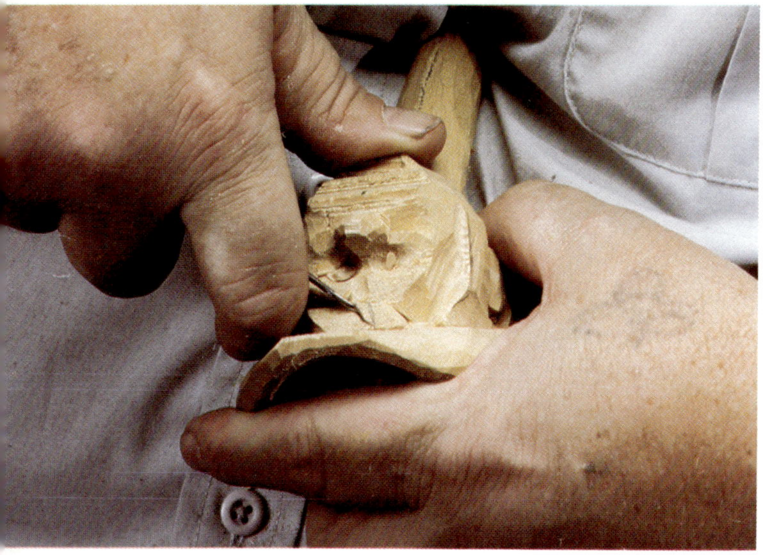

Use a knife to cut these out.

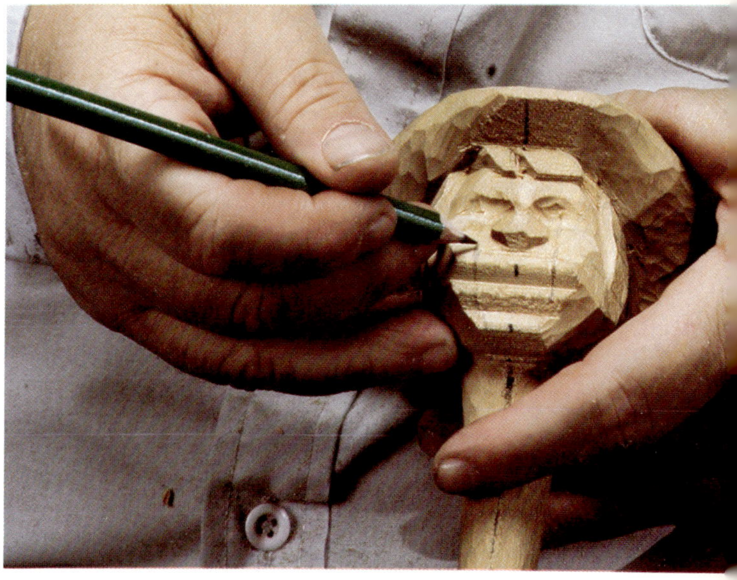

Define the mouth. As a rule of thumb, the corners of the mouth are parallel to the pupils of the eye. Draw the lines.

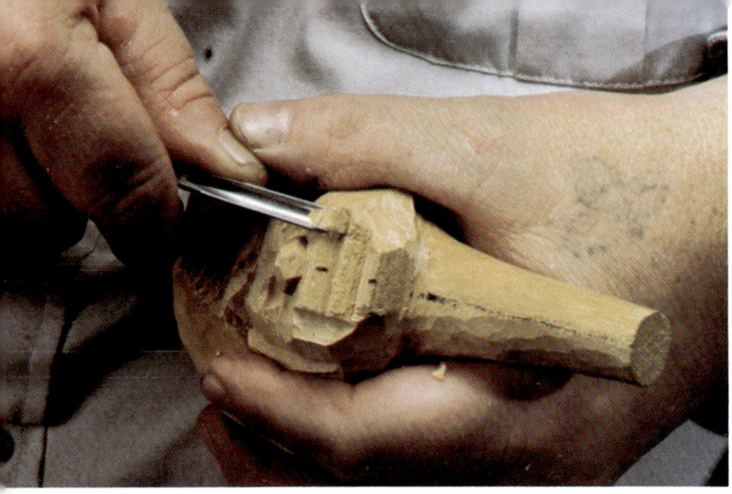

With a gouge, come down from beside the nose to the corner of the mouth.

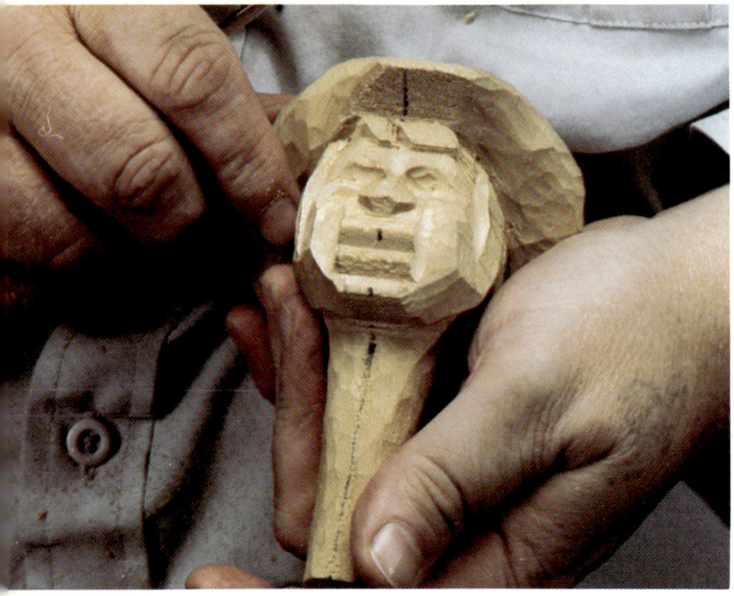

You can see how the gouge line gives the mouth its width and adds character to the face. When trying to make a face seem younger, as we are here, the gouge is generally better than the knife and should be used more.

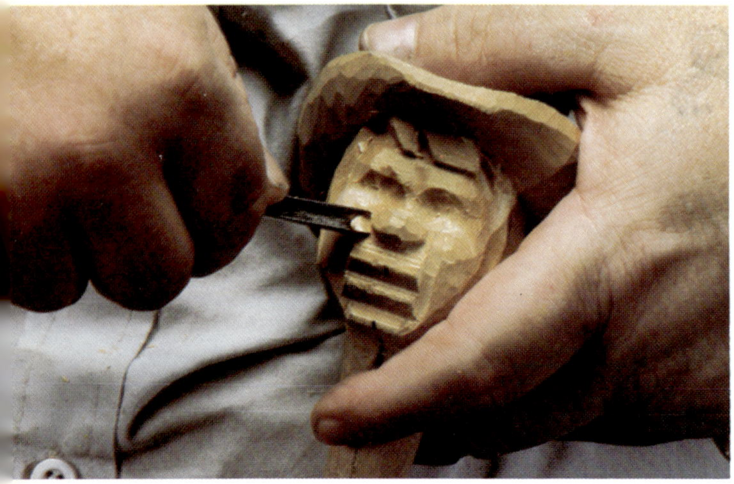

Continue the line into the nose to define the shape of the lip and cheek.

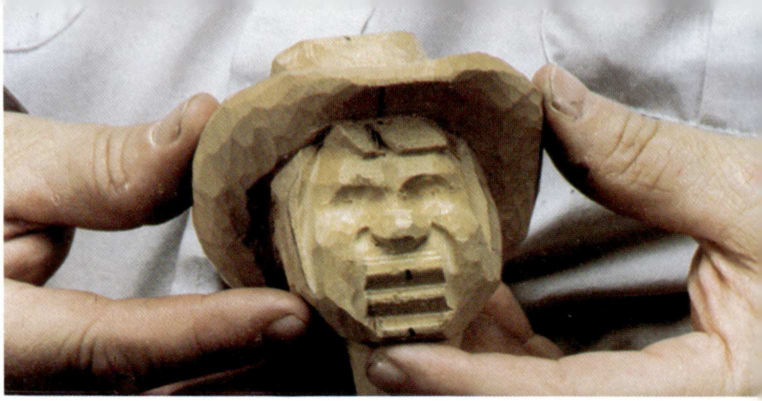

This is the result.

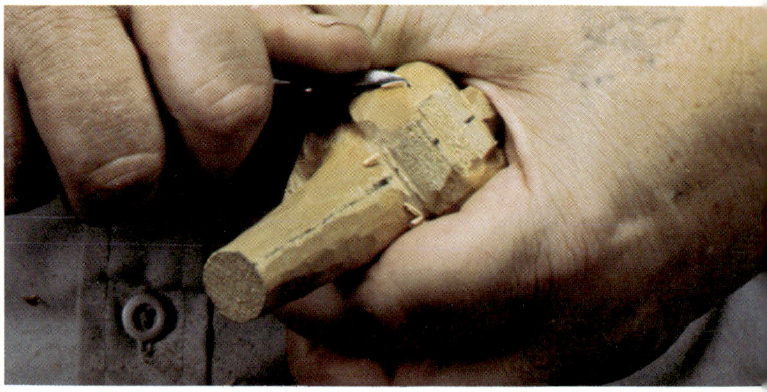

Round off the face and cheek.

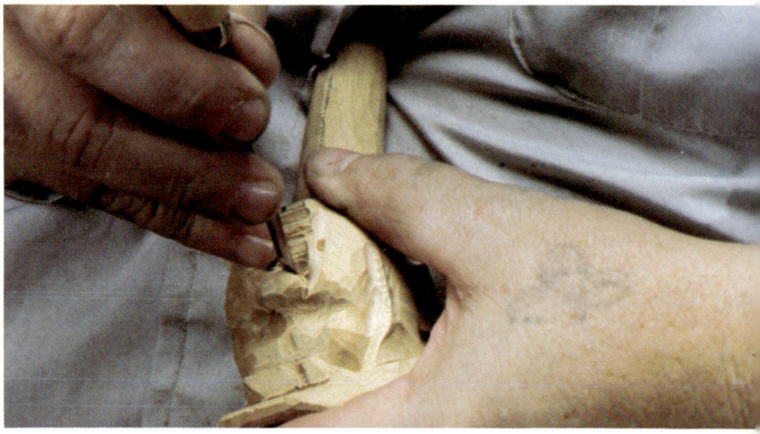

The nostrils are formed with a small flat gouge. Go from the front of the nose toward the lip, pushing gently.

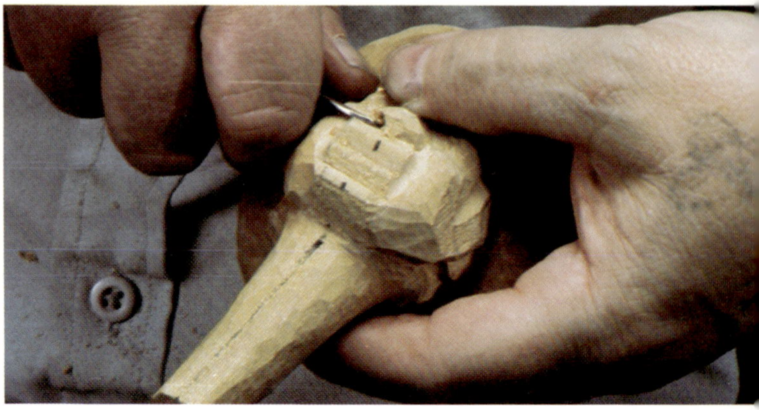

Cut off the shaving with a knife.

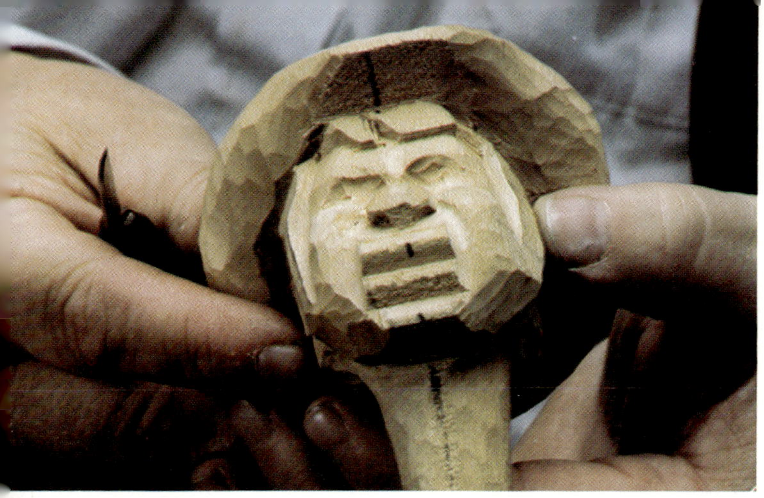

The nostrils.

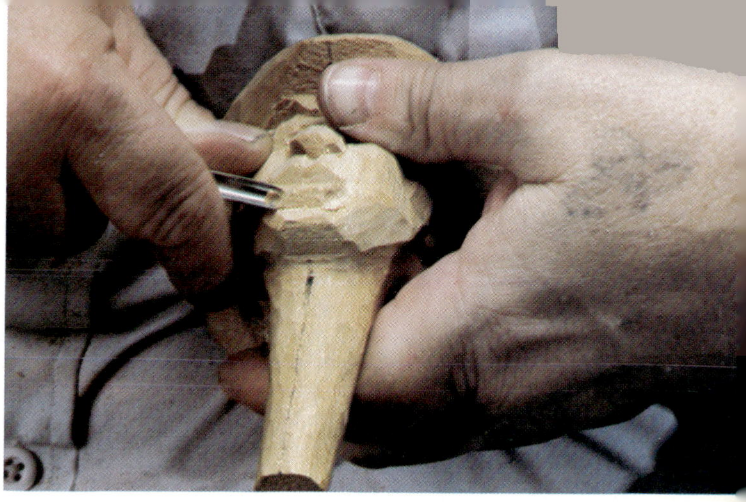

Use a gouge to form the groove under the bottom lip.

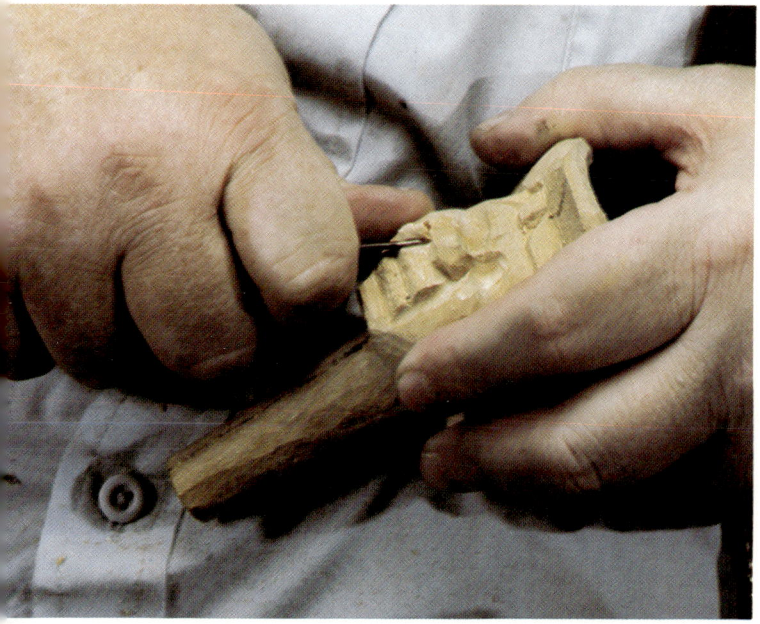

Trim the upper lip with the knife.

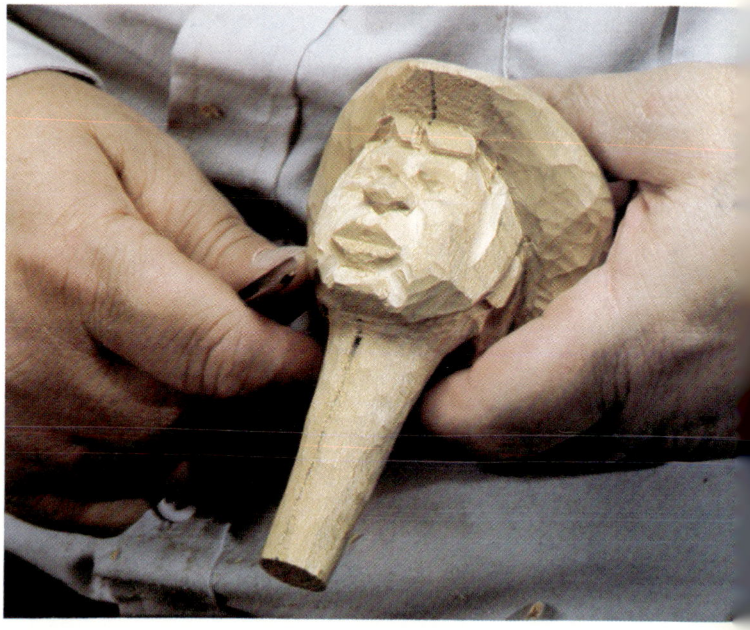

Continue with the gouge on either side of the chin to bring it out.

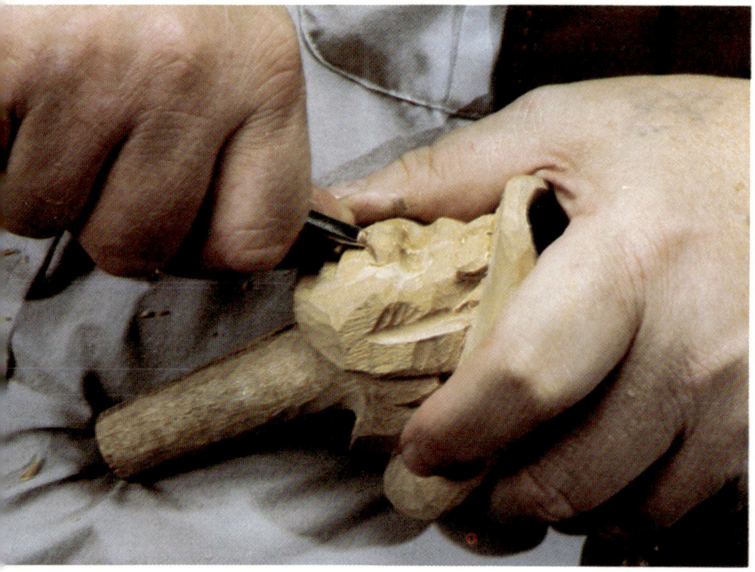

With a gouge, carve the "fairy's fingerprint" between the upper lip and the nose.

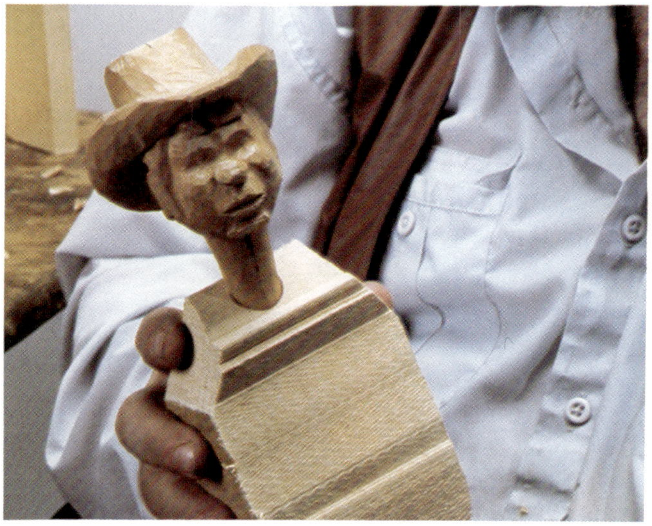

With the head almost finished we can begin to fit it to the body. Right now the neck is much too long. Mark the neck so we will know how deeply it goes into the body.

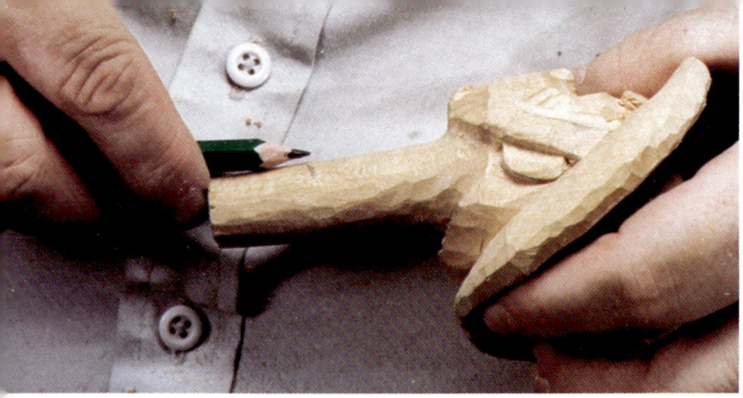

Use a pencil as a depth gauge.

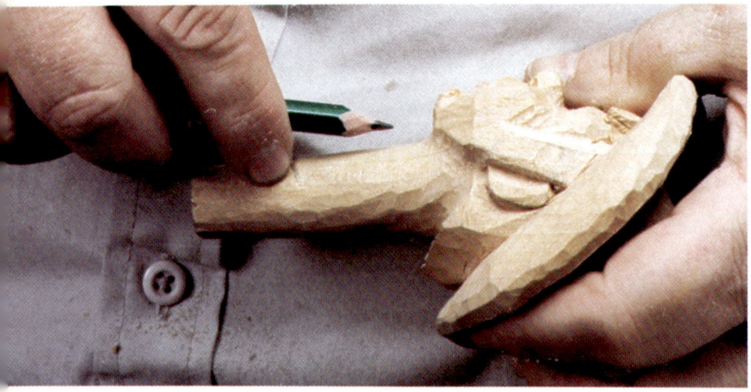

By moving it up the neck you can determine how much neck will show, and where to cut the neck.

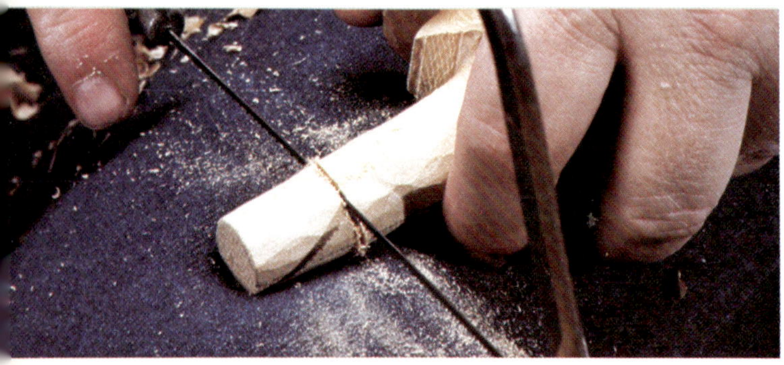

Cut the neck with a coping saw.

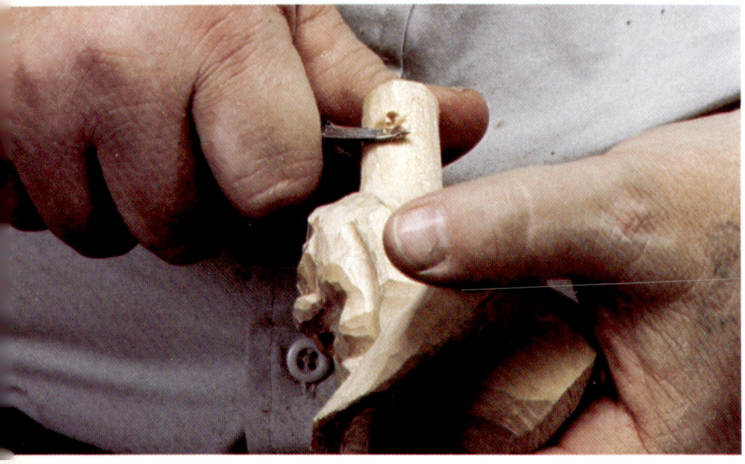

With its new length we need to refit the neck in the hole. First trim it down. Go around and around to keep the roundness of the neck.

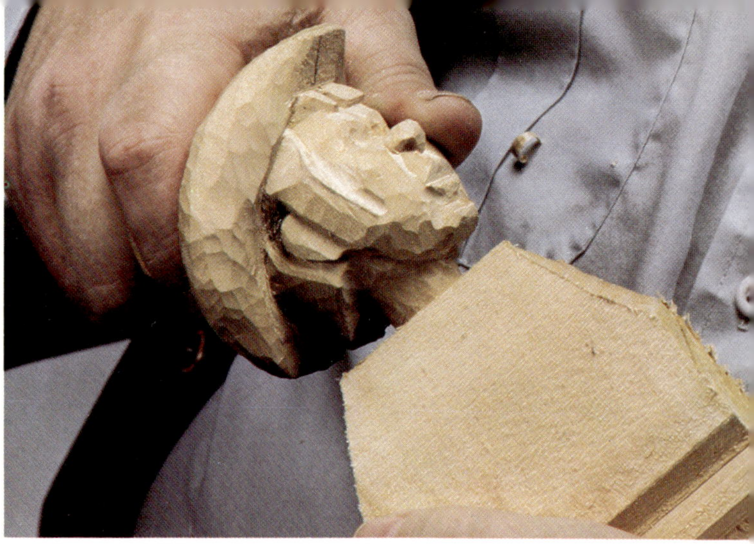

Put the head in the hole and rotate it with some pressure, but not enough to break the hat! Remove the head and as before look for shiny places. These are high spots and need to be trimmed.

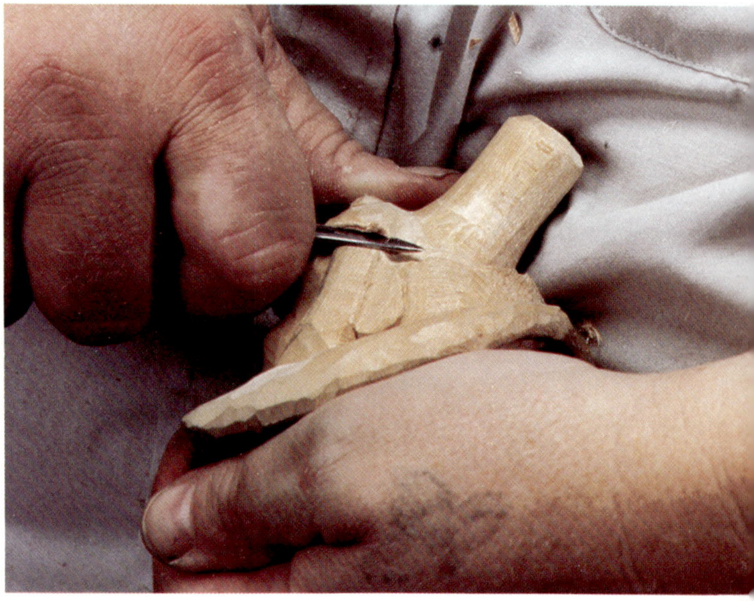

The face needs a little trimming for proportionality. Begin with the sideburns.

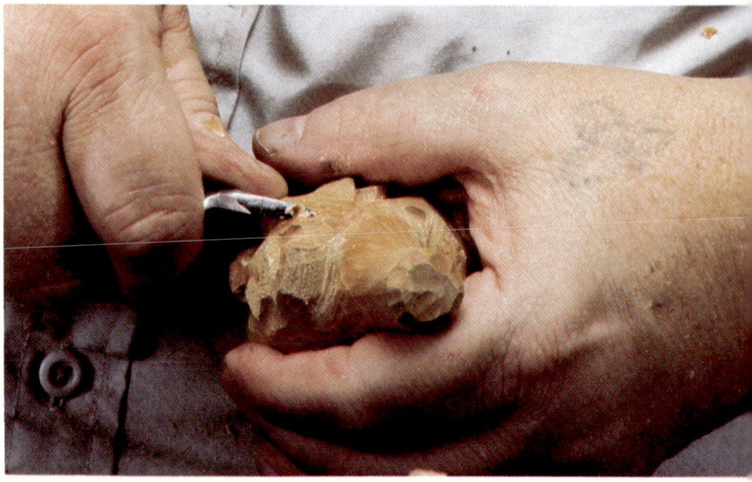

And continue around the face.

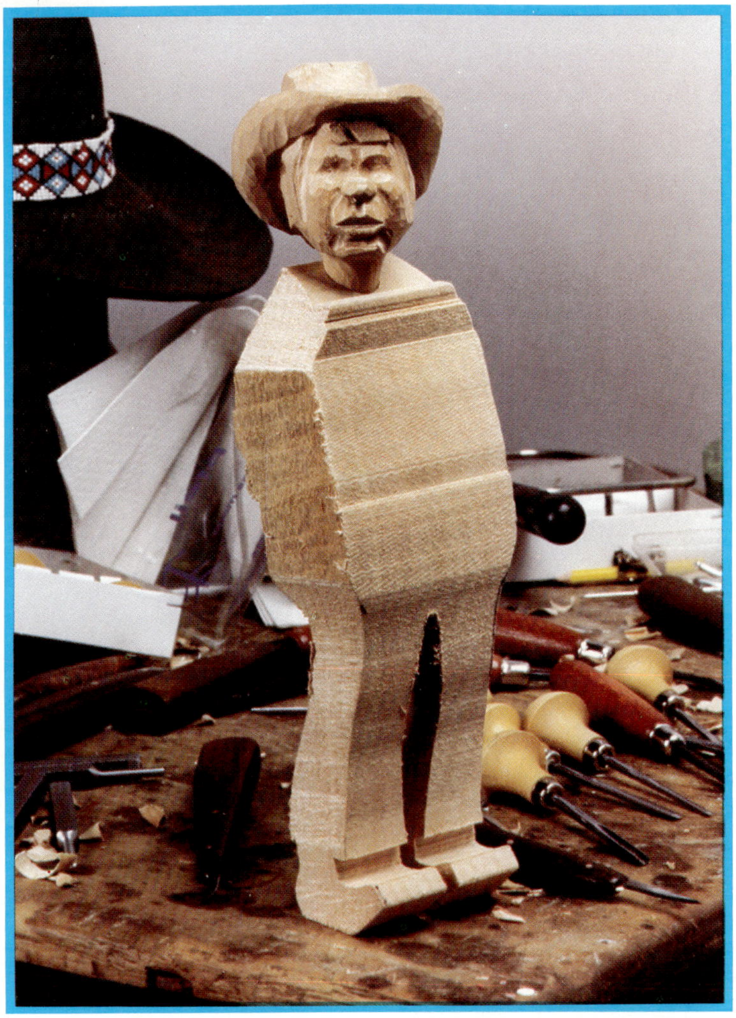

When drawing the body on the wood, it is good to have the head in place to maintain the proper proportions.

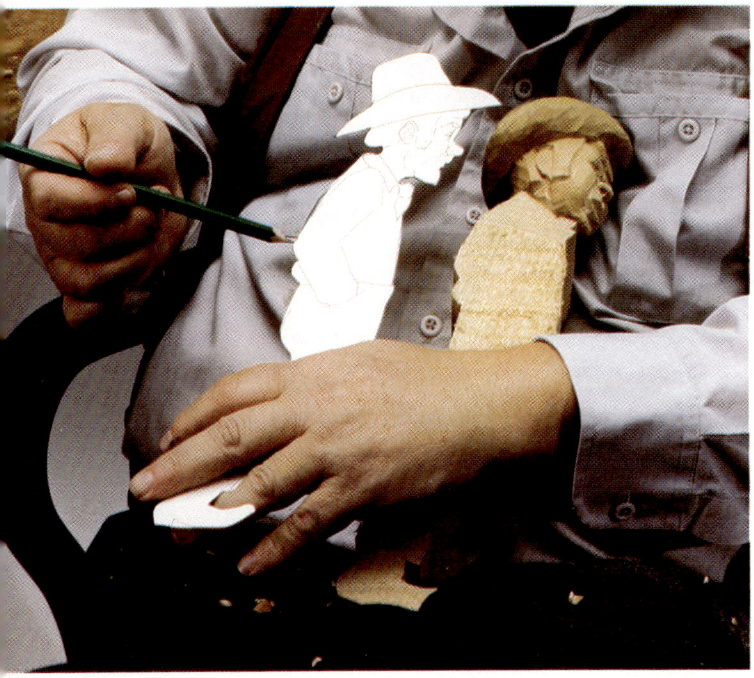

Reference to the pattern helps keep things in perspective. If you have a copier you can make two or three copies and actually cut out the piece you need and lay it on the carving to draw it in.

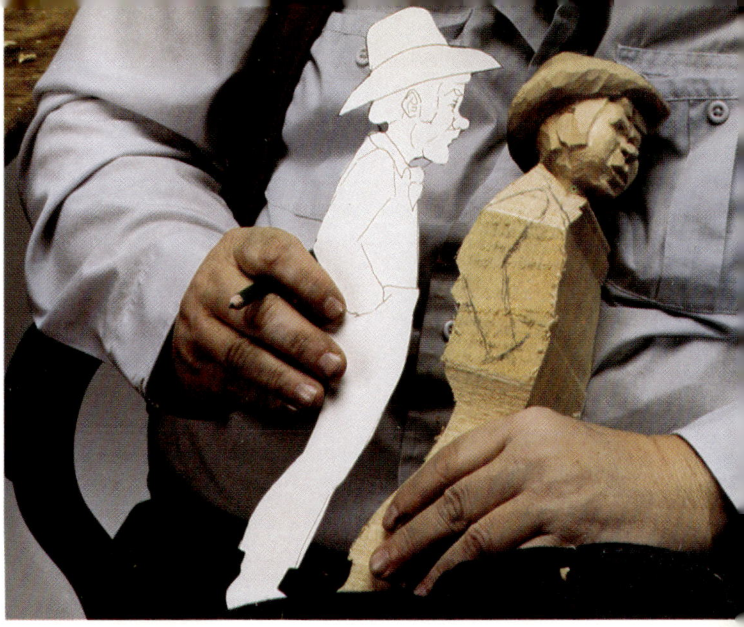

Begin on the side...

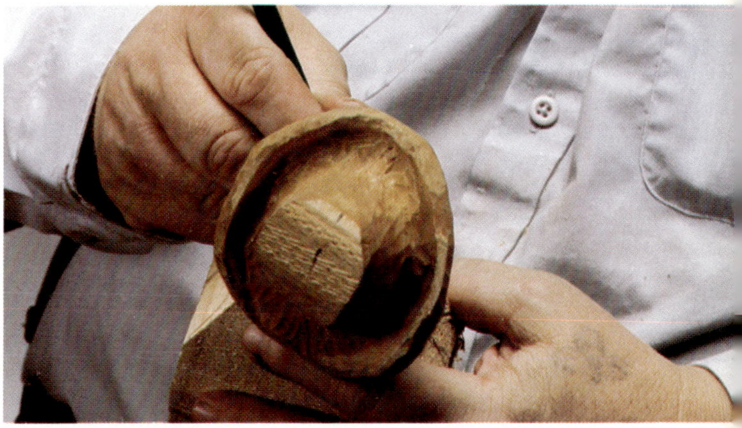

and continue to draw in details...

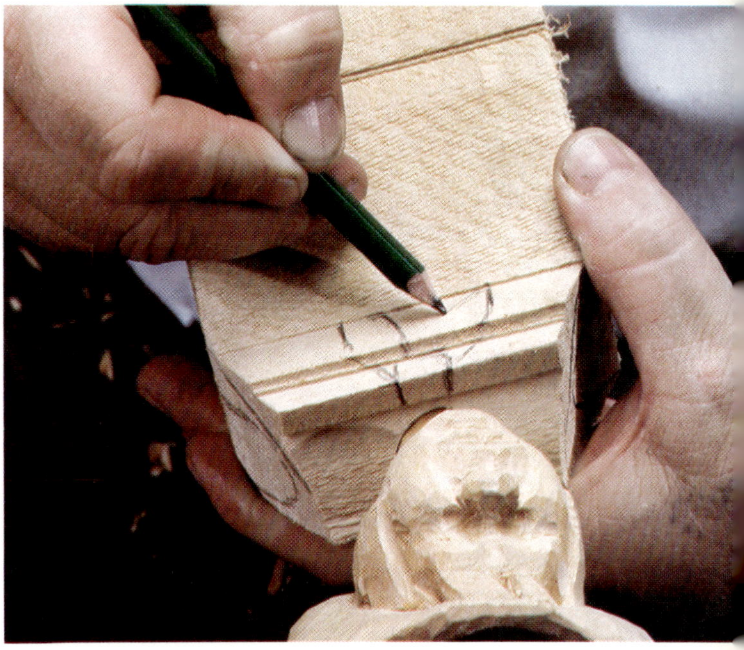

like the neckerchief. Don't make the two sides of the neckerchief the same or symmetrical.

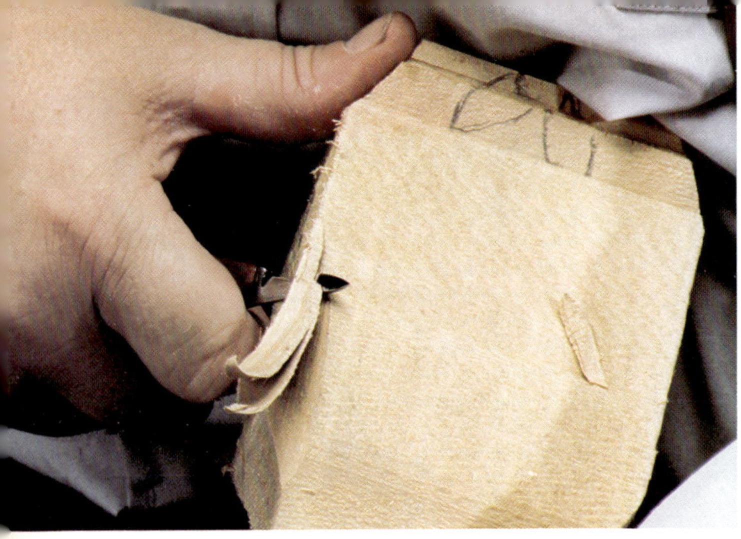

Use a knife to knock off the corners.

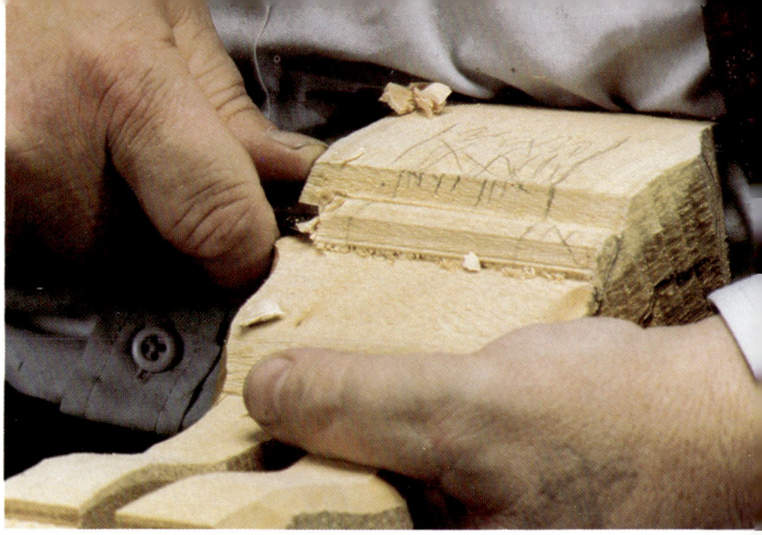

The ridge below the arms is the bloused part of the shirt. Remove the excess wood from behind the arms, using a gouge.

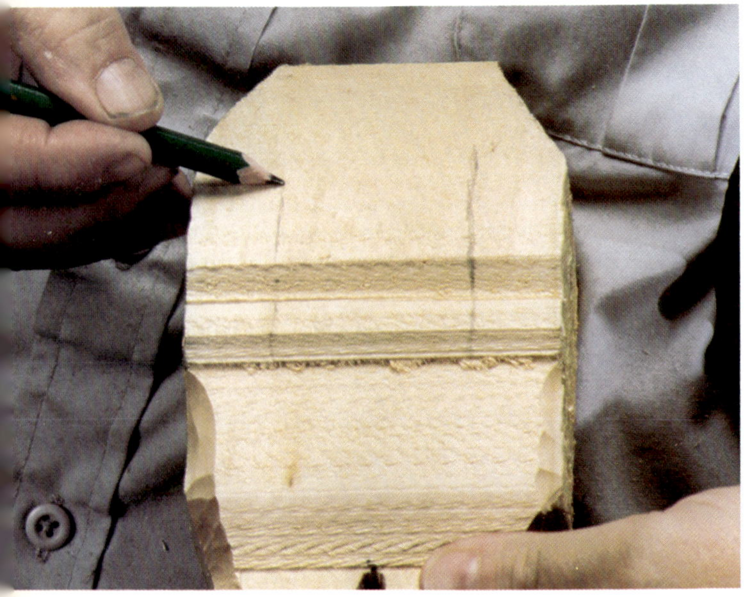

Mark the back of the arms...

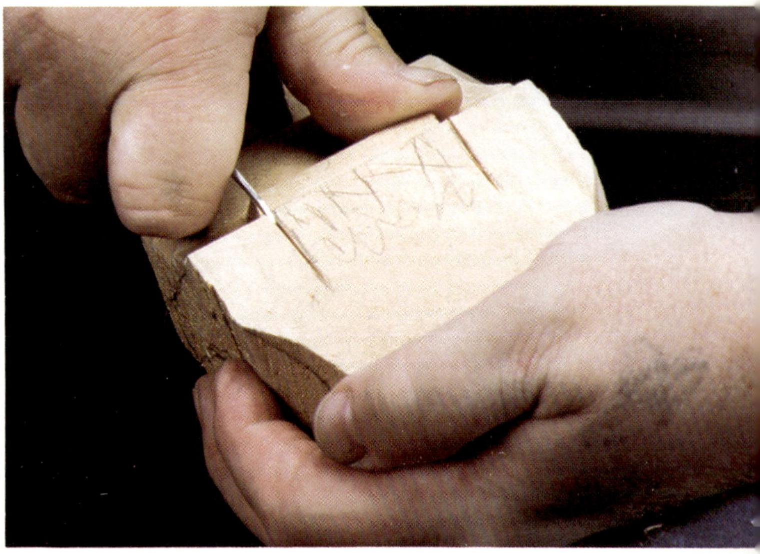

Cut stops in the back lines of the arms...

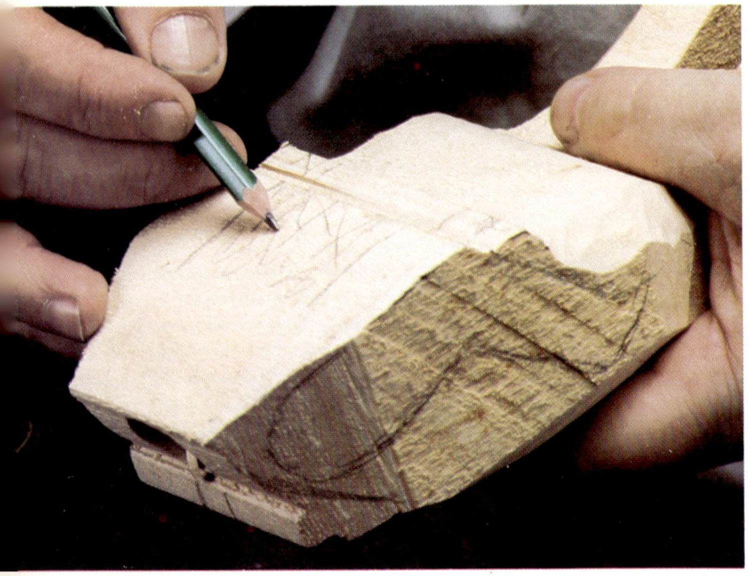

and the space between them to be removed.

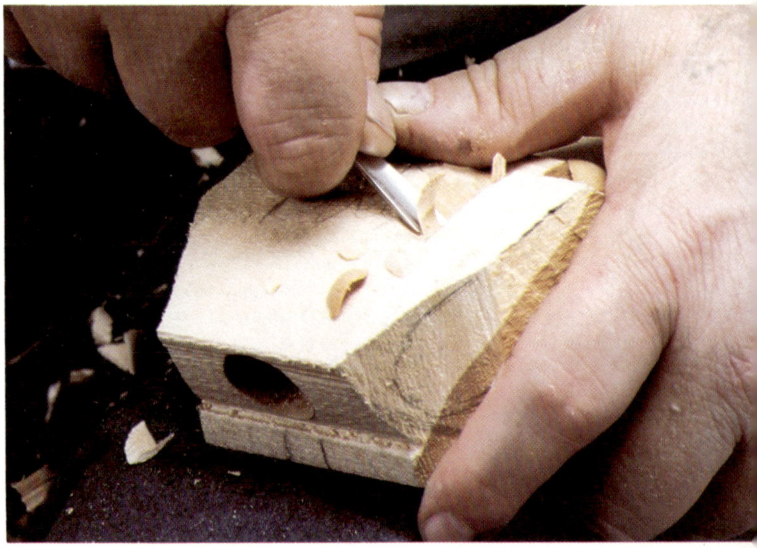

and remove the excess between them. Begin by cutting into the stops with a gouge.

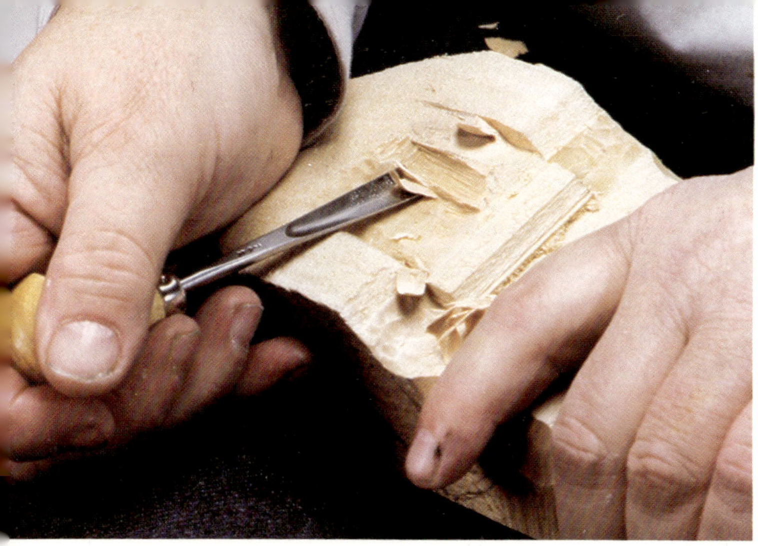

Then remove the large area between.

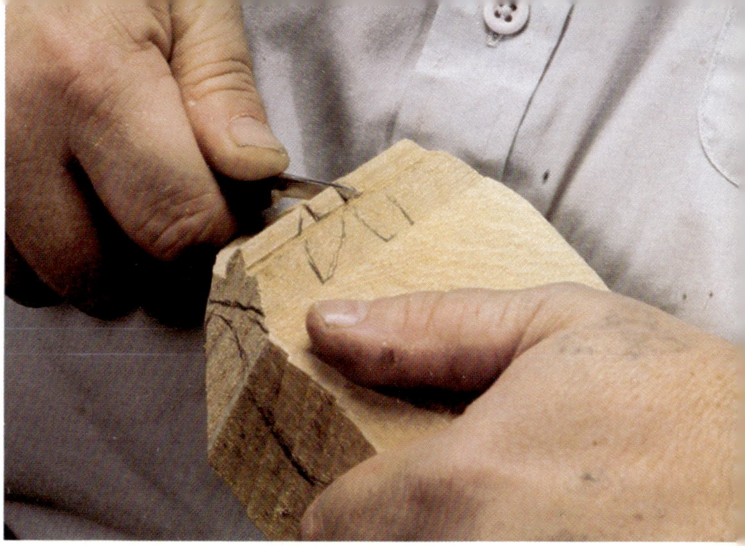

In the front, cut a stop on both sides of the knot of the neckerchief.

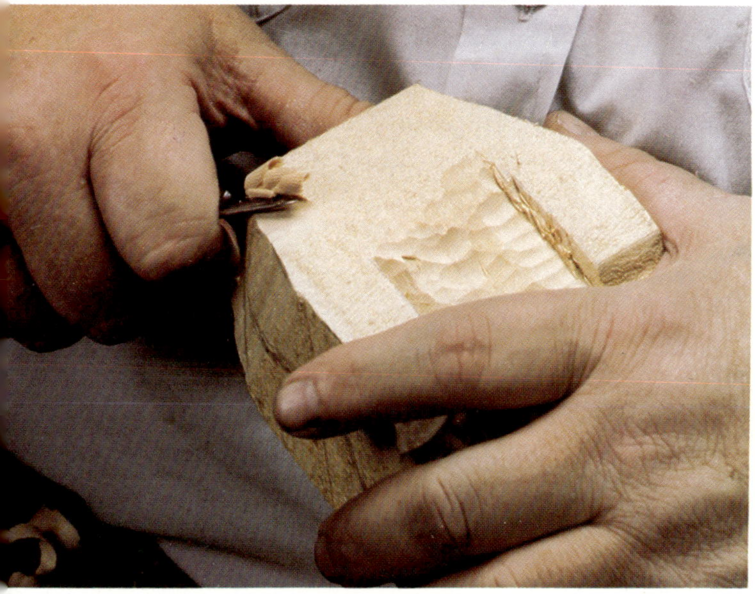

Trim the shoulders up to the neck.

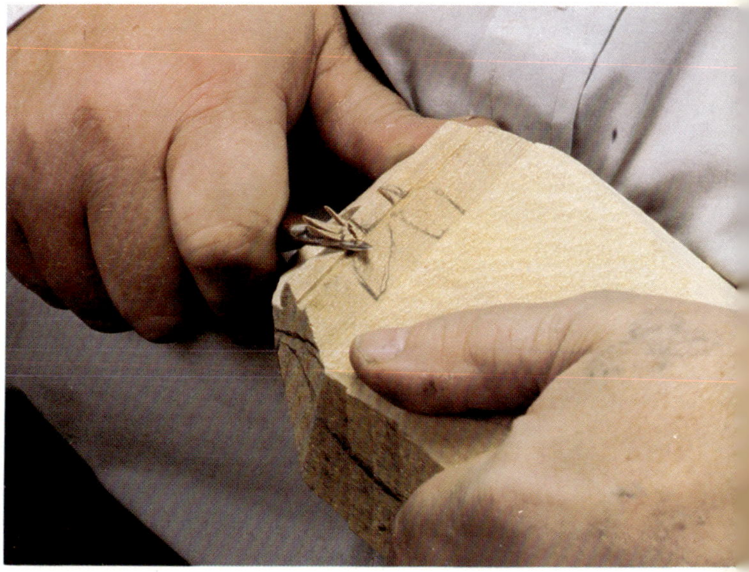

Cut back into it from the sides.

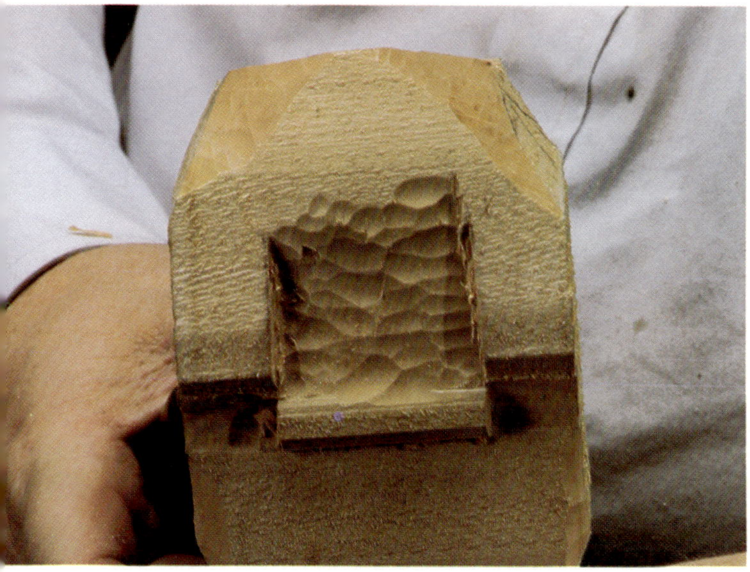

The back view so far.

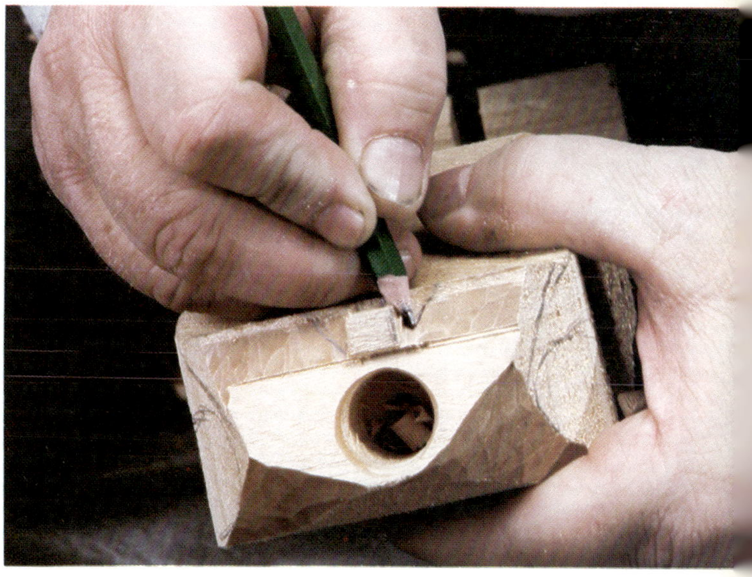

Redraw the line of the neckerchief.

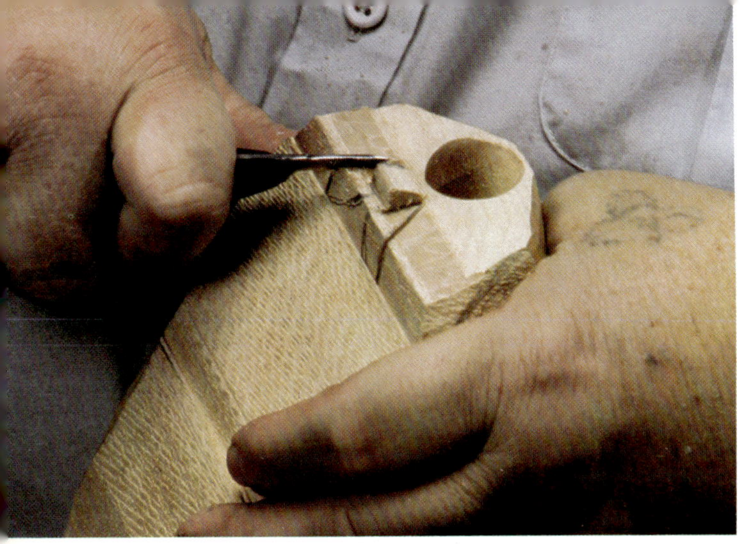

Cut stops down the edges of the neckerchief...

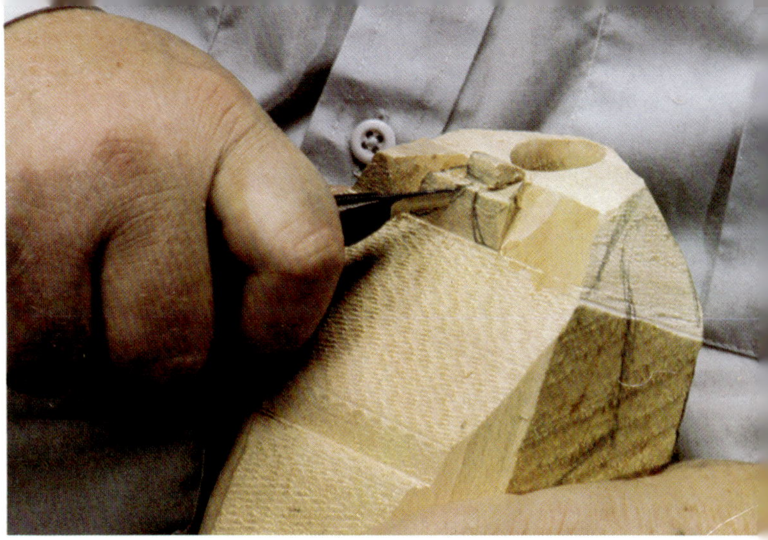

Cut stops on inside lines of the neckerchief.

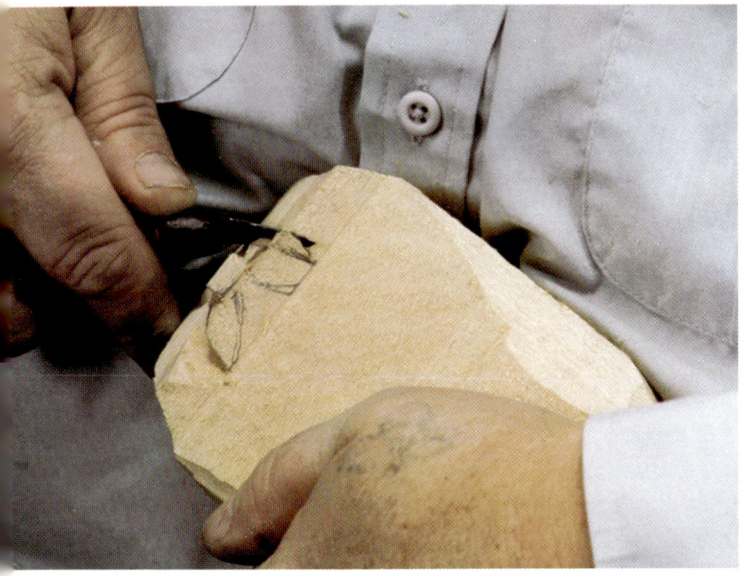

and trim back to it from the shoulder.

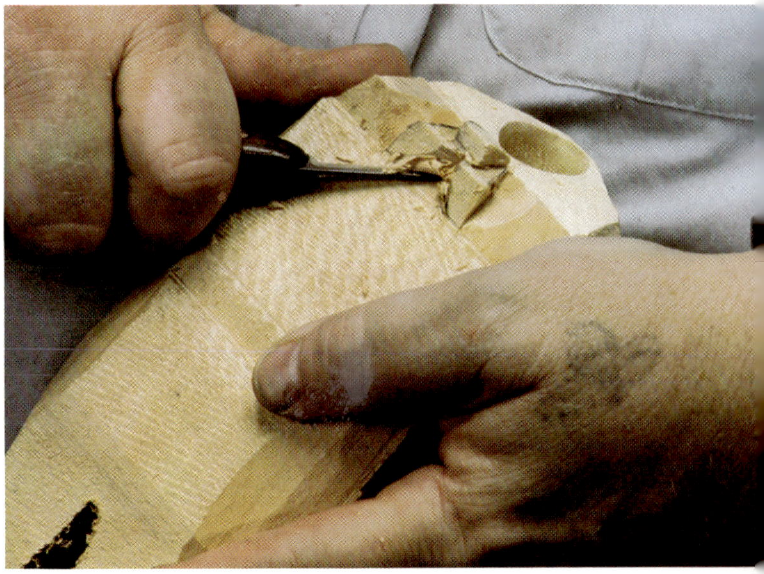

Clean out the space in between.

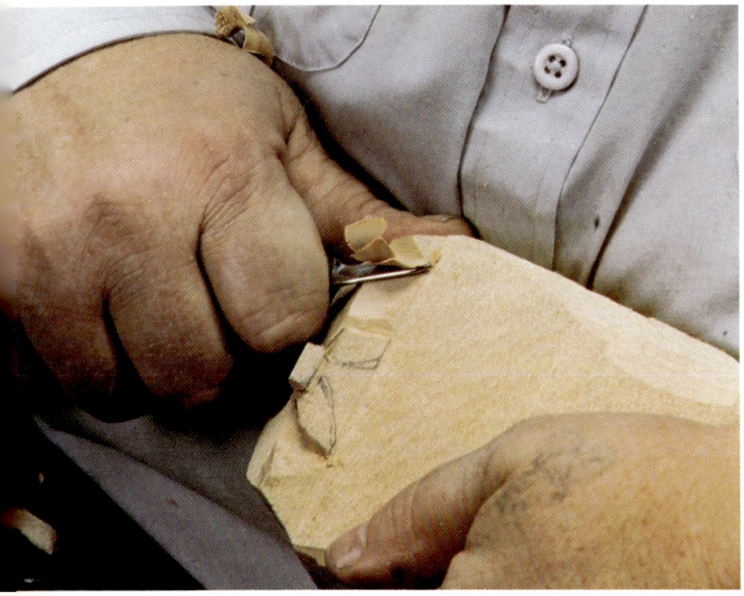

Trim the shoulder moving out from the neckerchief.

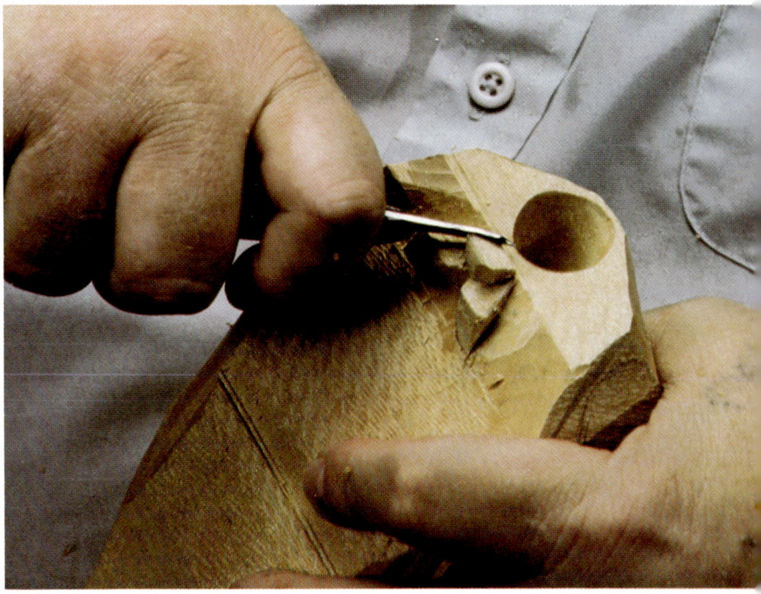

Round off the neckerchief to make it more realistic.

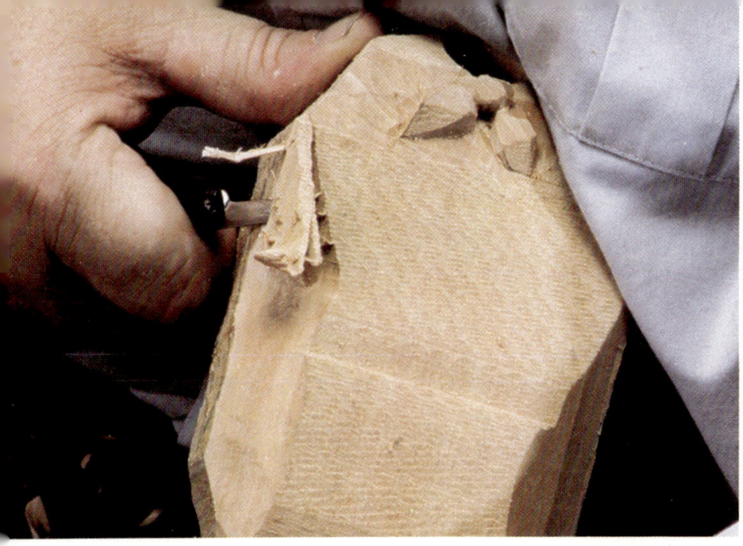

Knock off the edge of the body in front of the arms.

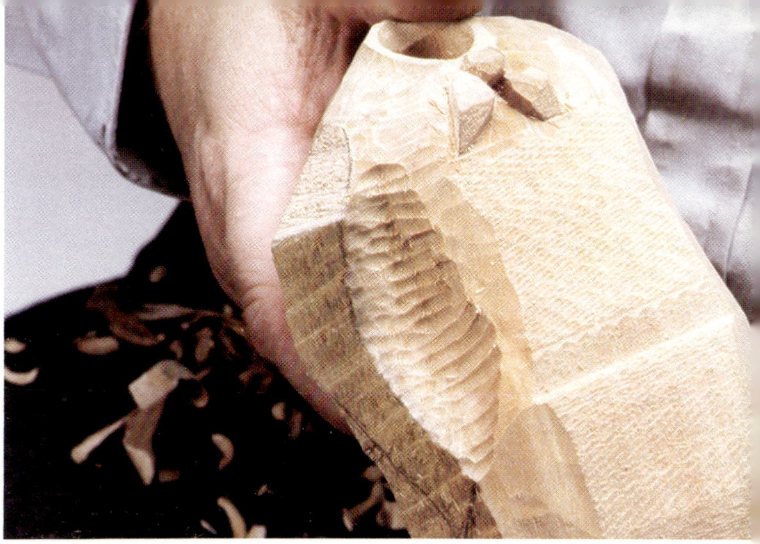

This is the effect of this gouging. Do the same on the other side.

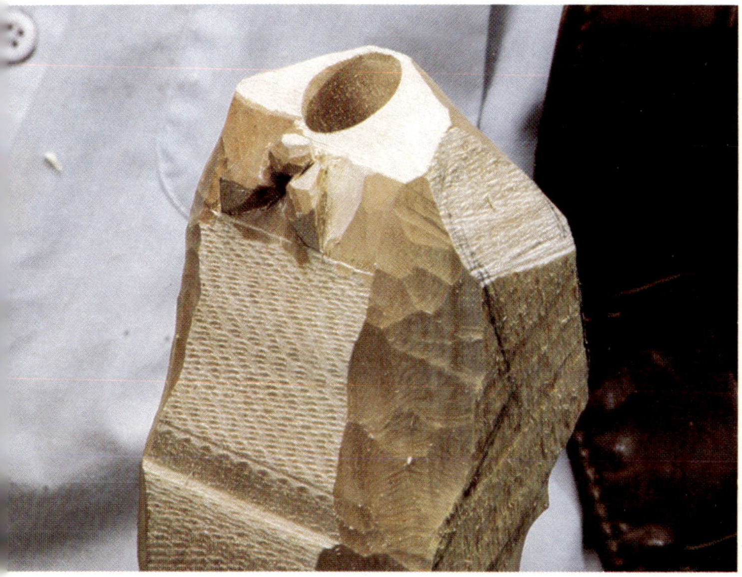

The upper body so far.

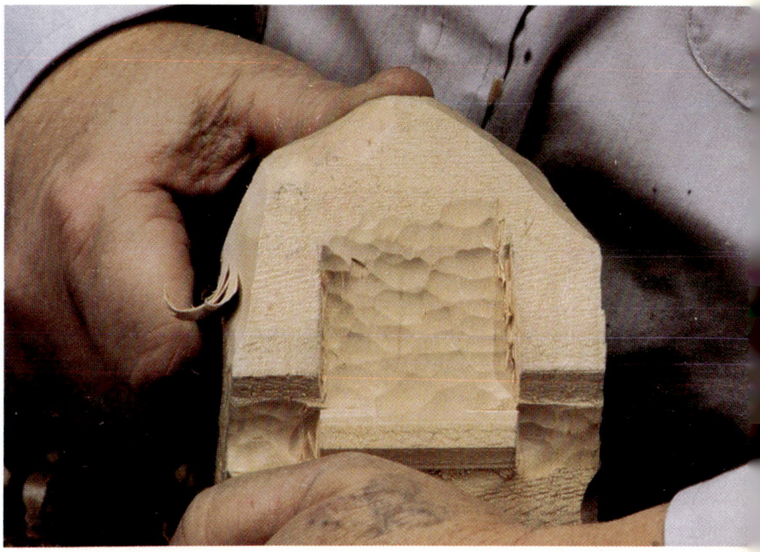

The shoulders are out of balance, so I'll carve a straight line from the elbow to the shoulder.

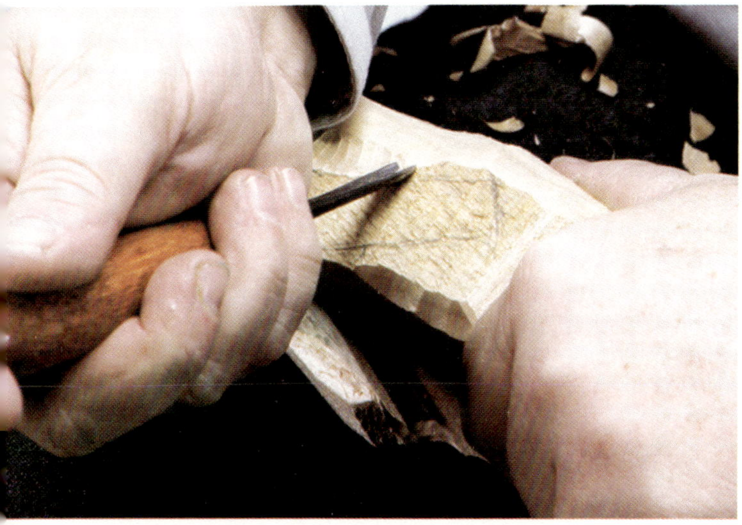

Round the area in front of the arm using a chisel and go against the grain. Notice that the thumb of my left hand is hidden, and the stroke is short and curved to reduce the threat of injury.

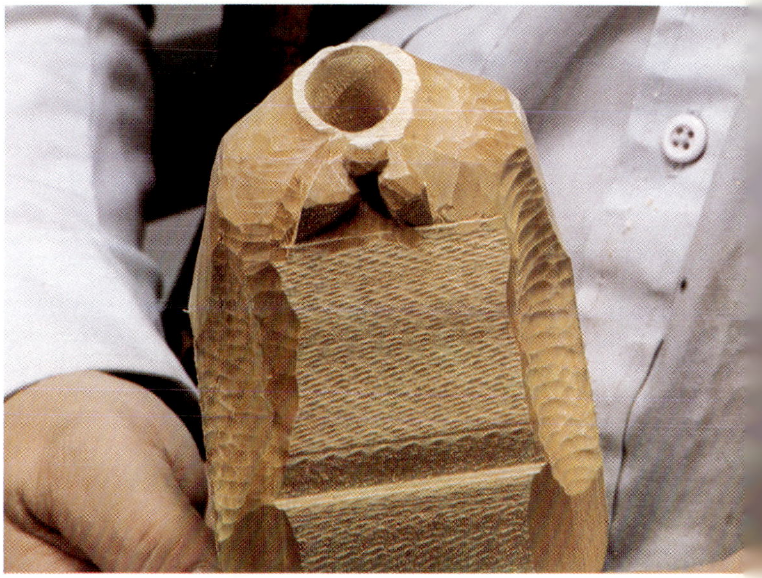

This brings them into symmetry.

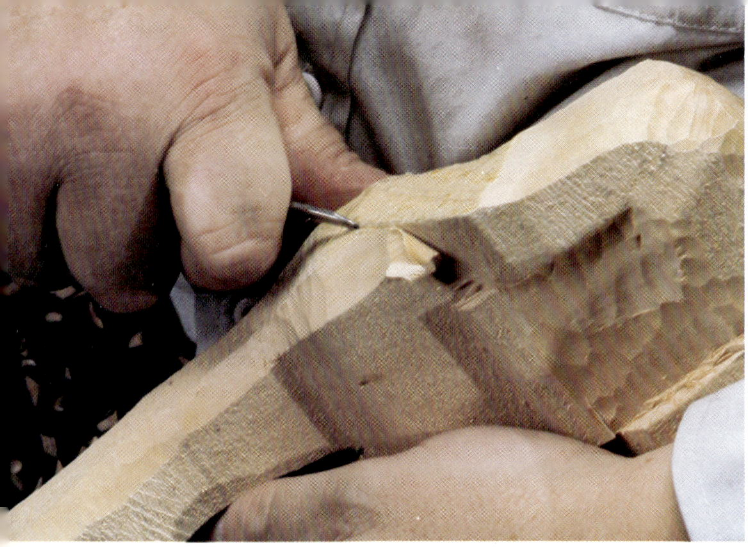

We need to define the line of the forearm as it goes into the trousers. Cut a stop along the line.

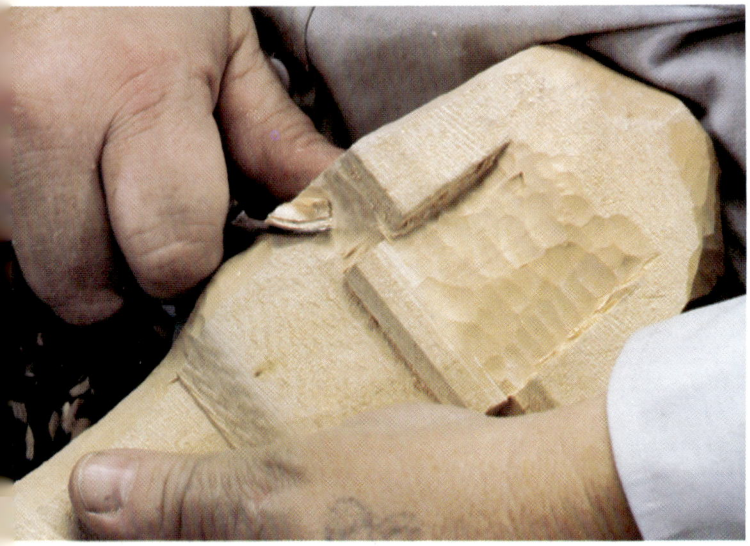

Cut back to it. Continue this process until you get the...

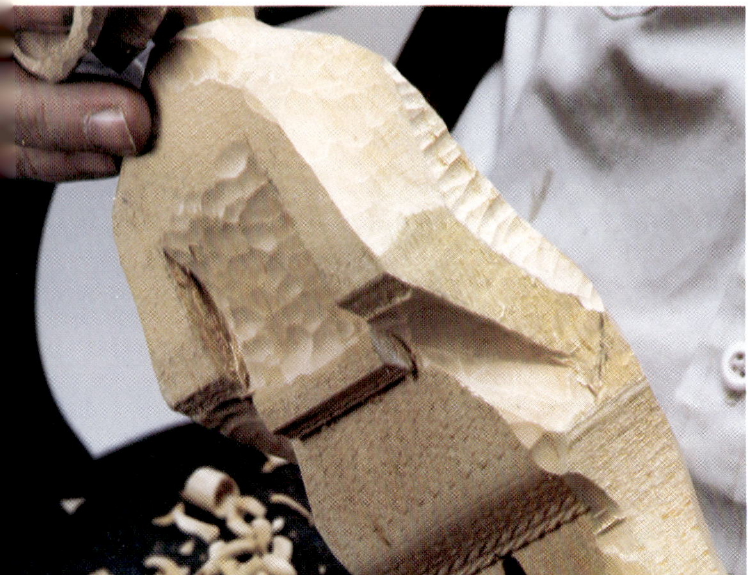

shape you want.

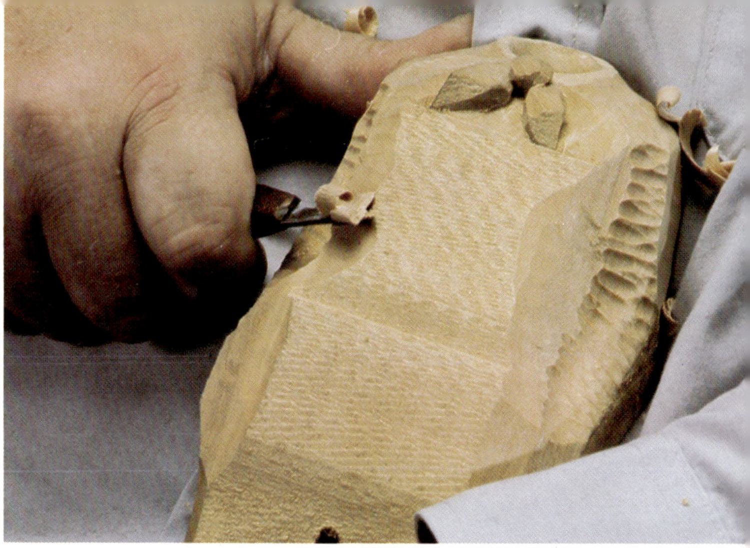

Round up the front corners of the shirt.

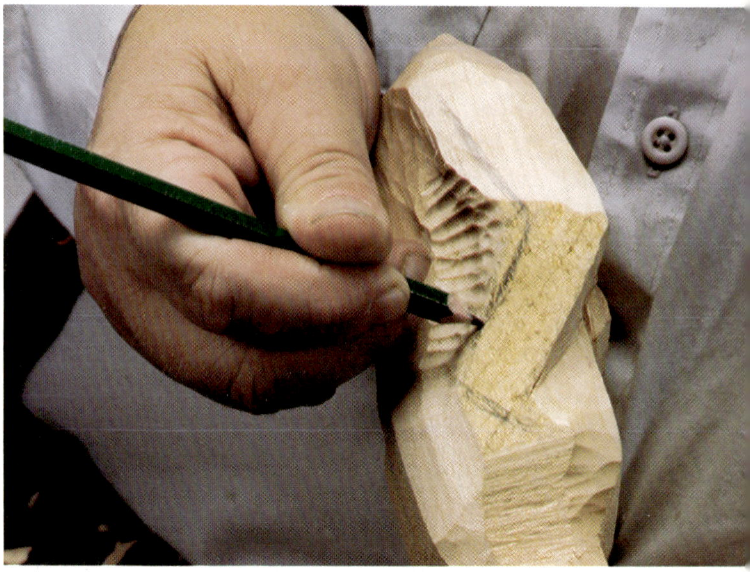

Draw in the thickness of the arms.

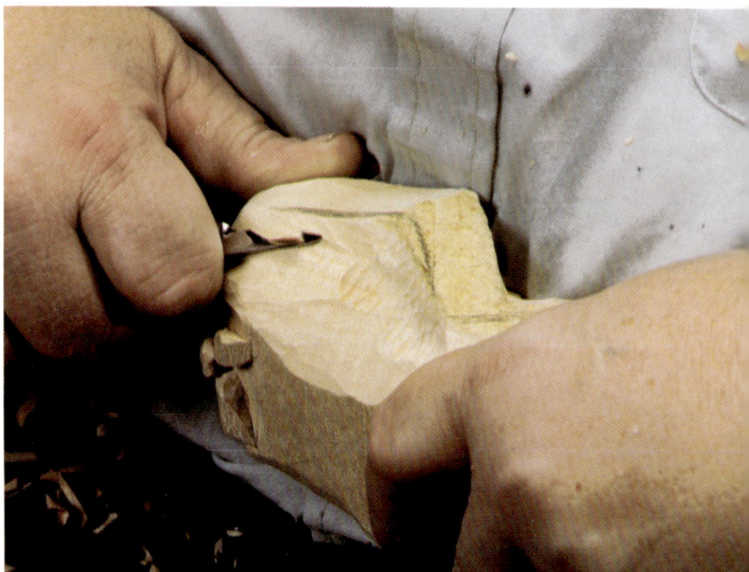

Trim away the excess with a knife and

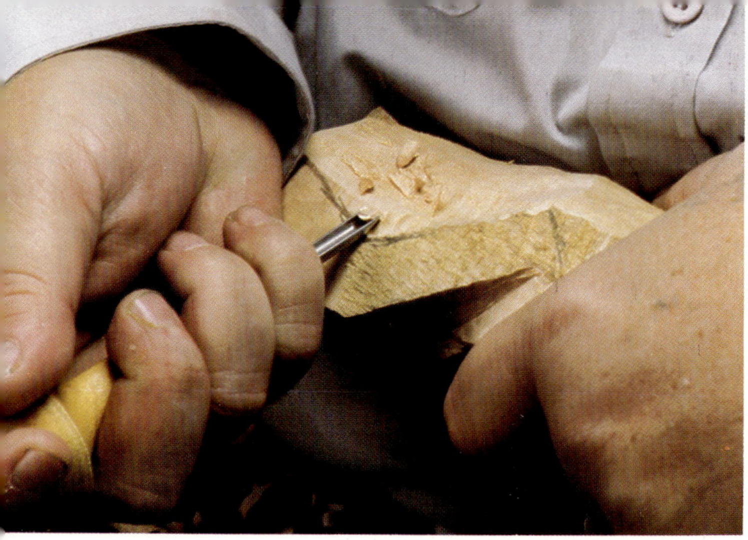

a gouge.

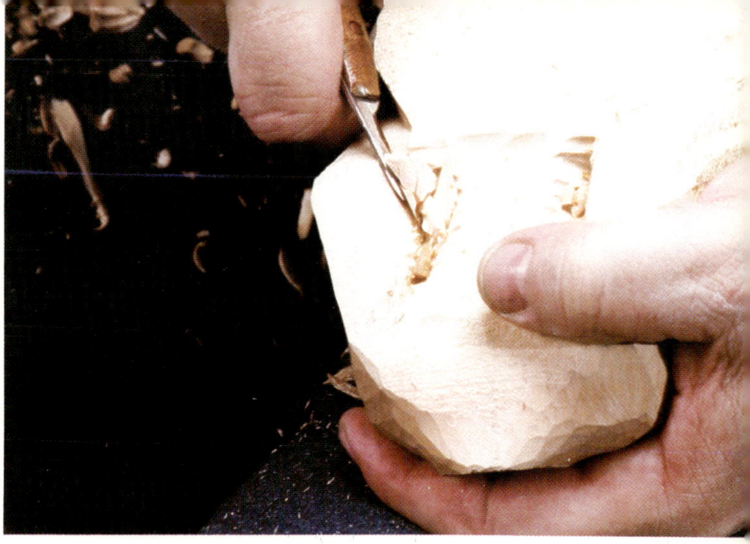

Trim the inside back of the arms into the body.

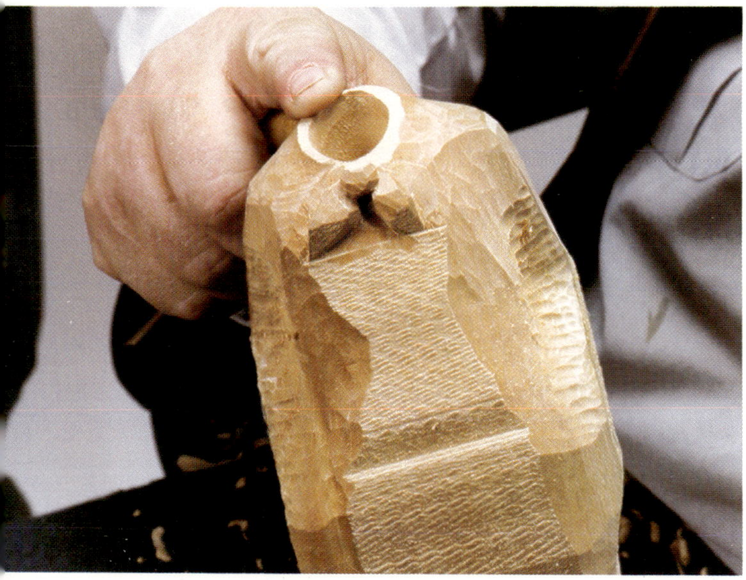

The front of the arms.

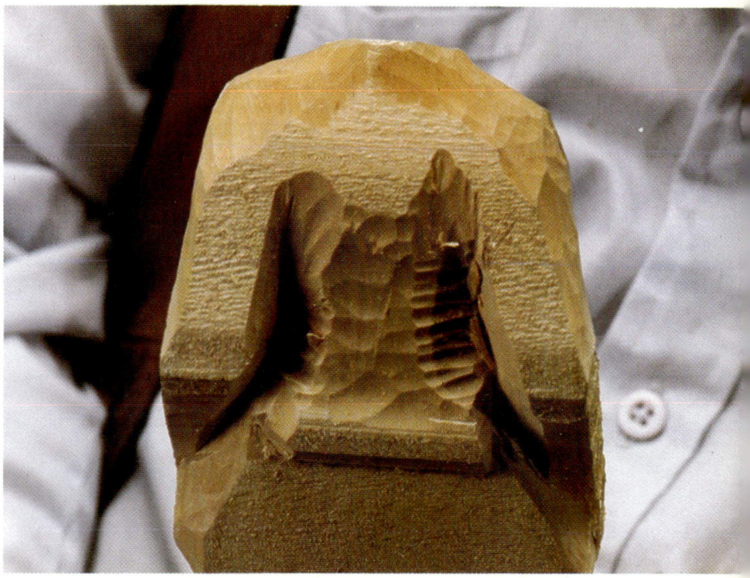

The back so far.

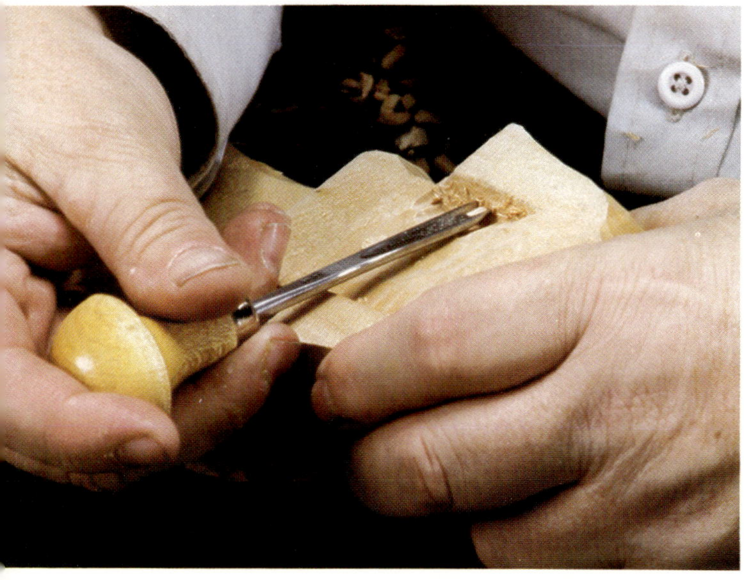

Using a gouge continue shaping the upper body to the arms in the back.

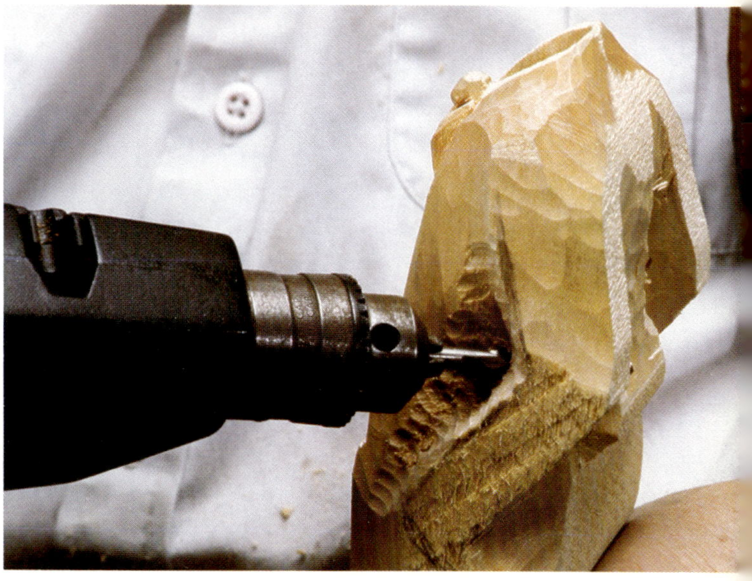

We want to drill a hole between the body and the arm to open the space up. Go in here...

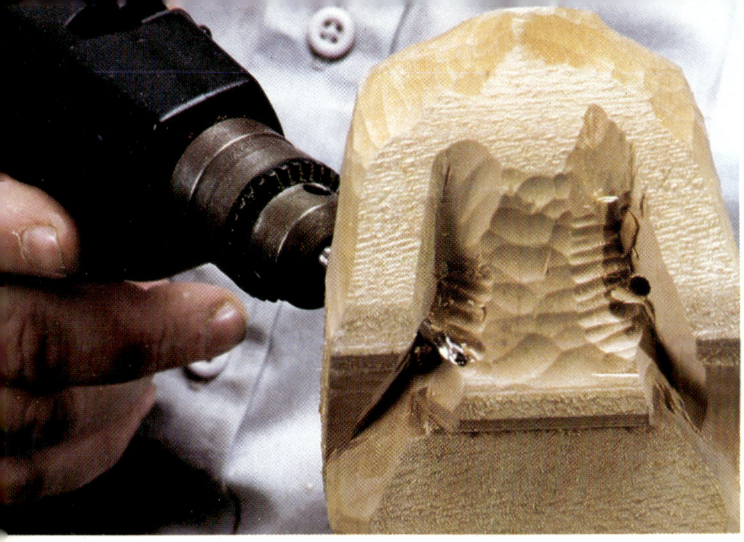
and come out there.

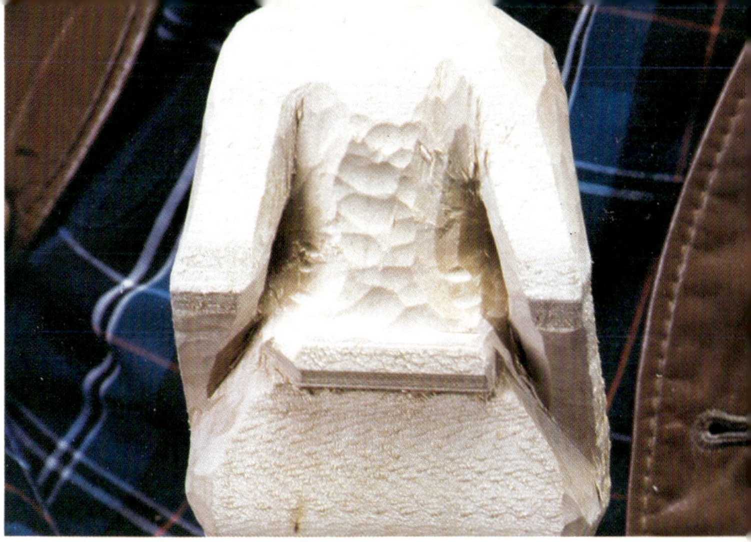
Your object is to get the back to look something like this ...

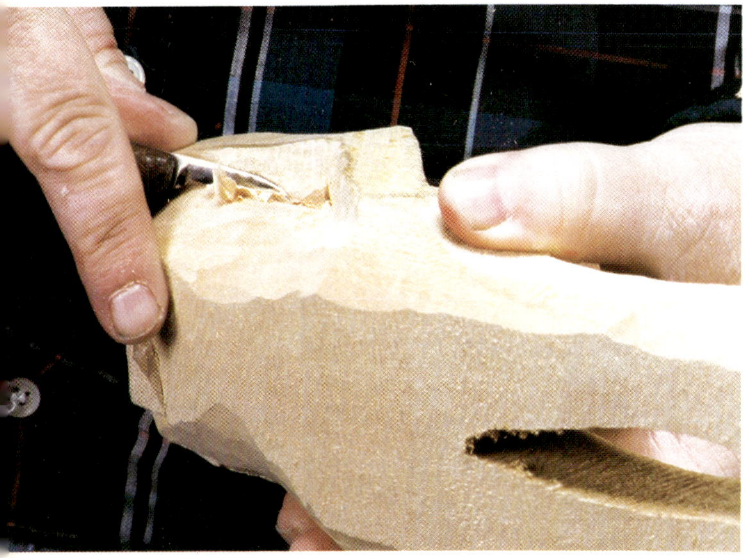
Open up the area between the arm and the body.

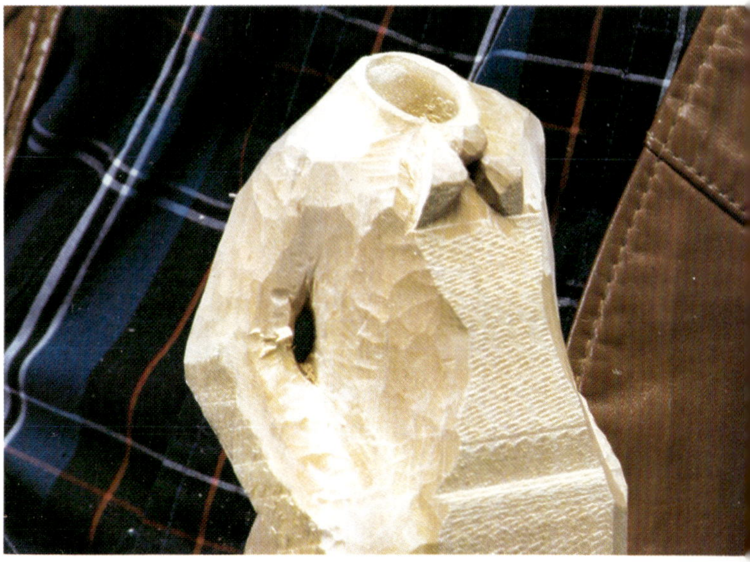
and the front like this.

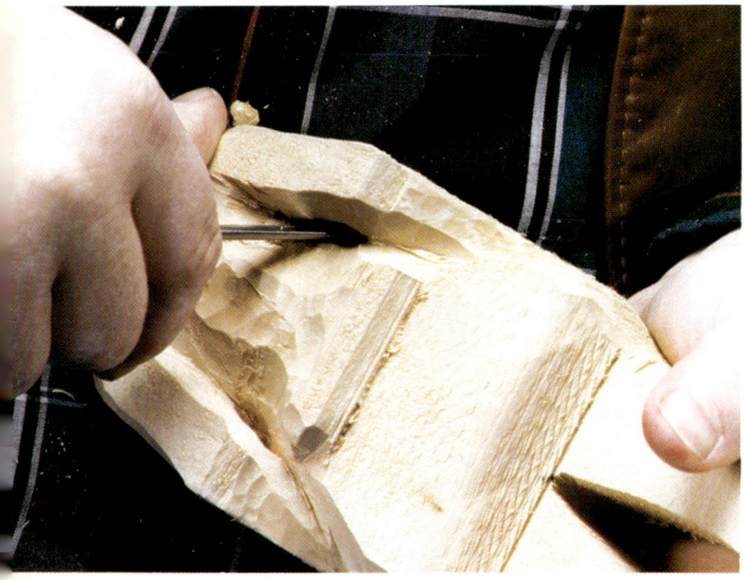
This area is not easy to get into. After using a knife for a bit I switched to a narrow flat gouge, which seemed to work better.

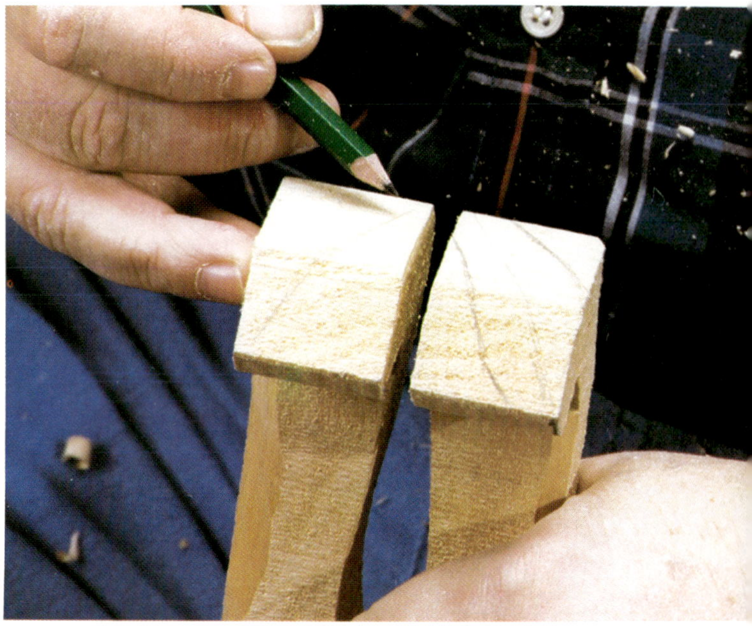
On the bottom, draw a line down the center of the foot...

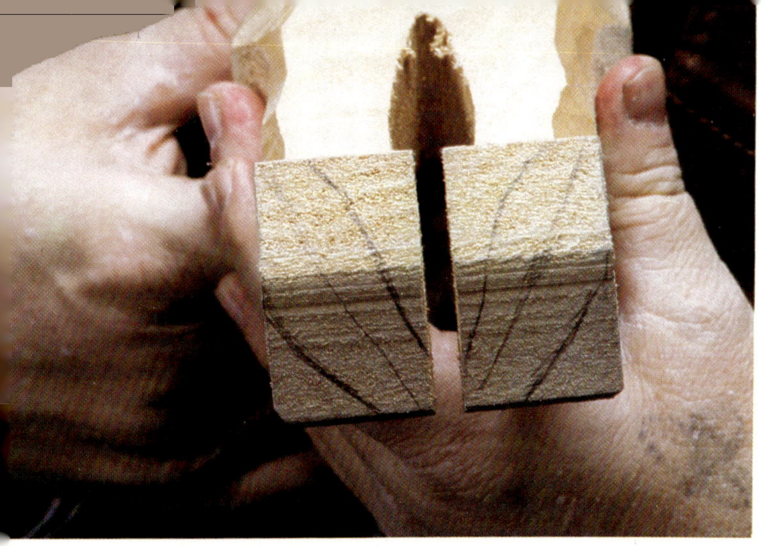

then outline the shape of the boot.

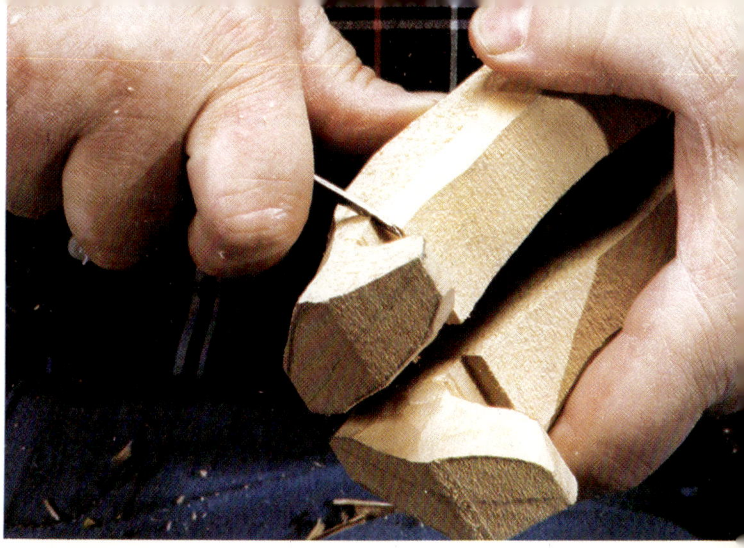

Go around the pant legs with stops...

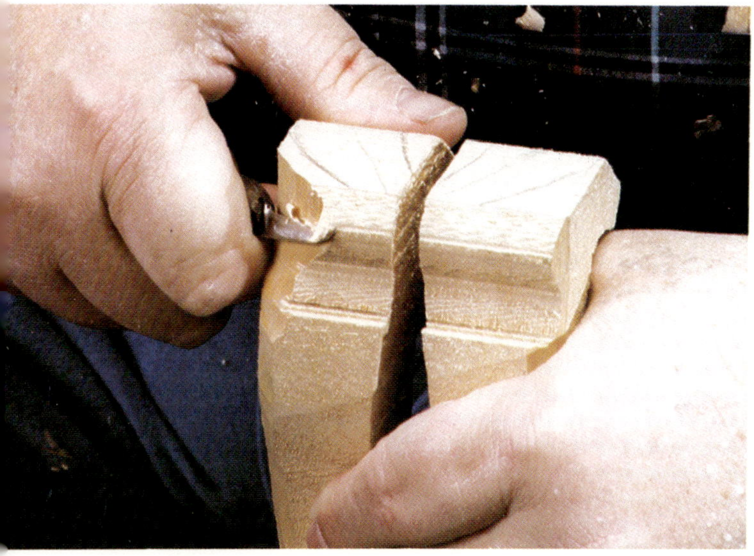

Trim to the outline of the boot. Since we're going with the grain the wood just pops off.

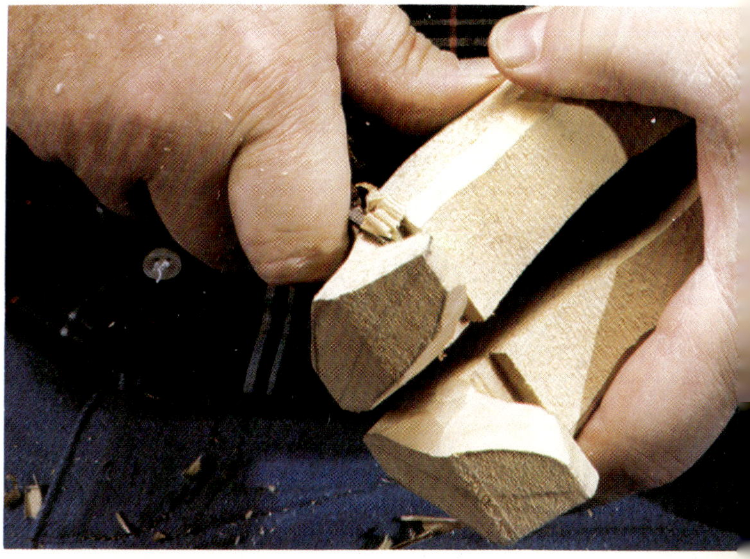

and trim back to them from the boots, knocking off the corners of the boots.

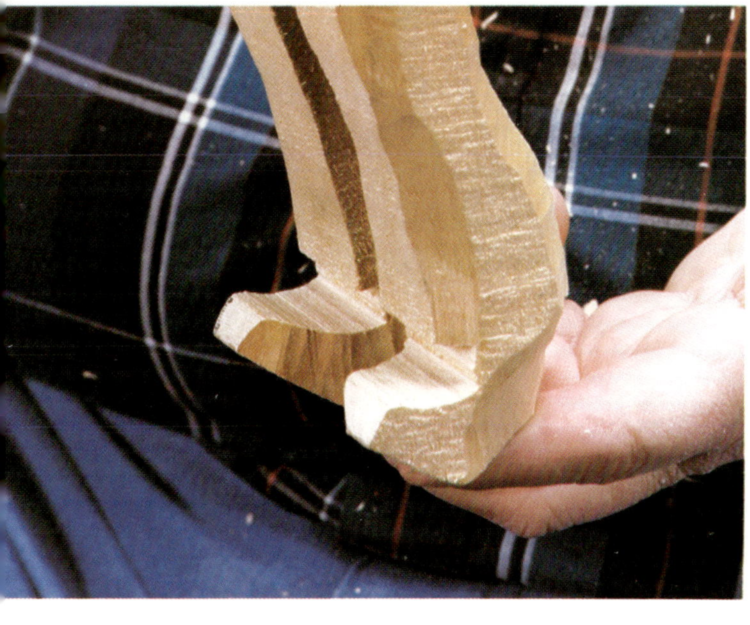

The roughed out boots.

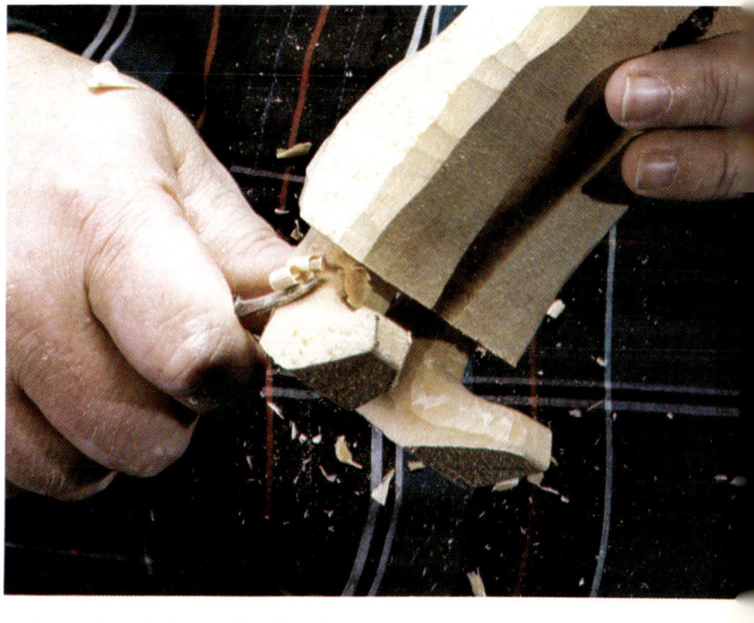

Round and shape the boots.

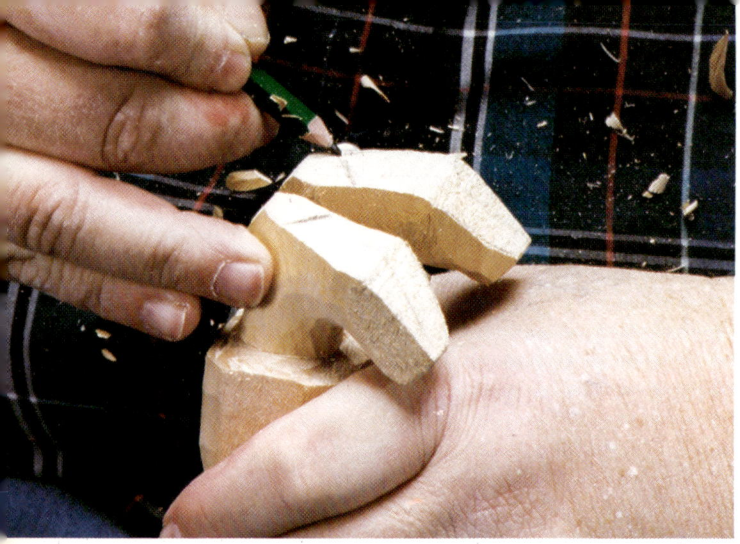

Mark heels on the boots.

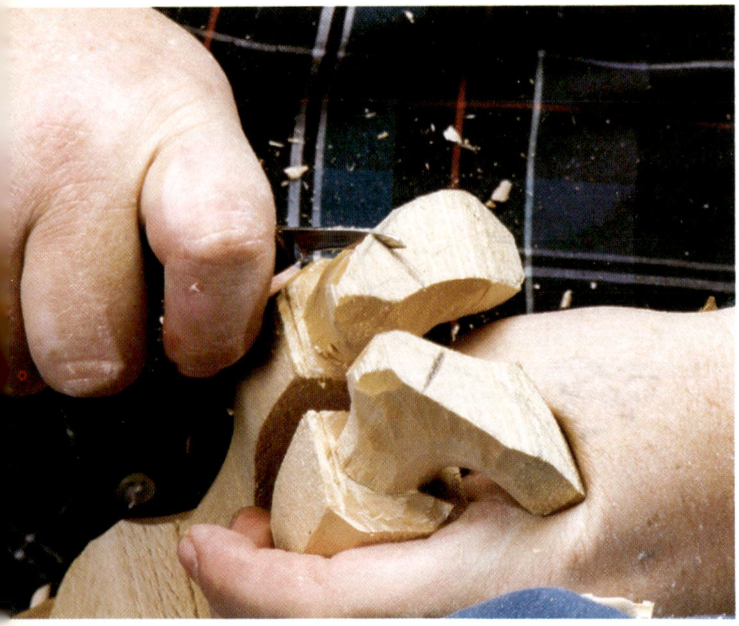

Cut a stop at the outer corner of the heel...

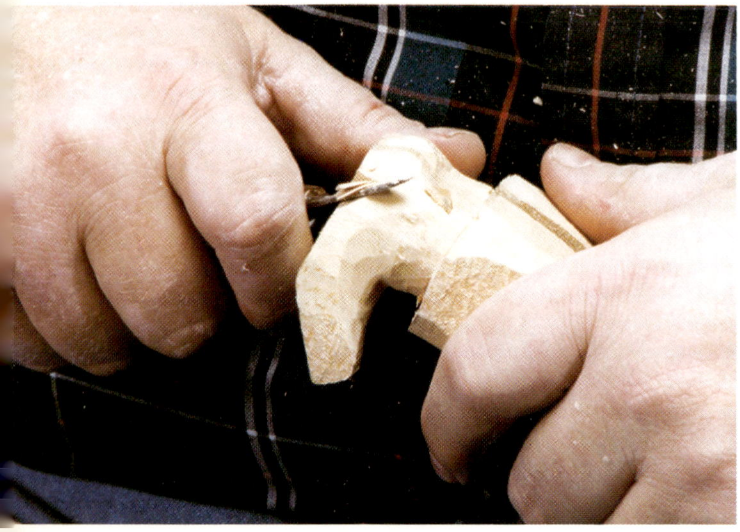

and cut back to it. These are kind of high-heeled boots, so make this cut deep.

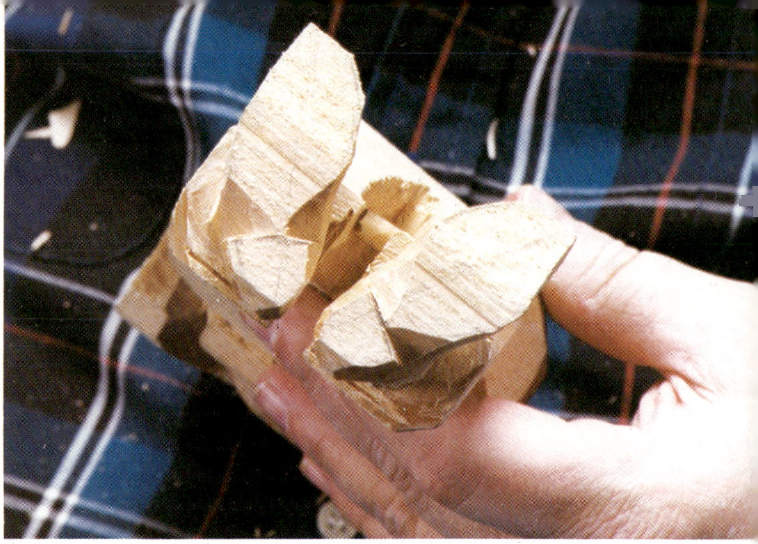

Trim the inside corners too,but don't go all the way across the heel. Having it connected to the sole will give the piece a little more stability.

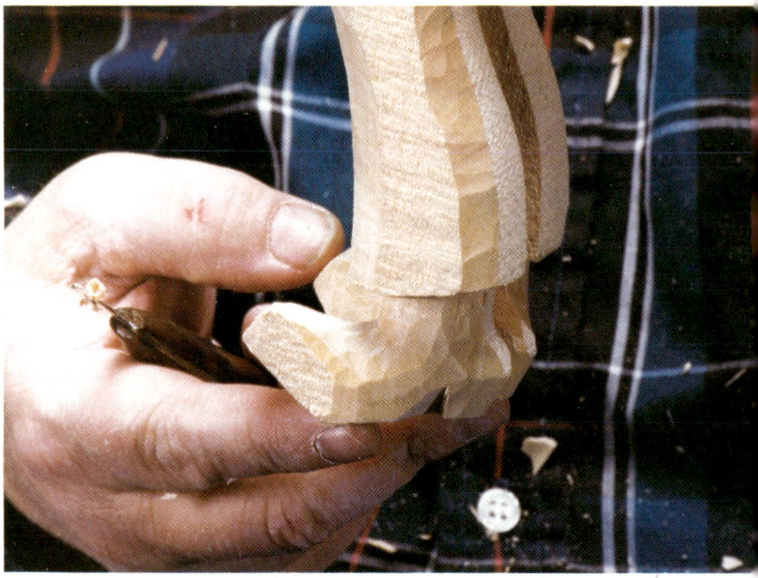

Taper the heel in good western fashion.

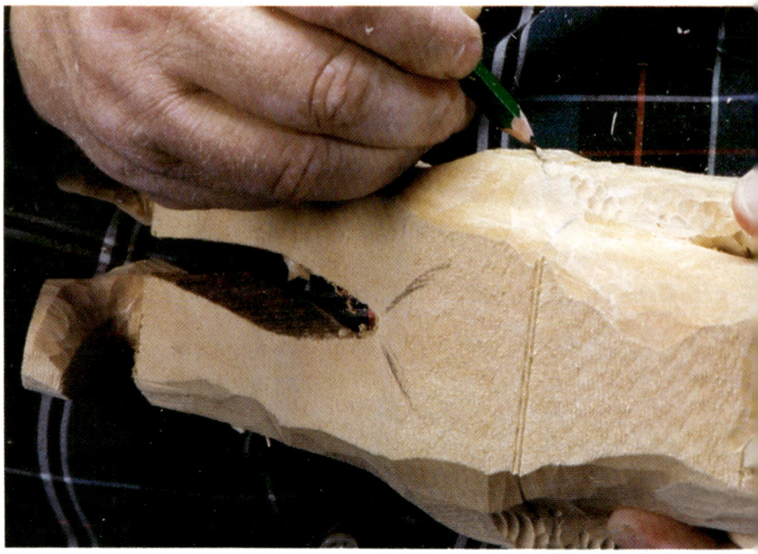

Draw the crotch, waistline, and pockets on the pants.

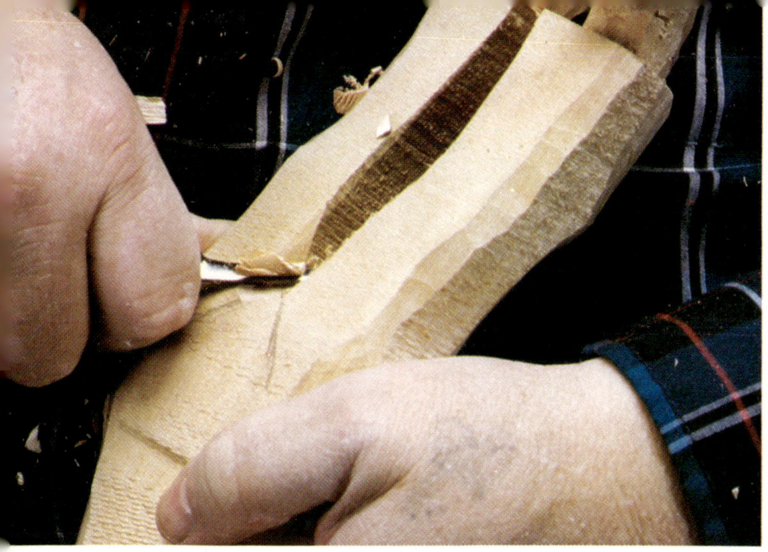

Beginning at the crotch, round the leg.

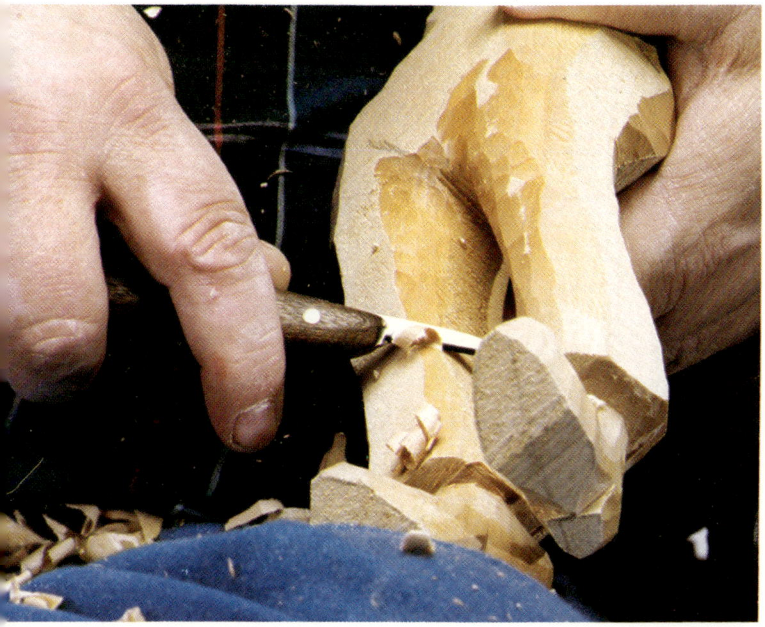

After knocking off the corners, round the front of the leg.

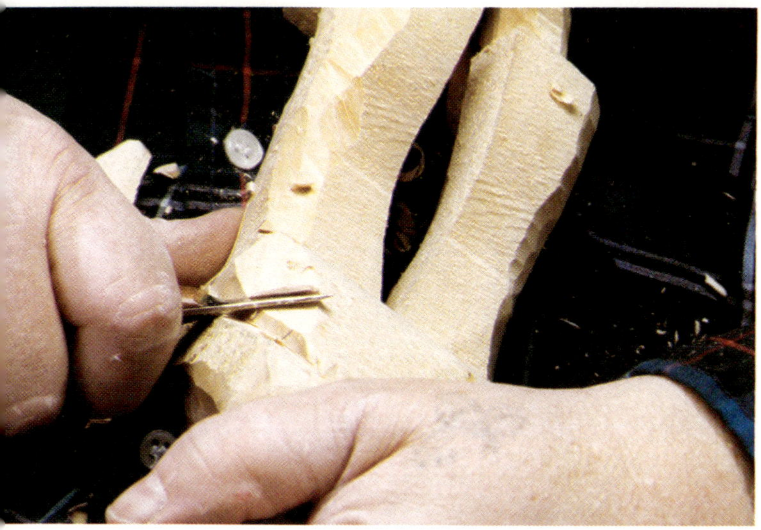

Continue on the back, rounding up to the waist and down to the boot.

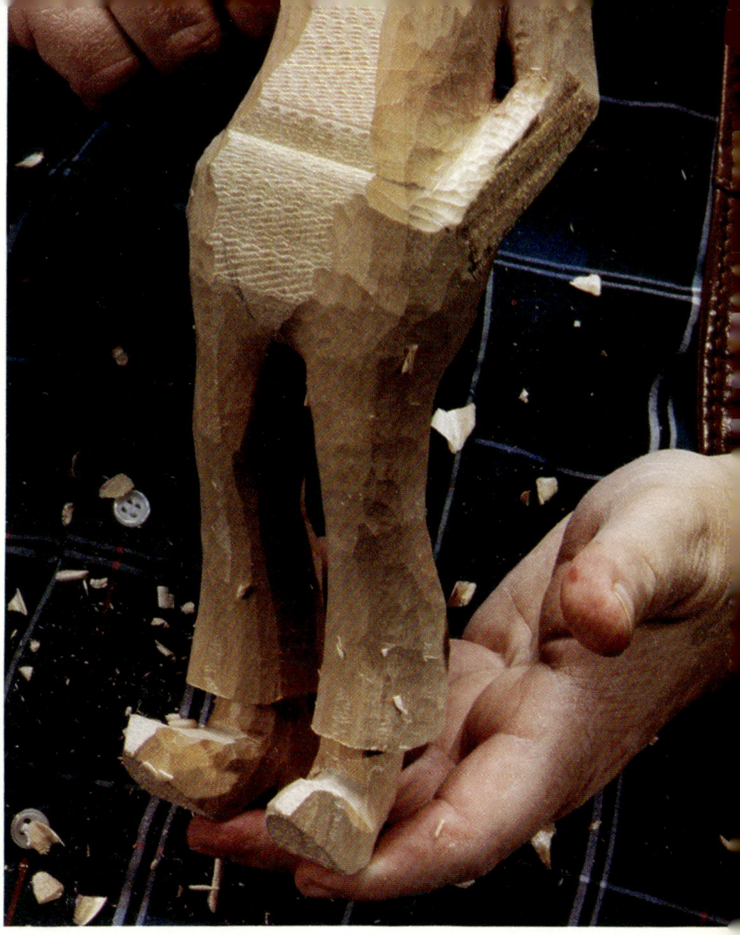

The pants so far, front...

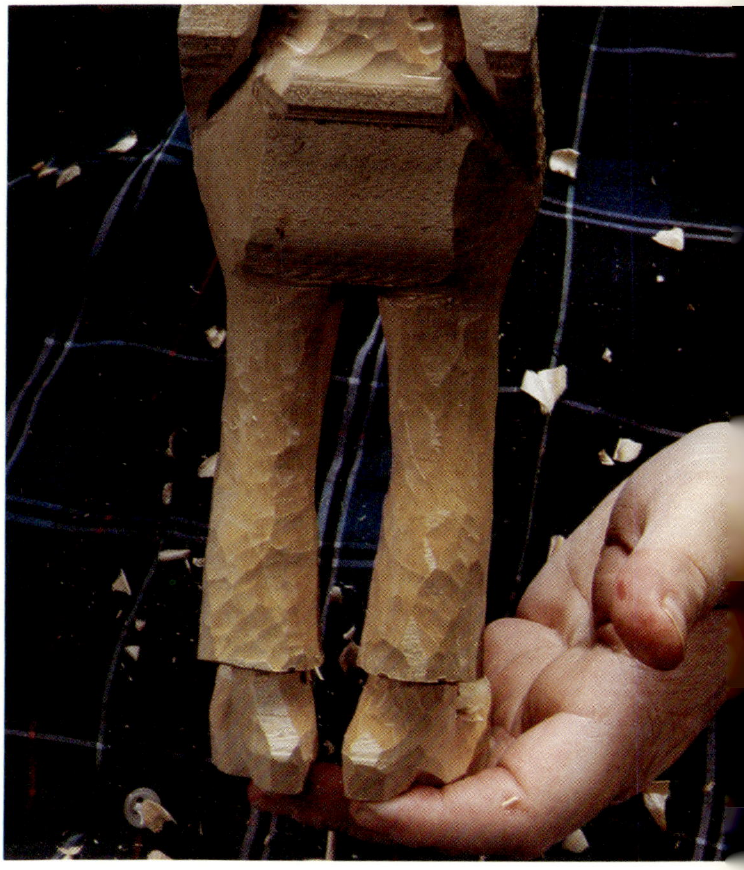

and back.

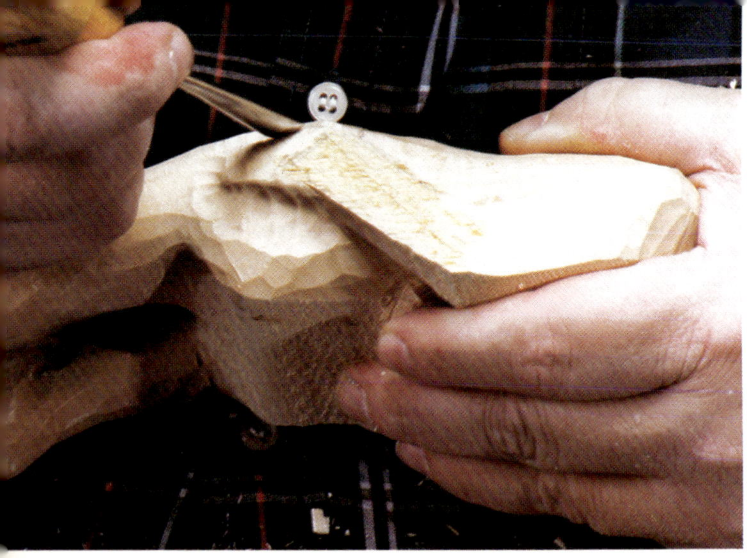

Use a gouge to bring out the pockets so they look like the cowboys hands are inside of them.

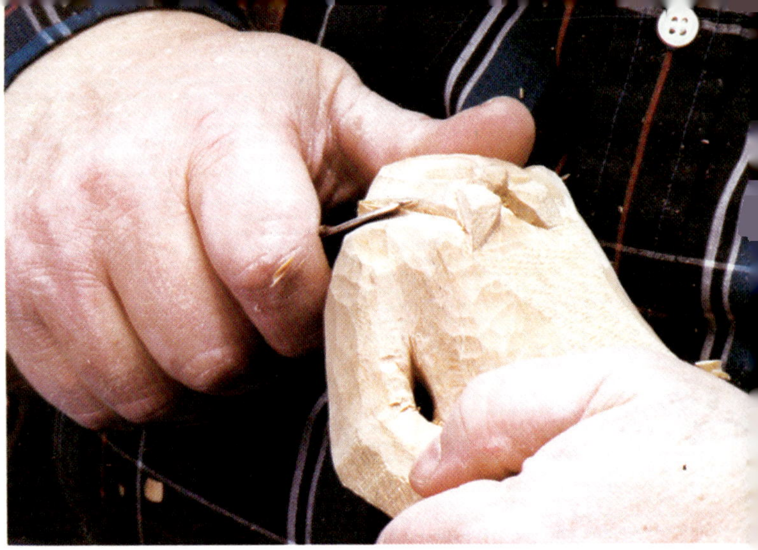

Make your collar strong and thick. This allows you to shape it later.

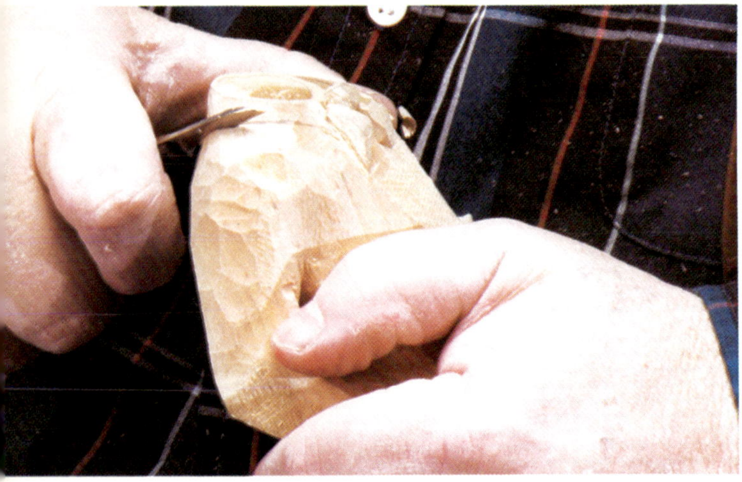

Think about how you want the shirt to look. Options include a vest, suspenders, double or single breasted shirt, paneled shirt or pull-over shirt. It should fit in with the other figures. With a kid like this, I think he should be dressed in a kind of overly macho way. While I'm deciding, I'll draw in the collar and cut a stop in the line.

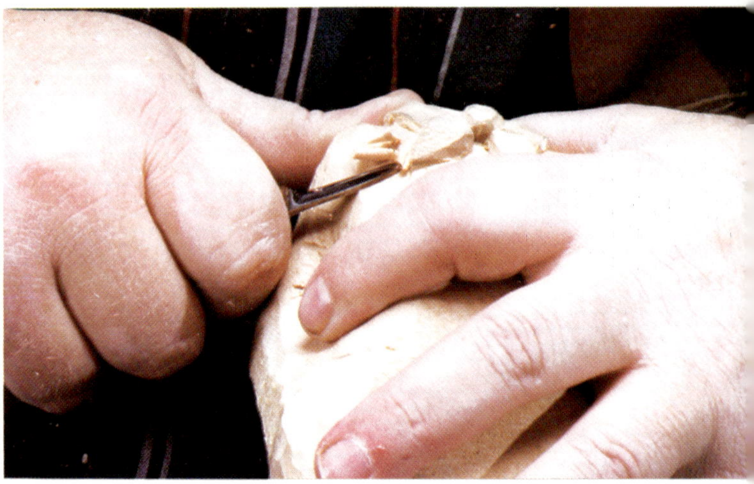

After defining the collar, the shoulders will be too high. Go back and trim them down.

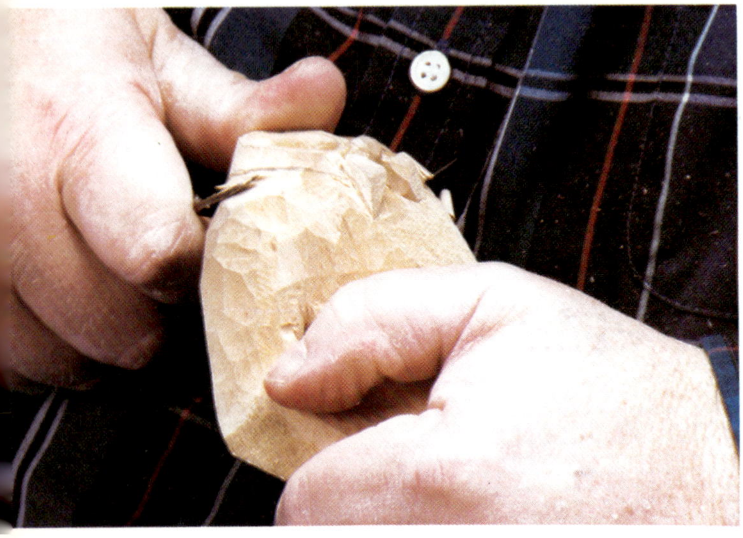

Cut back to it.

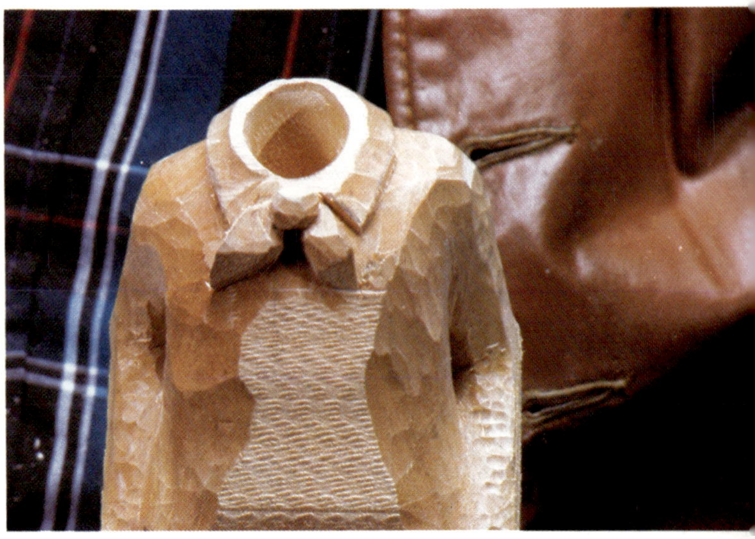

Here you can see one shoulder before shaping and one after. You can get a lot of body language out of the shoulders. By simply putting one lower than the other, or one forward and the other back, the carving can take on a whole different character.

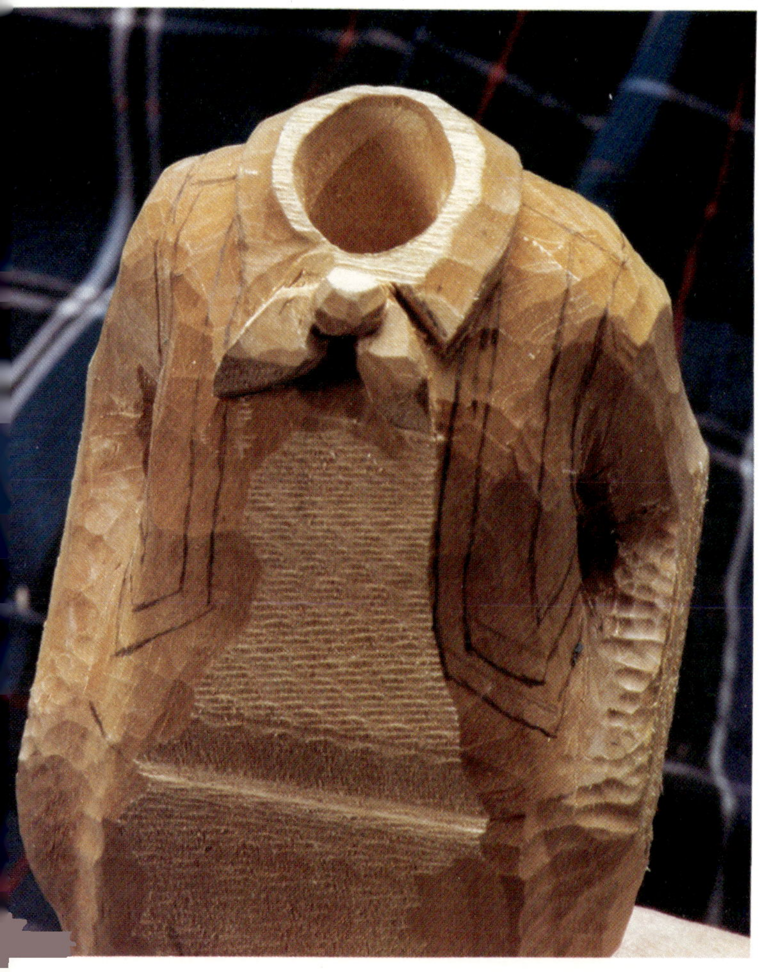

I've decided to go with an open leather vest, with a little tooling or Indian beadwork down the front and across the back.

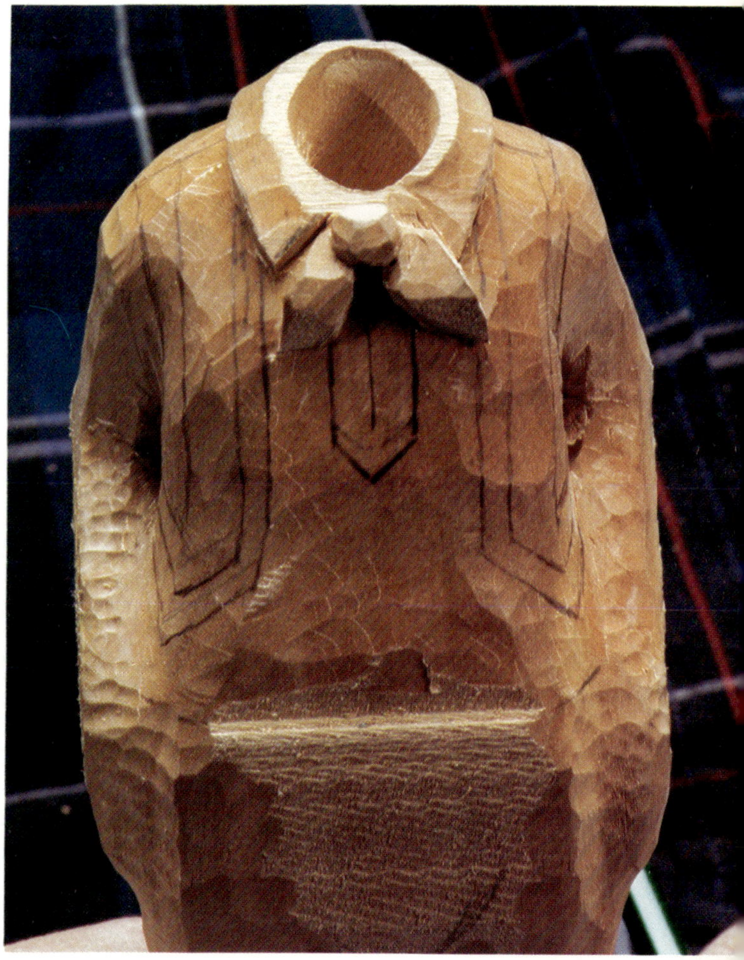

Draw in the details of the shirt.

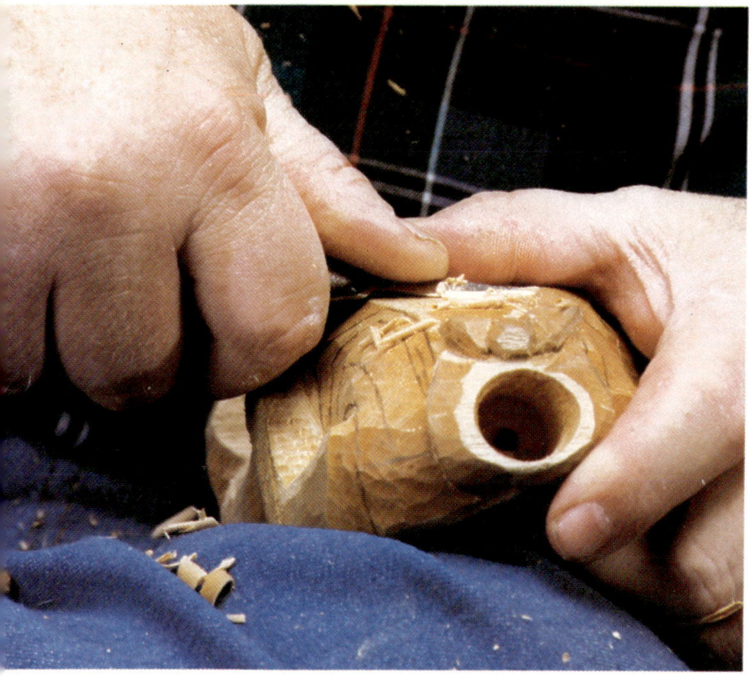

Go over the figure and dress it up. Remove lines that are confusing or unnecessary.

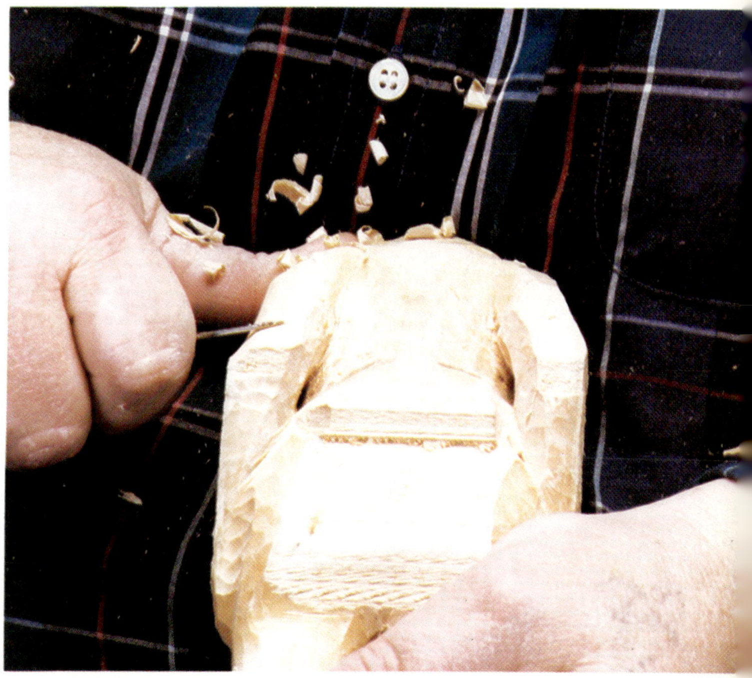

Round off the arms, reducing them in size until they are proportional.

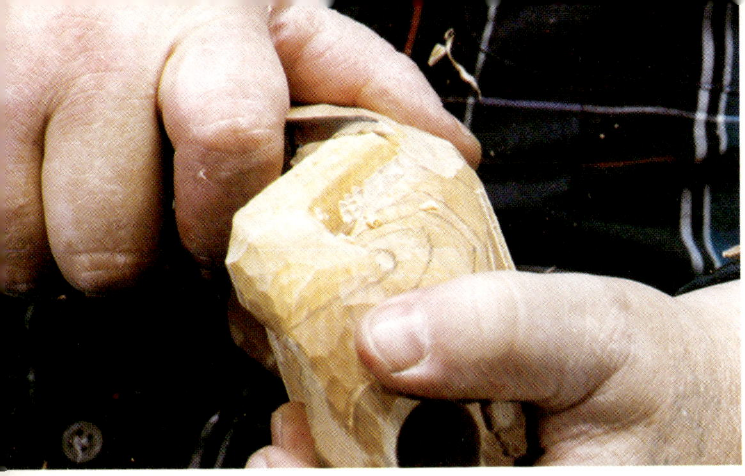

Before you go very far define the pocket line. Make a stop,

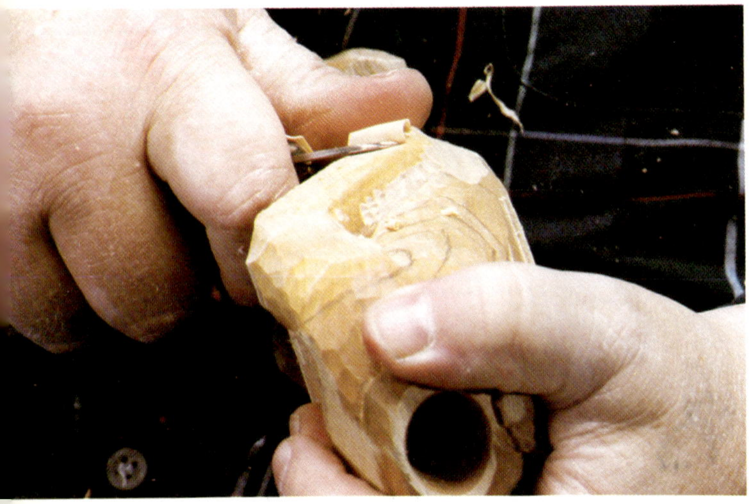

and trim the sleeve back to it. If you don't define the pocket line early on, you are likely to carry the sleeve too far and spoil the effect you are seeking.

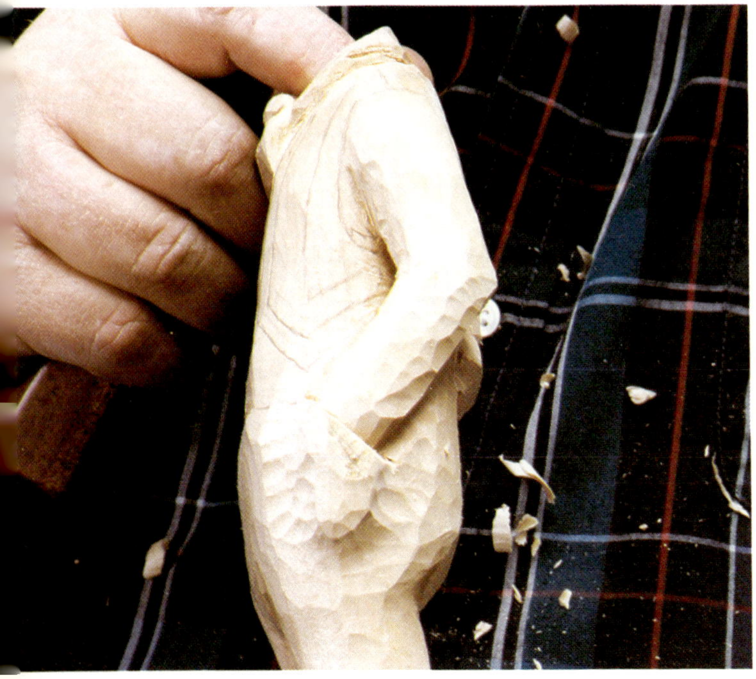

The arm so far.

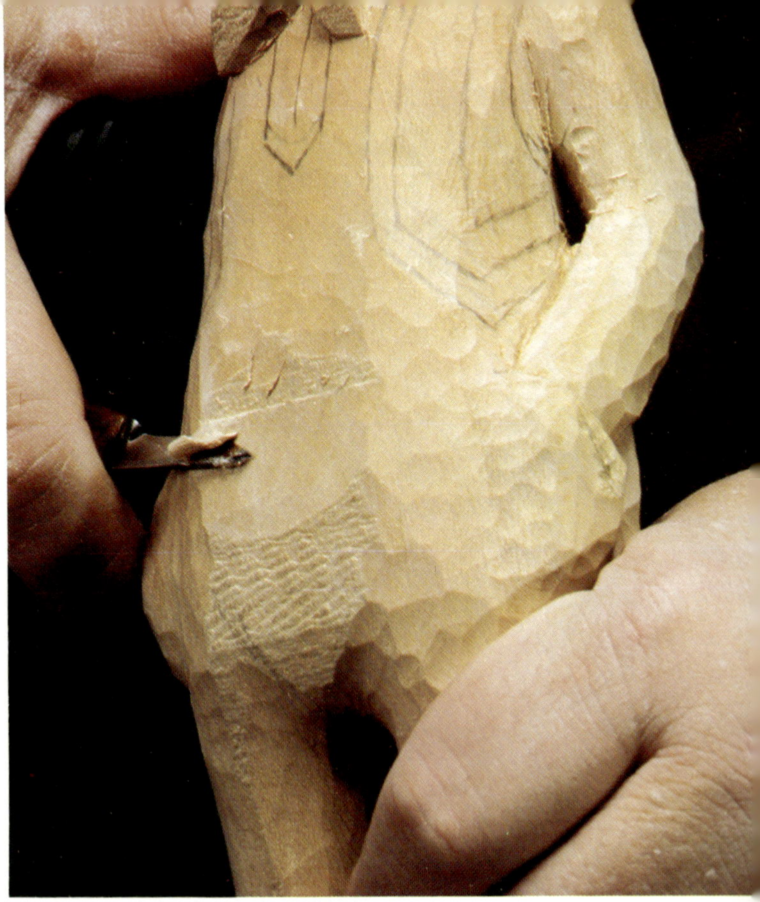

I need to make an adjustment to the pants. First I cut away the saw cut from the pattern.

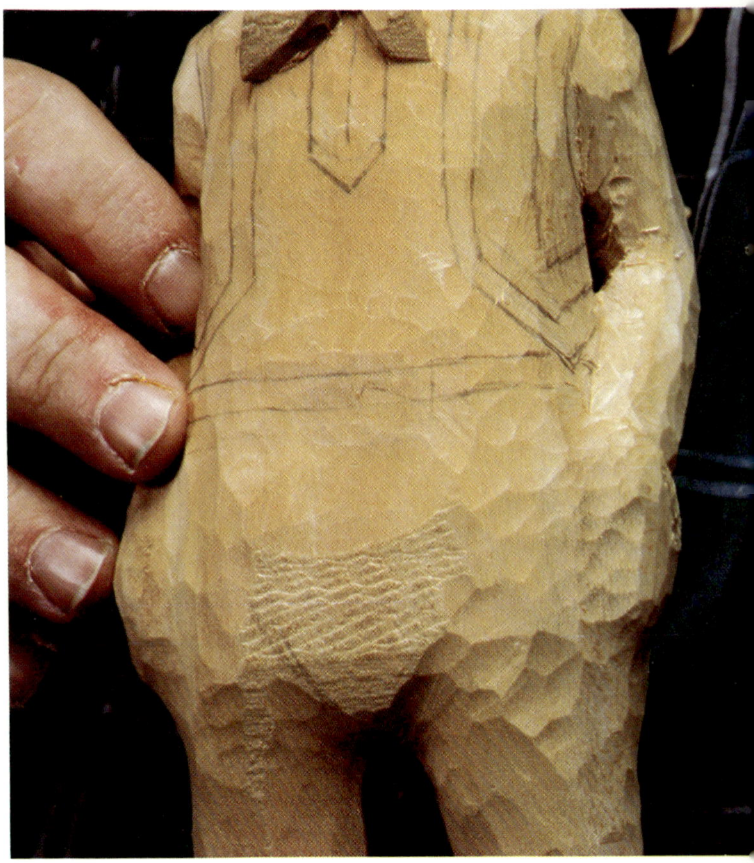

Then I draw in the new line for the top of the pants.

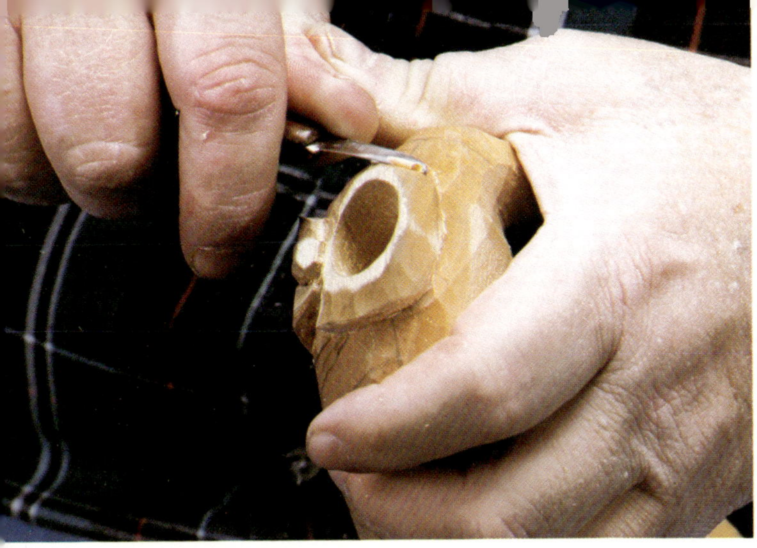

Trim the collar, giving it a natural, concave look as it rises from shoulder to the neck.

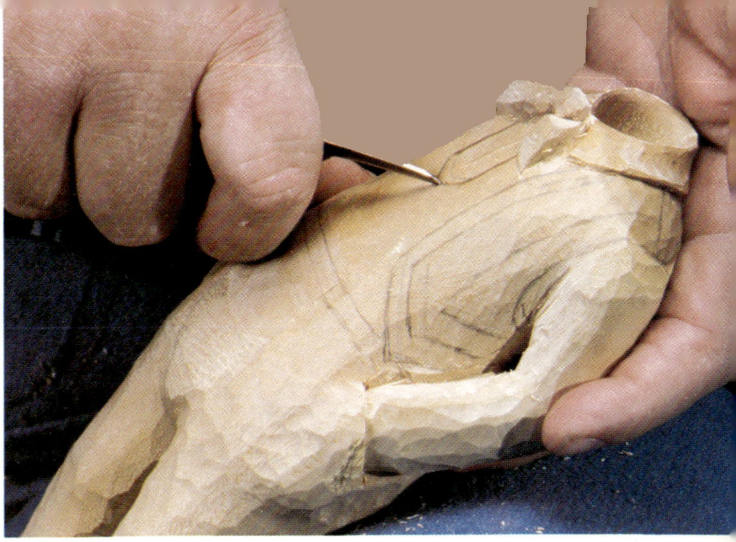

Cut a stop around the gusset of the shirt...

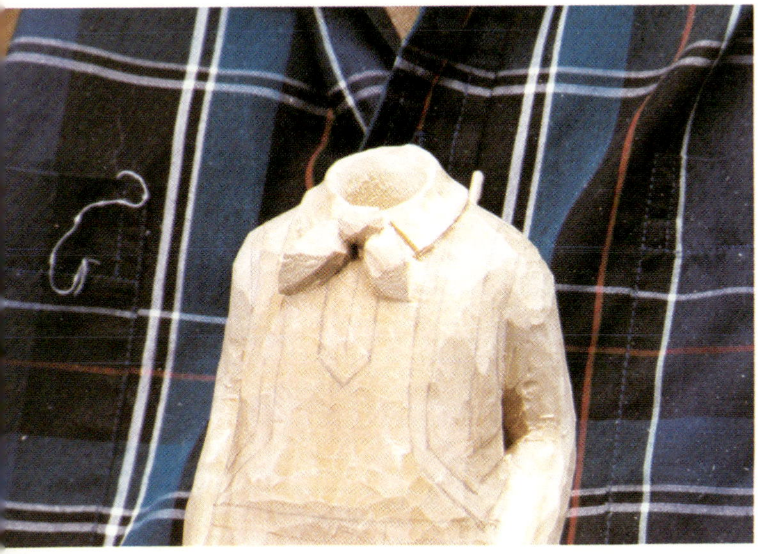

The shaped collar.

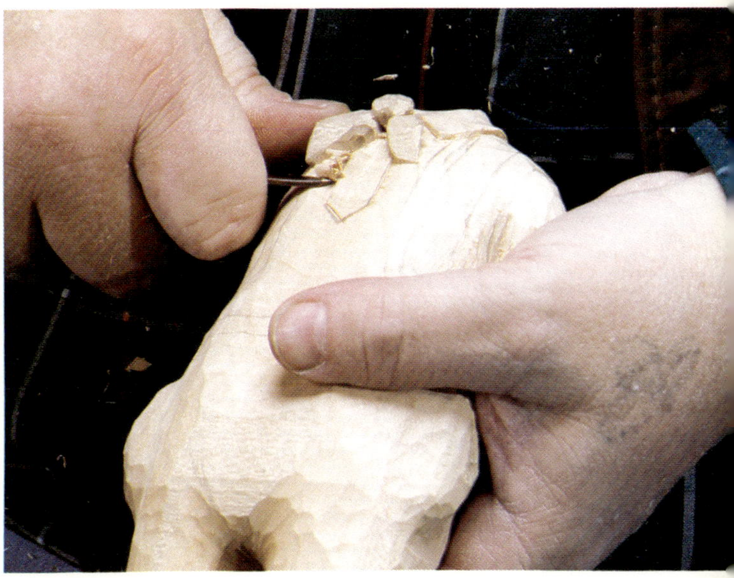

and trim around it.

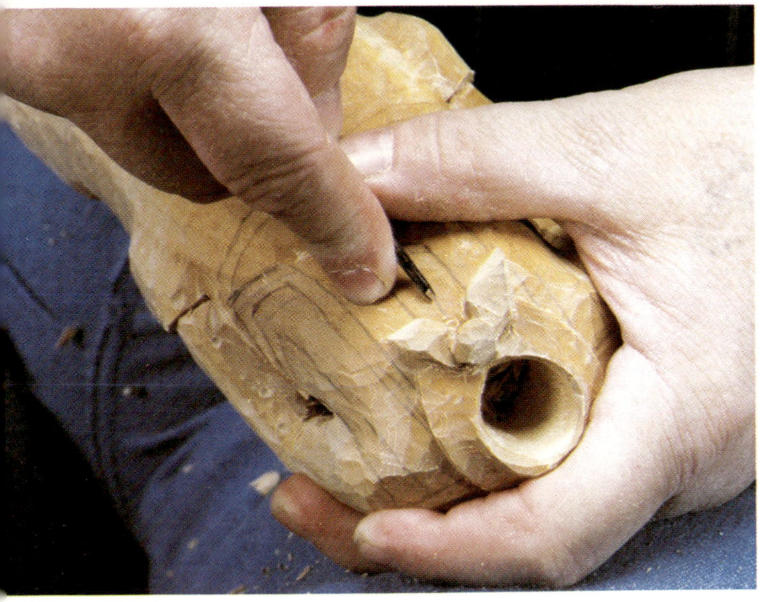

Use a veiner to follow the line of the opening of the shirt.

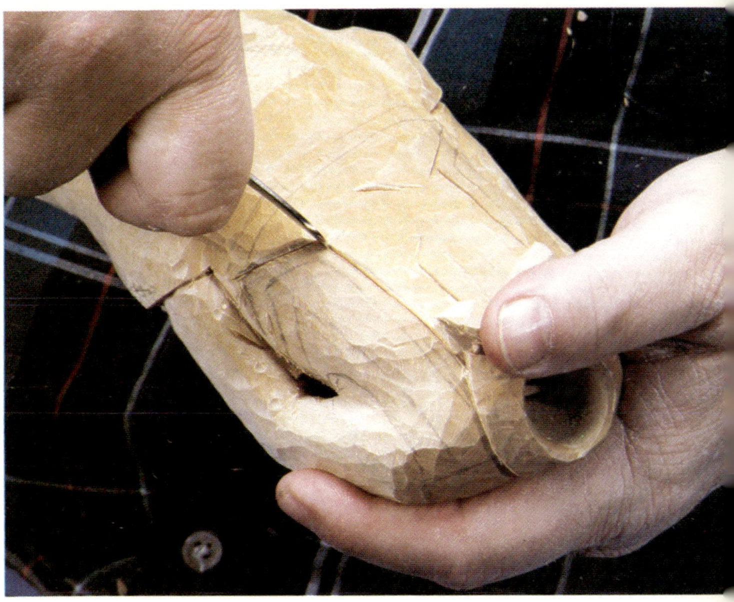

Cut a stop around the line of the vest...

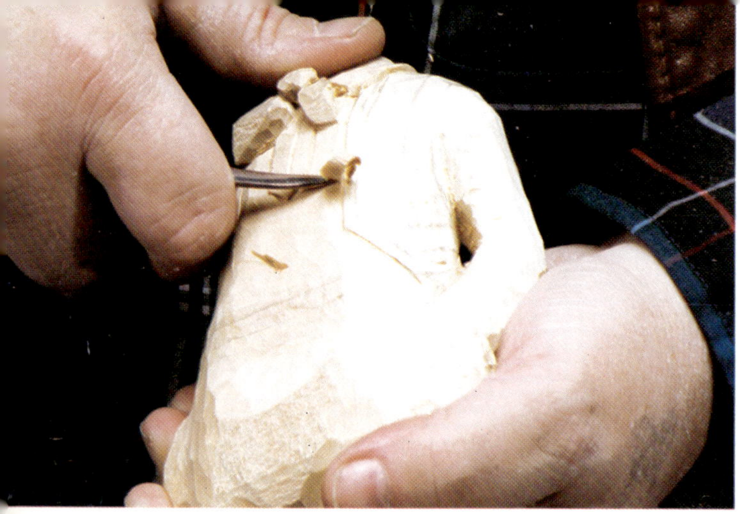

and trim along the line from the shirt.

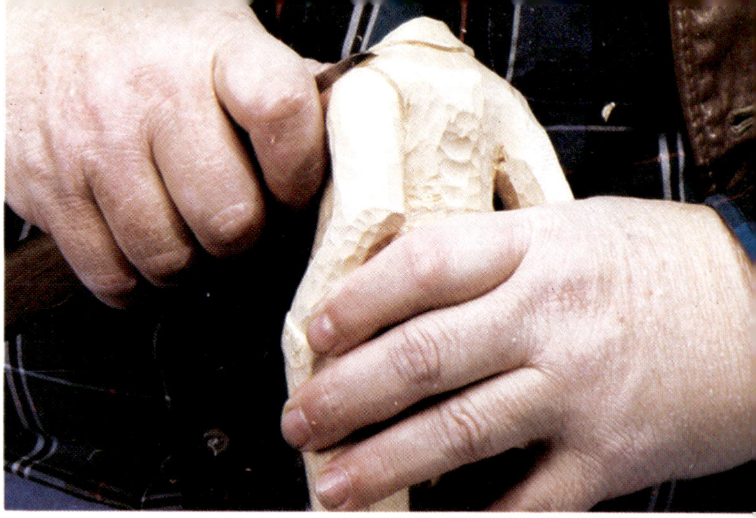

Continue the vest line around the arm, over the shoulder, and around the back. Cut a stop and trim back into it from the shirt.

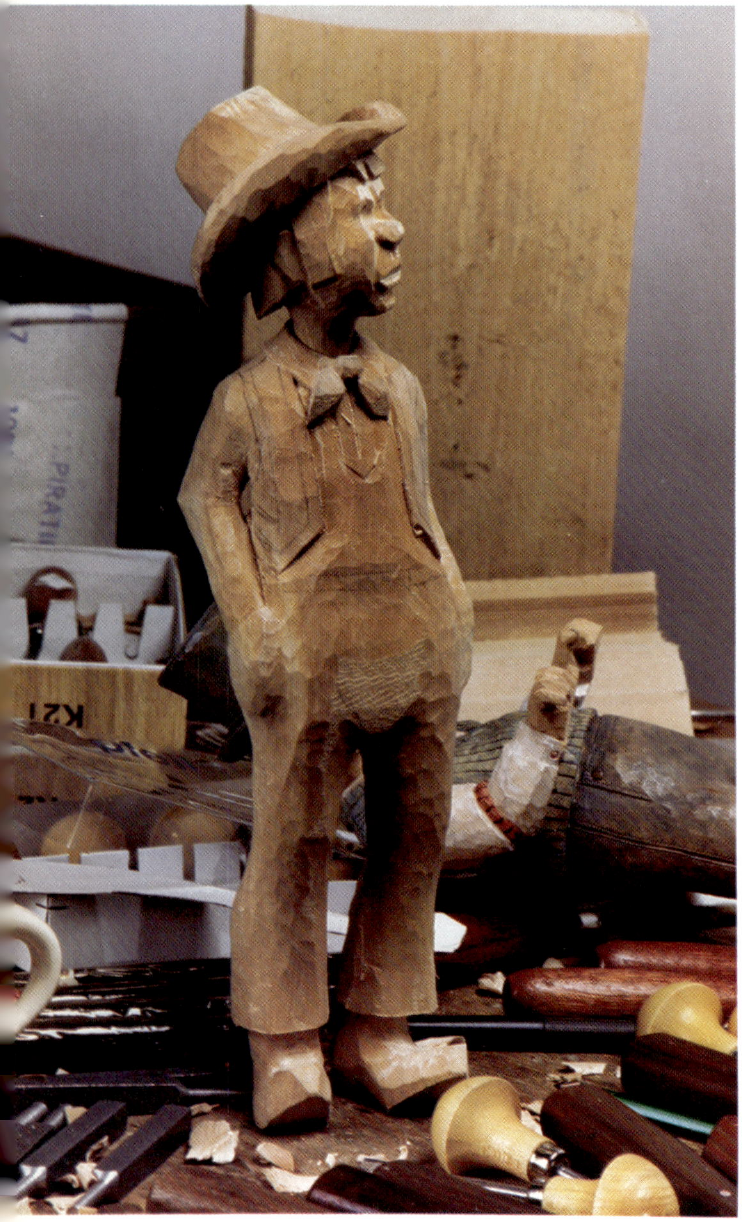

A test fitting showing the front of the vest.

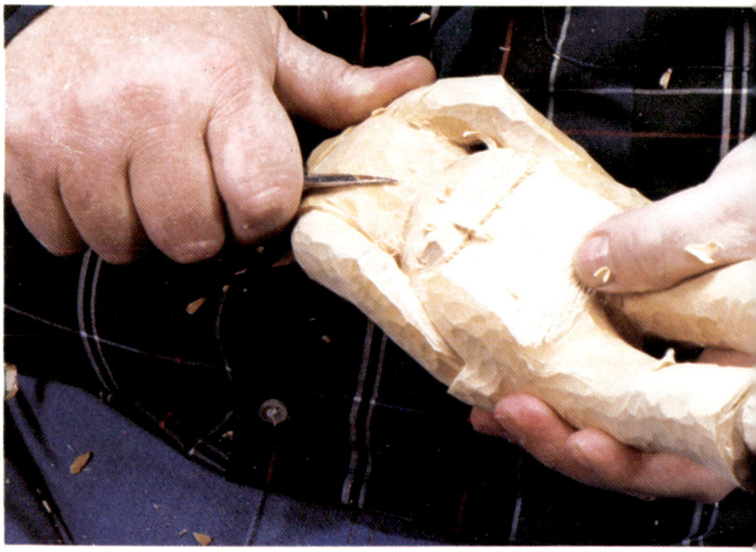

Clean up the back.

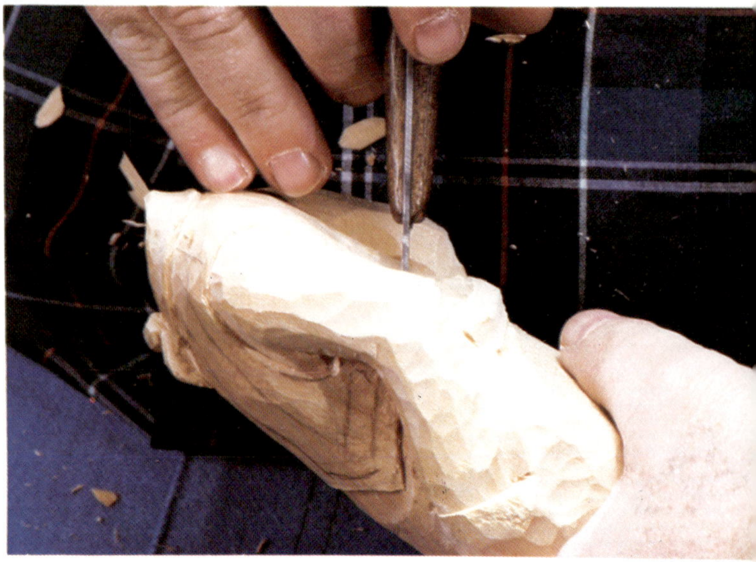

Before cutting a stop in the bottom of the vest in the back, check the line out to make sure it is a continuation of the line in front.

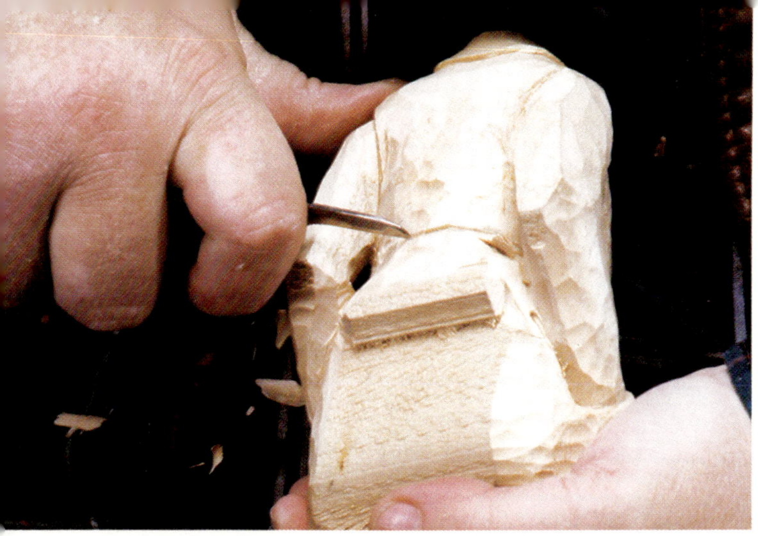

When the line is set, cut a stop in it.

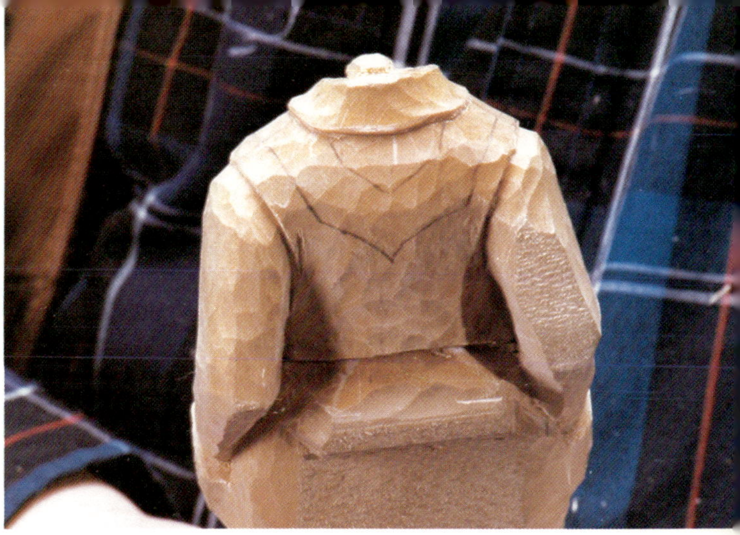

Draw in the decorative pattern of the vest, continuing it over the shoulder and onto the back.

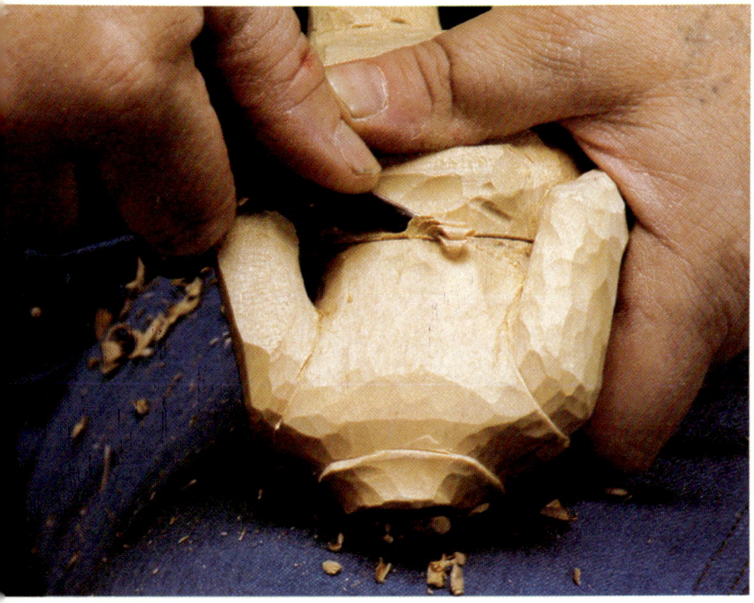

Trim back from the shirt.

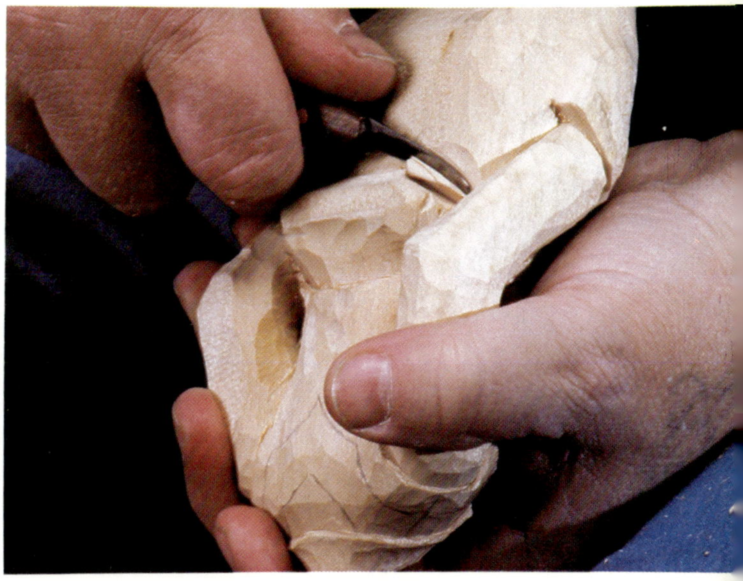

Trim the roll of the shirt in the back.

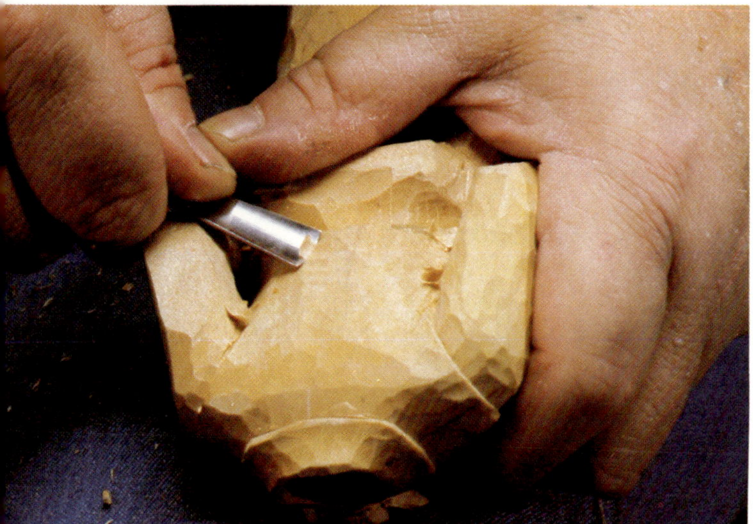

Clean up and shape the back. Sometimes when the grain seems to be going in both directions, the only way you can get it clean is with a flat gouge.

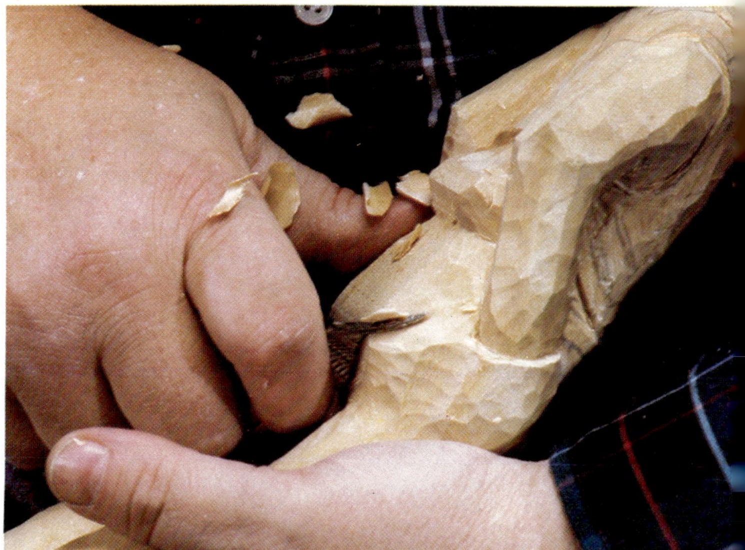

His rear-end is a bit large, so we need to do some cosmetic surgery.

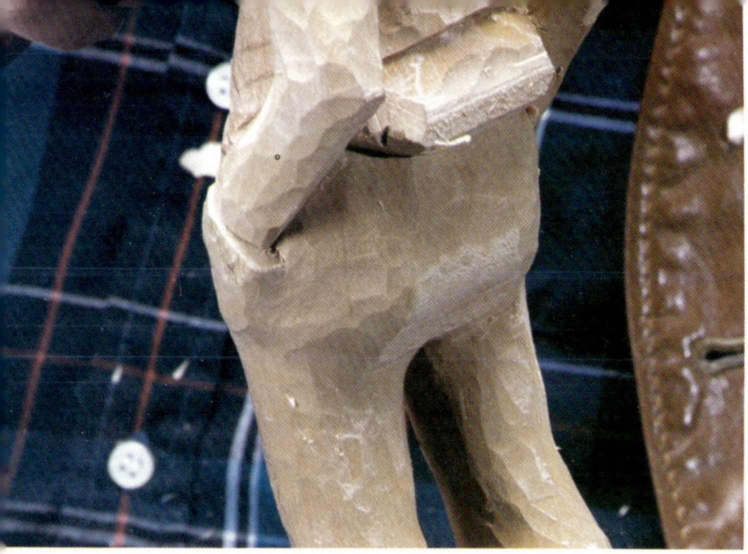

By taking some excess wood off of each side and shaping it overall, things come into proportion. If only it were so easy for us mere humans!

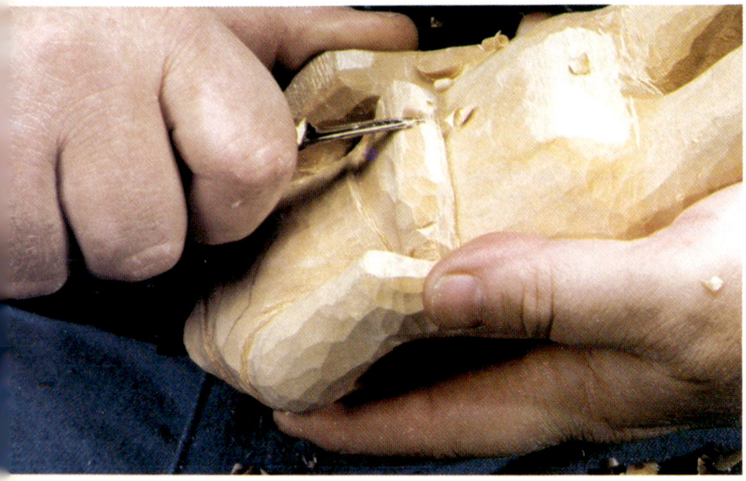

Go back and round off the exposed tail of the shirt, making it look more believable.

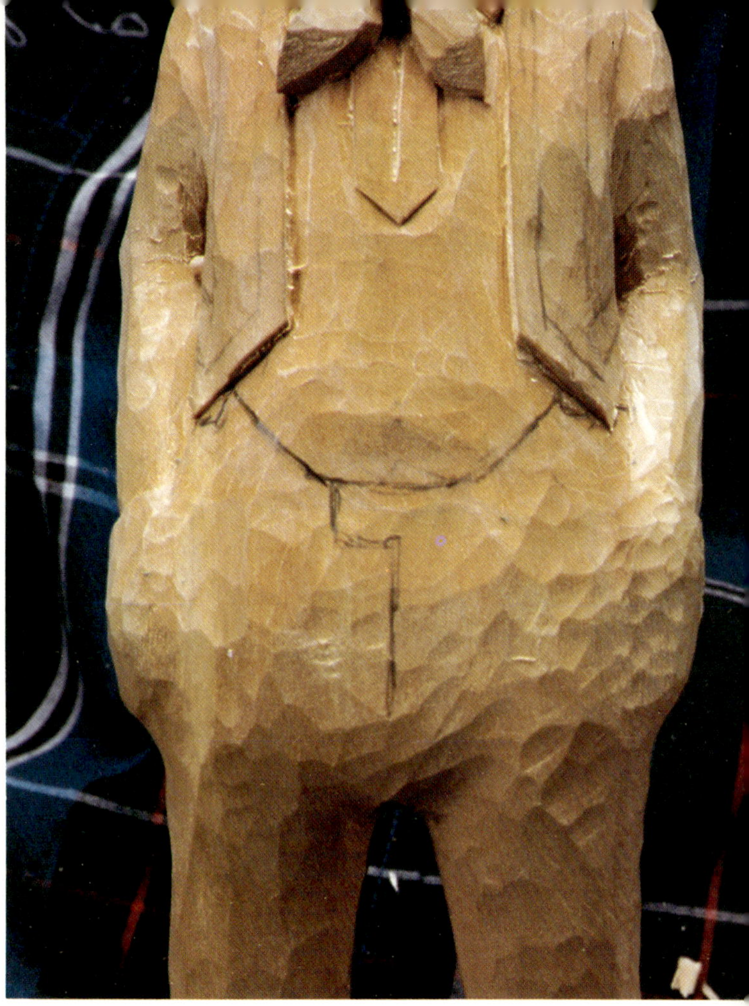

Sometimes things just don't look right. Here the pants were riding too high, and were unbelievable. I erased their line with the knife and redrew it in a way that looked better. The nice thing about wood is that it erases pretty easily. In this case I let the pants ride lower by insinuating that suspenders are holding them up under the vest.

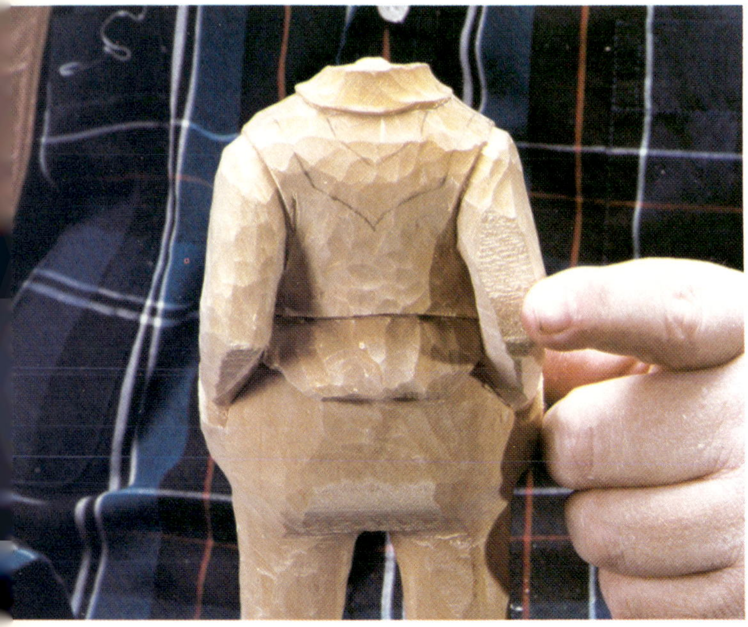

Put in a couple gentle folds, giving it this bloused look.

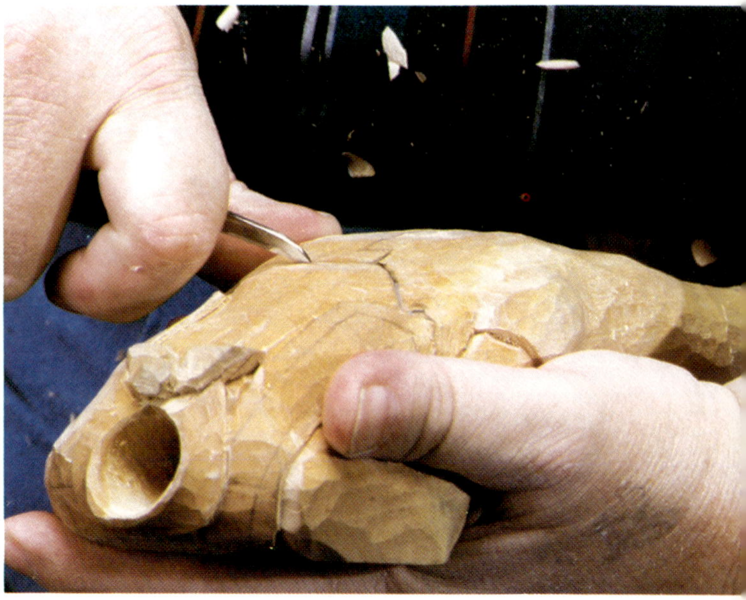

Cut a straight stop line along the top of the pants. Make it fairly deep so the shirt looks like it is rolling under.

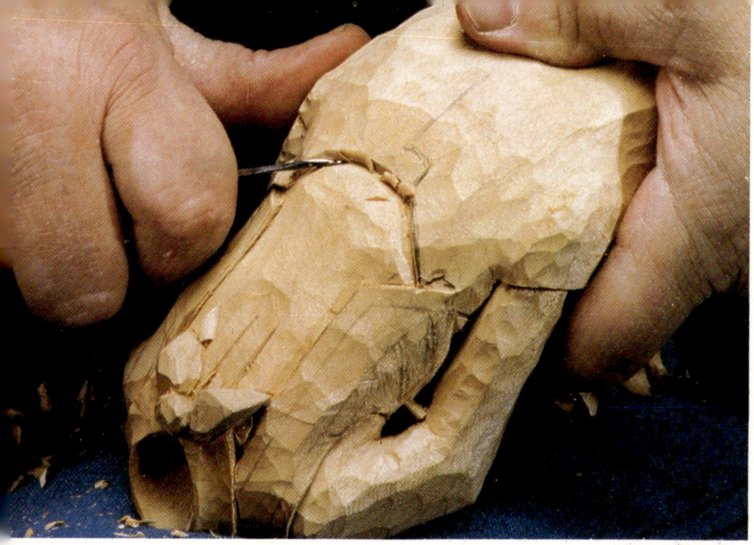

Trim back to it, getting the look you want.

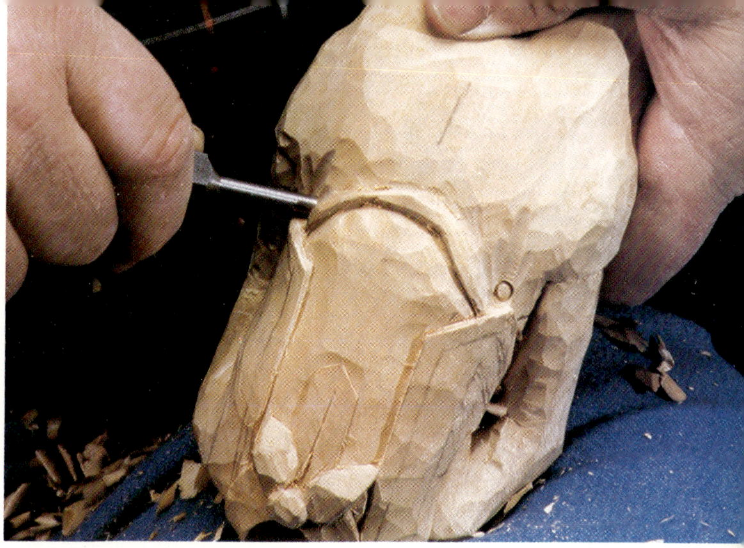

Place a suspender button just below the coat. Use a small eyepunch, pushing into the wood and turning.

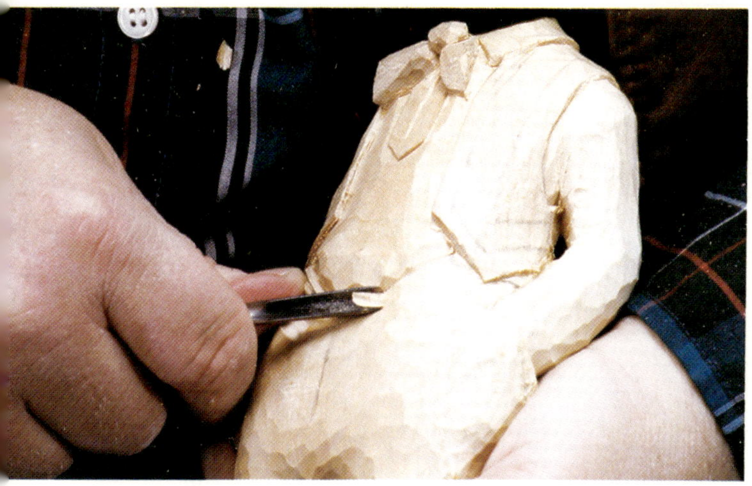

The other thing we need for the new look is to make the front of the pants concave. This is caused by the suspenders pulling up. Use a gouge to get this pulling effect.

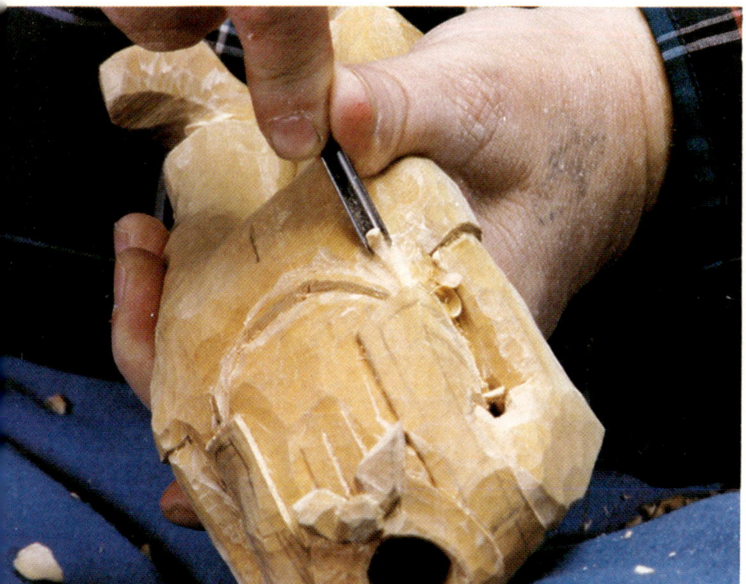

Add pull marks toward the suspenders with the gouge.

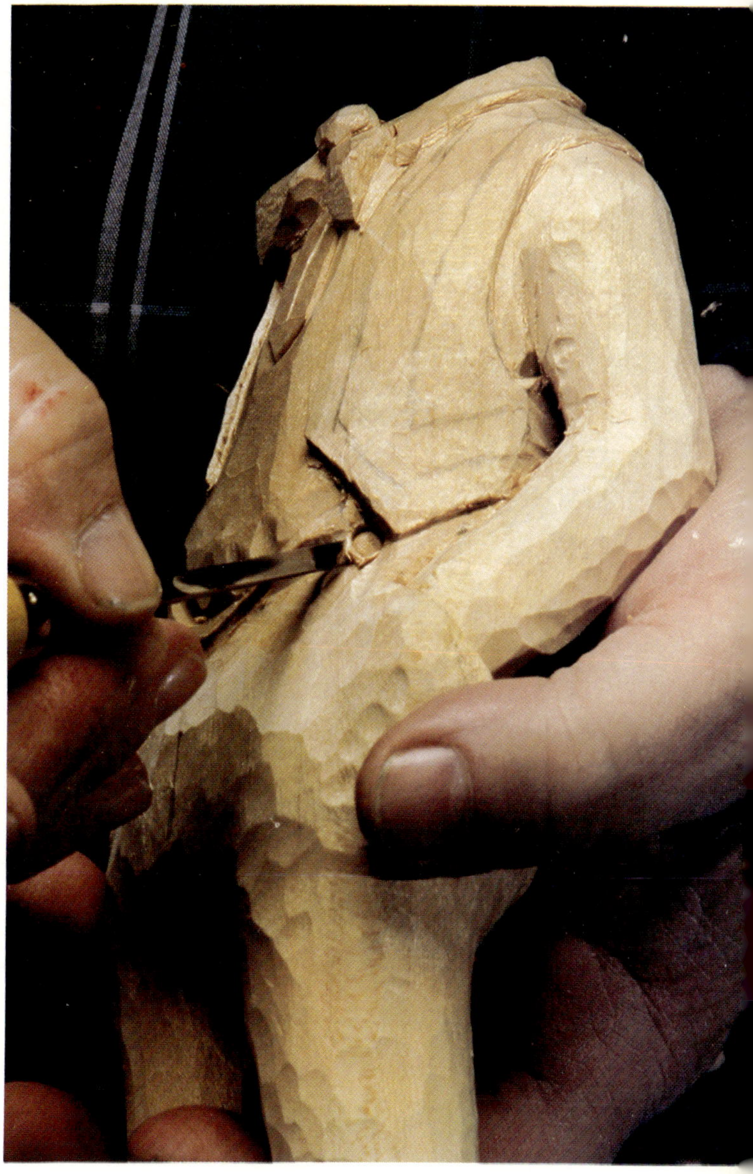

Go back with a gouge and cut into sides of the button to make it stand out more. After you do that it would be good to go over the button again with the eyepunch.

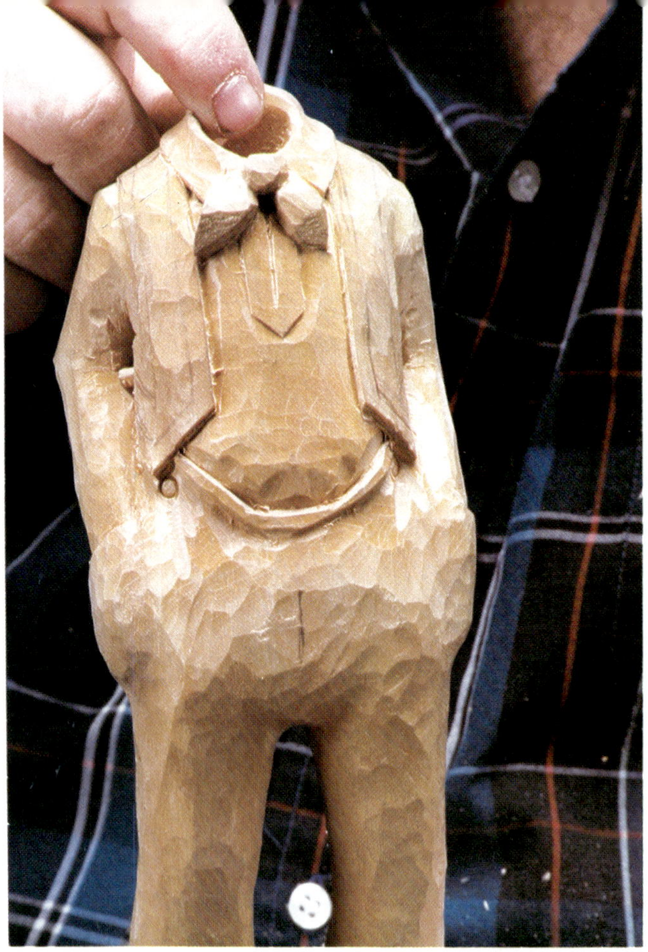

The front of the pants and the shirt.

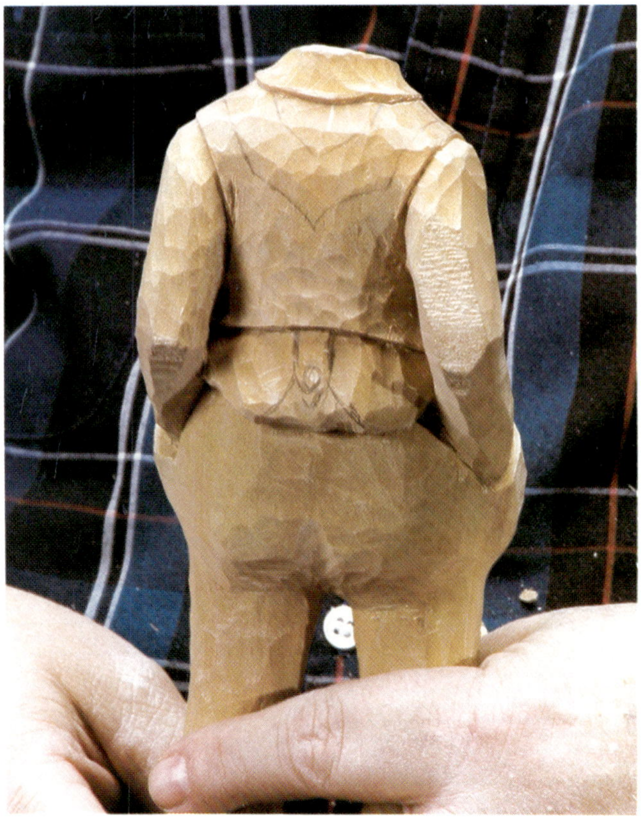

Adjust the design in the back to account for the addition of suspenders in the front.

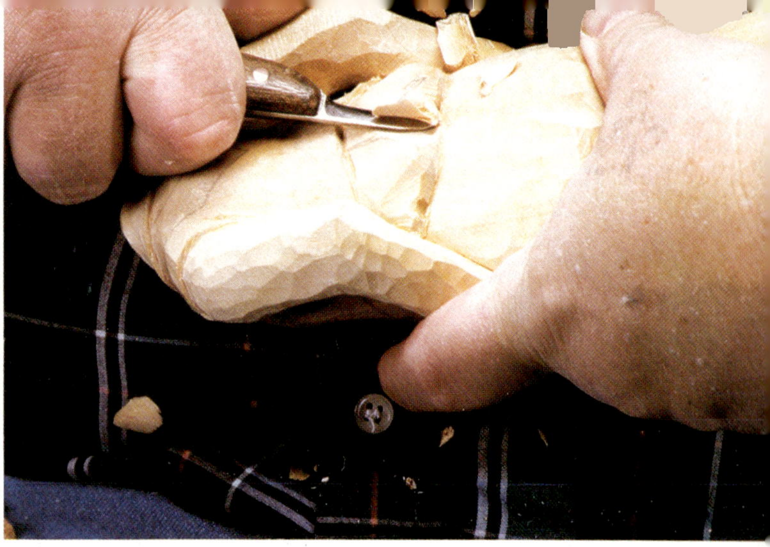

Cut out the area of the suspenders with a knife and gouge as needed.

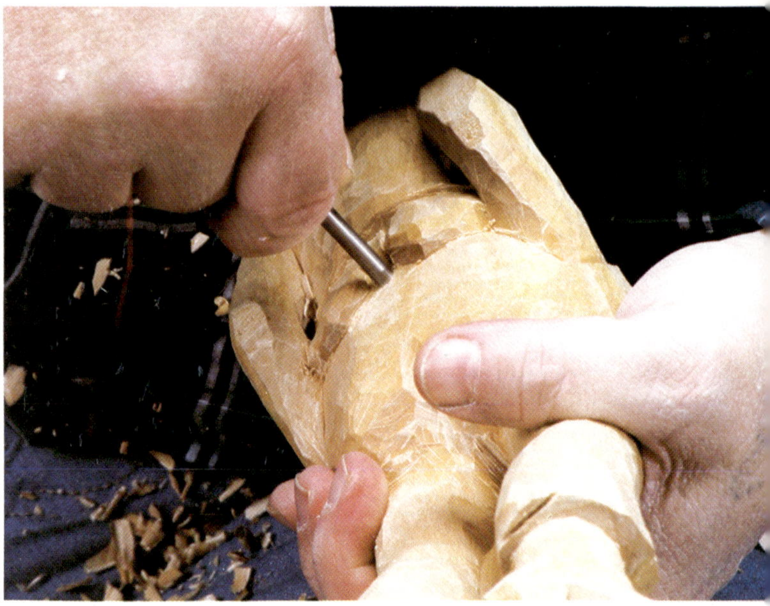

When the suspenders are formed, add a button.

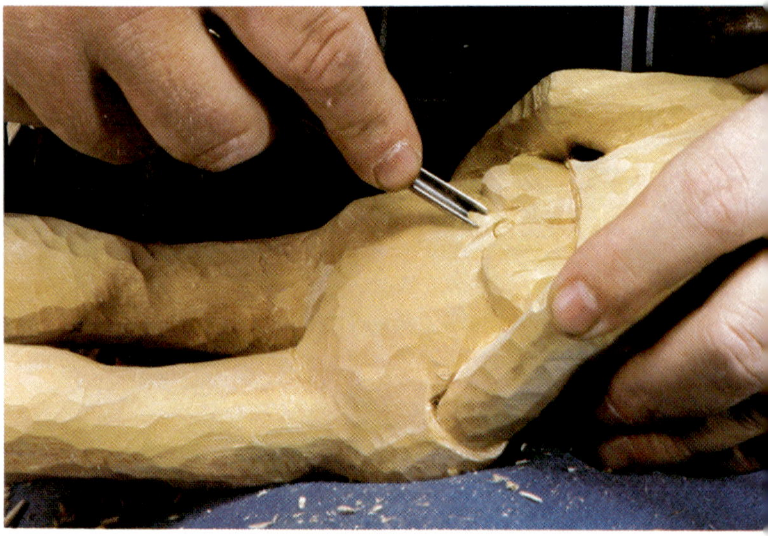

Add some stretch marks toward the button using a gouge.

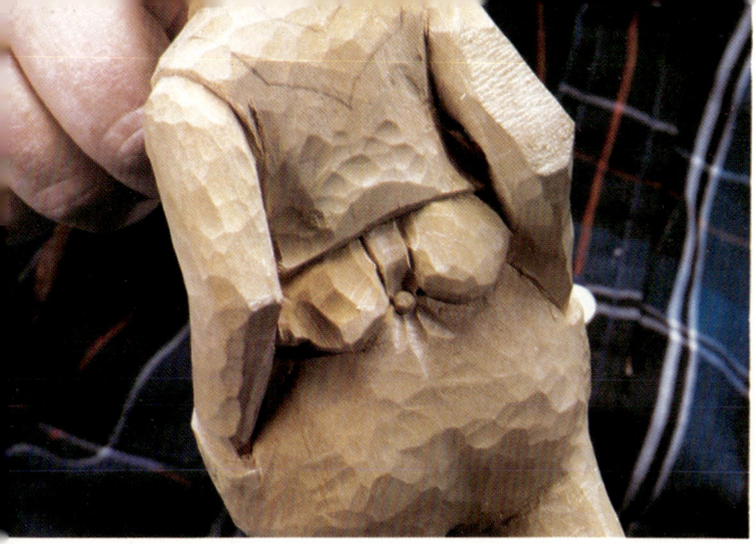

The shirt and suspenders in the back.

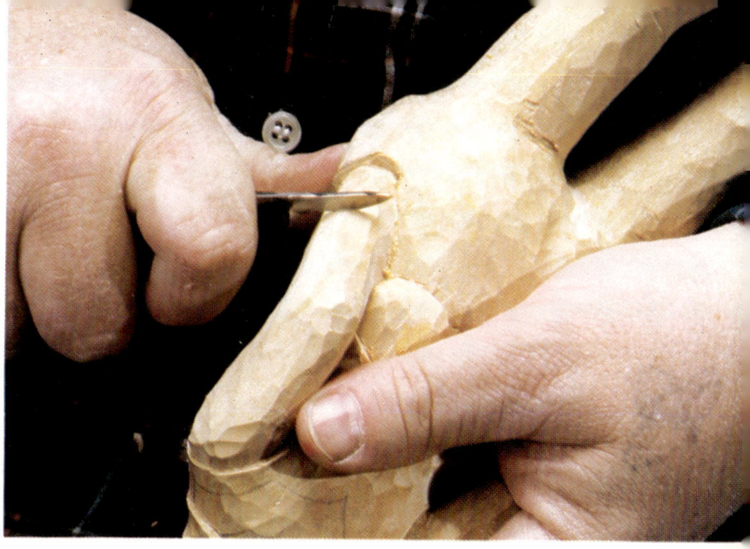

Make a stop at the top of the cuff, cutting straight in...

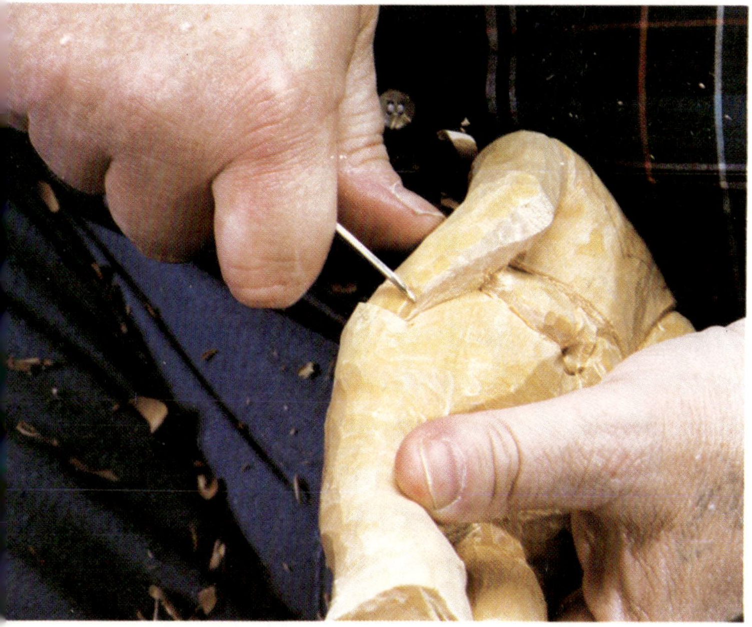

At the bottom of the sleeve make a straight cut...

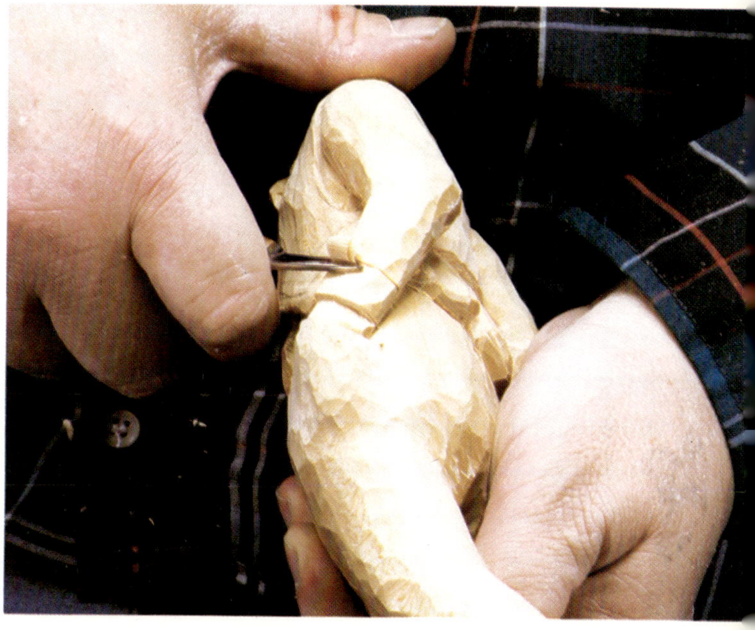

and back to it from cuff. It seems that you should trim from the sleeve, but in reality it just doesn't work to give you the bloused effect you seek.

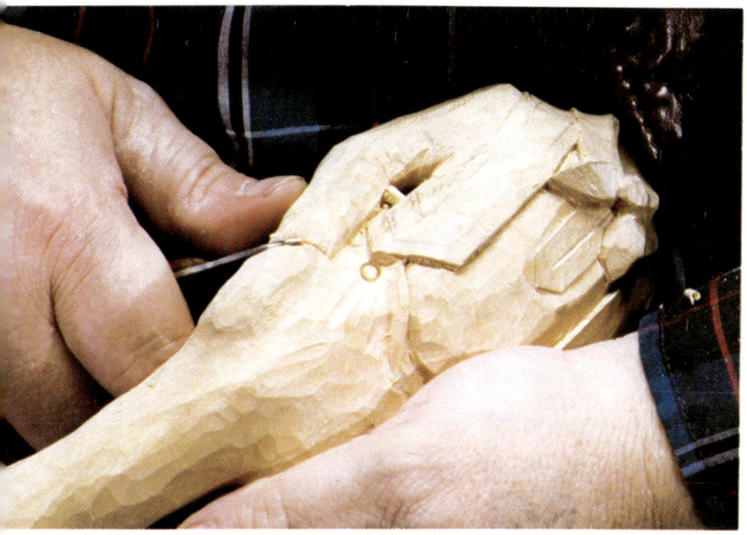

and trim back to it from the top of the pocket. This reveals just a little bit of the hand going into the pocket.

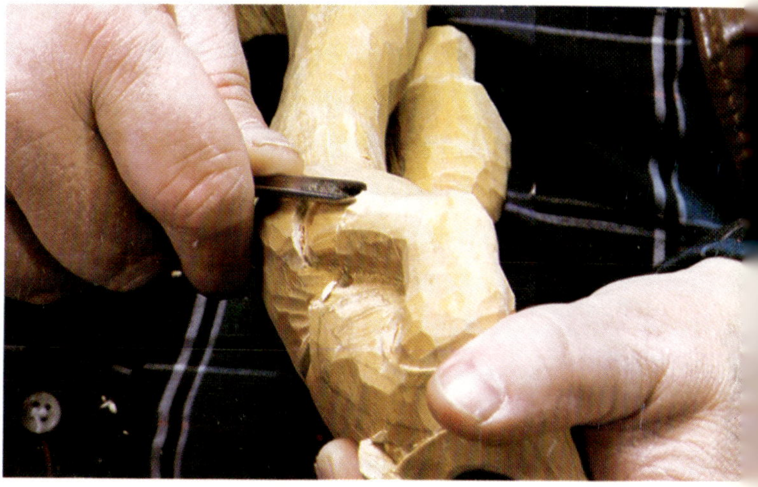

Use a gouge to make folds from the top of the cuff into the sleeve.

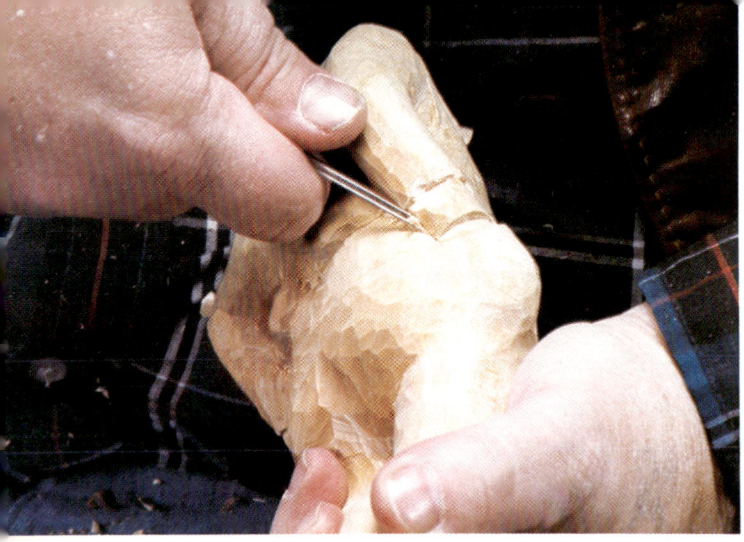

Use a veiner to make the line where the cuff comes together.

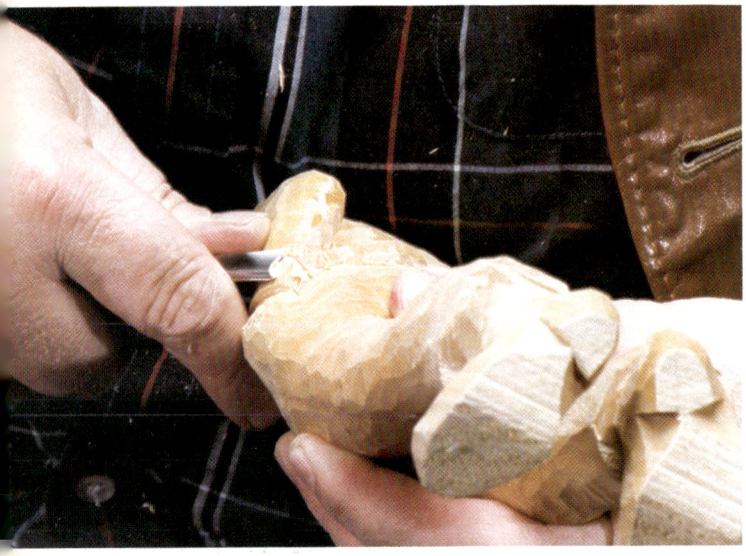

Gouge a little depression where the button will go.

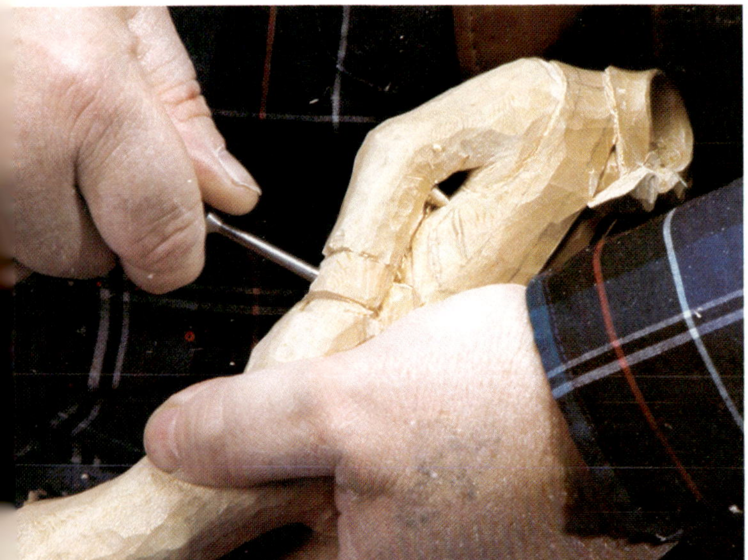

Put a button on the sleeve, using an eyepunch.

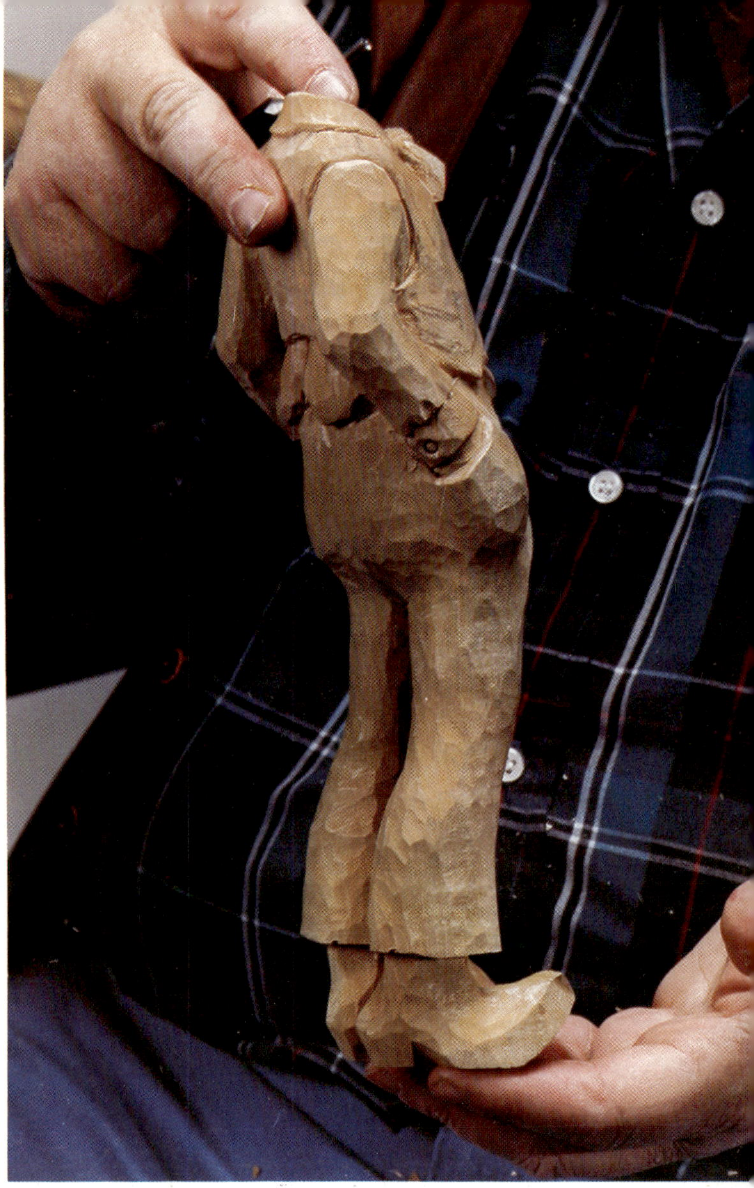

The finished sleeve.

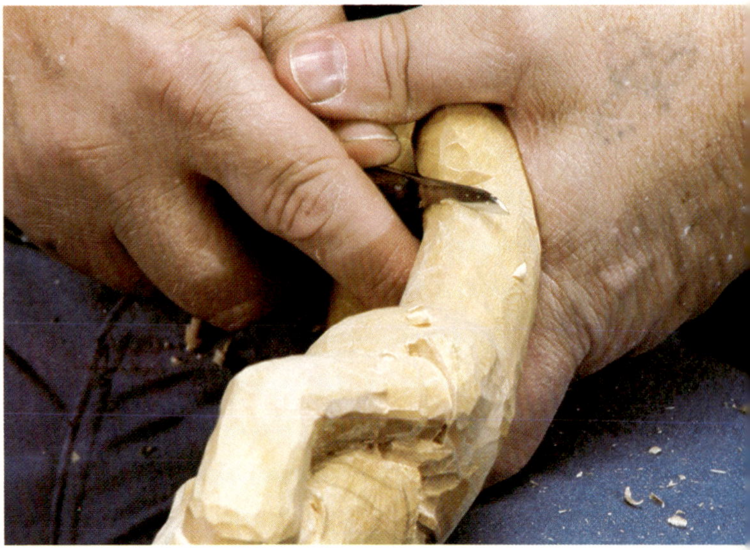

Add details to the body. Begin by using a knife to cut fold marks in the back of the knees and the elbows. These are done by cutting a slice with the knife, first one way...

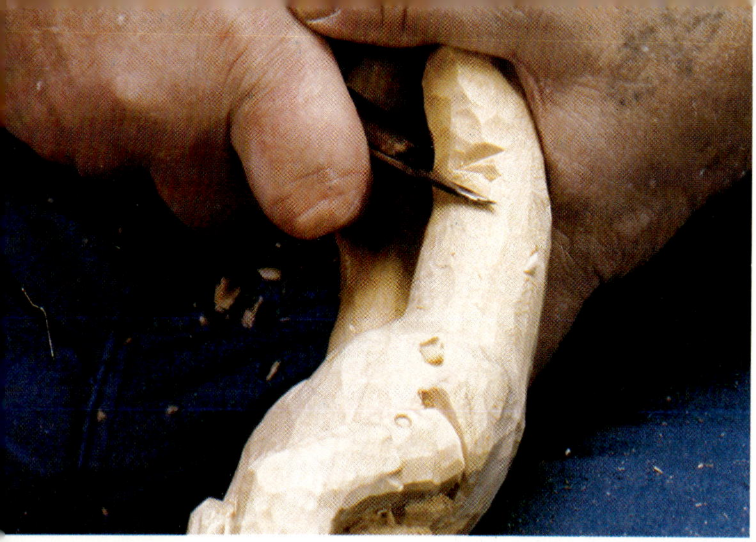

then the other.

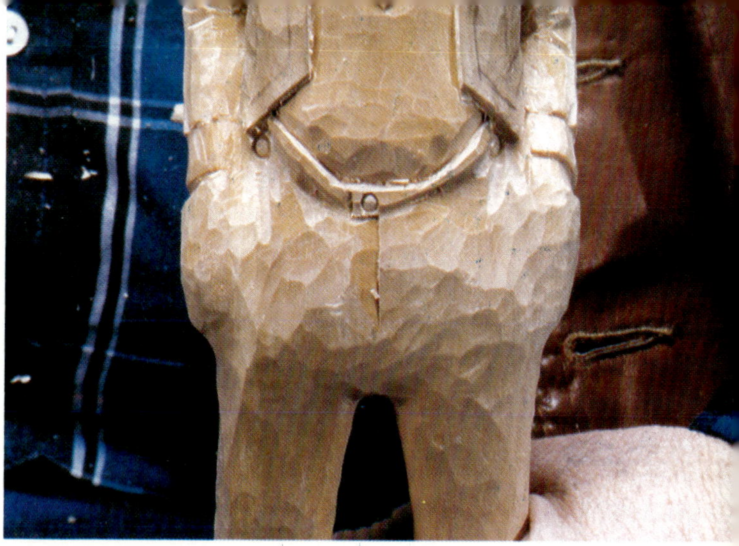

Add a line for the fly and a button in the front of the pants.

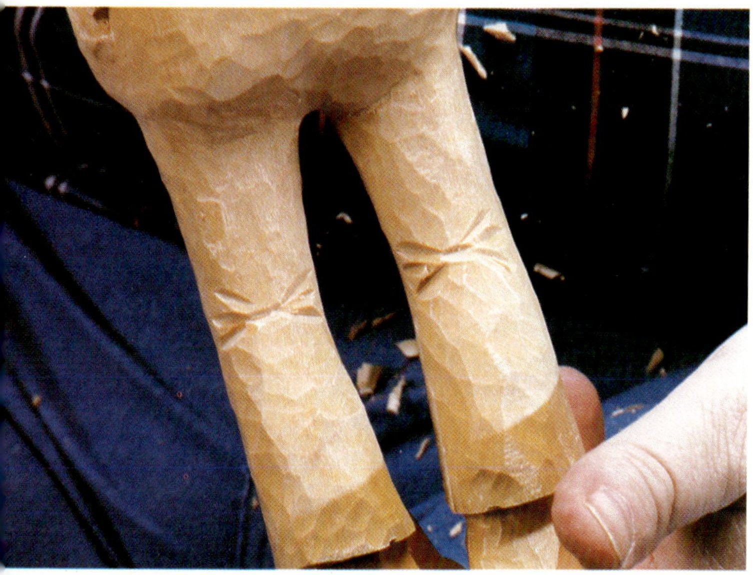

At the knees I often put three folds on either side of the back, and one between them.

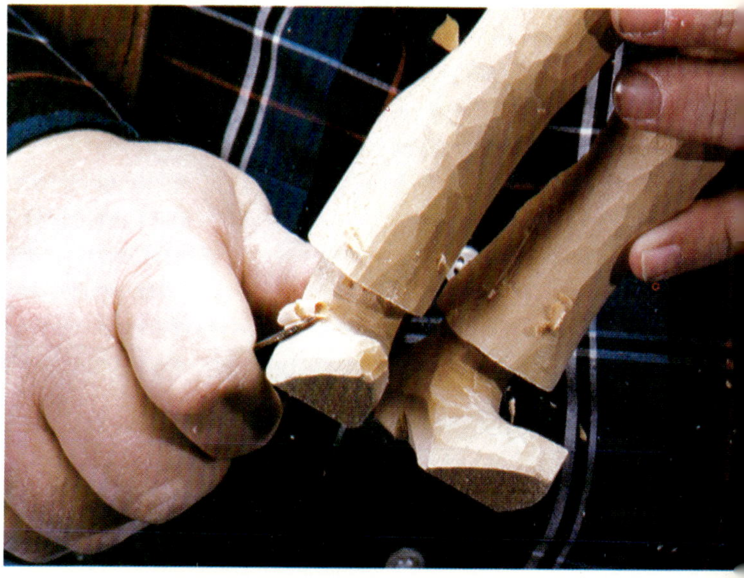

Shape and round the boots.

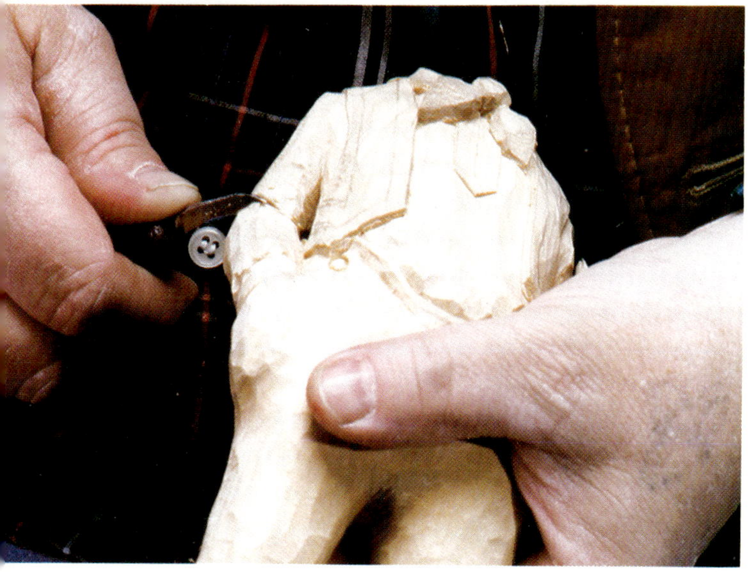

The same technique is used at the elbow.

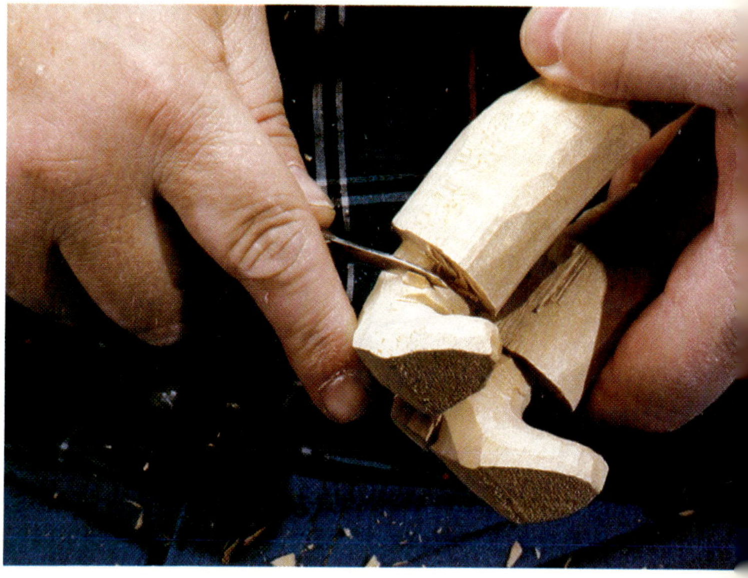

Put one crease across the instep of the boot, and another above it.

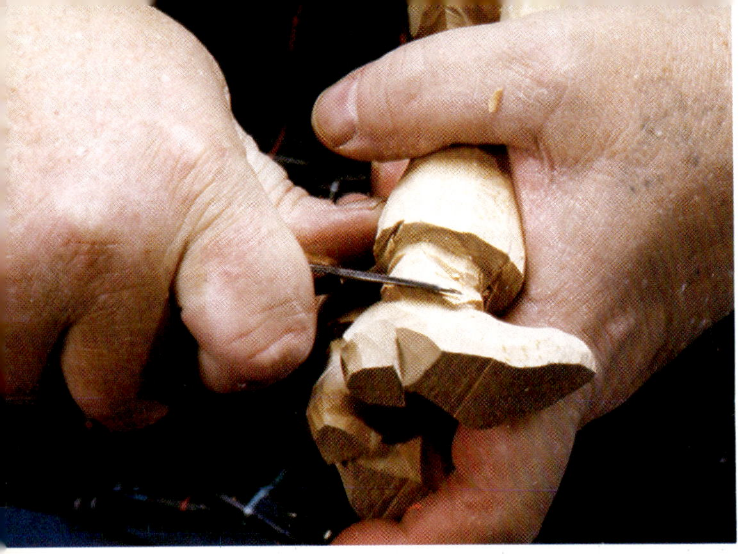

Also cut a double groove across the back of the boots, and a heavy crease across the ankles, both inside and outside.

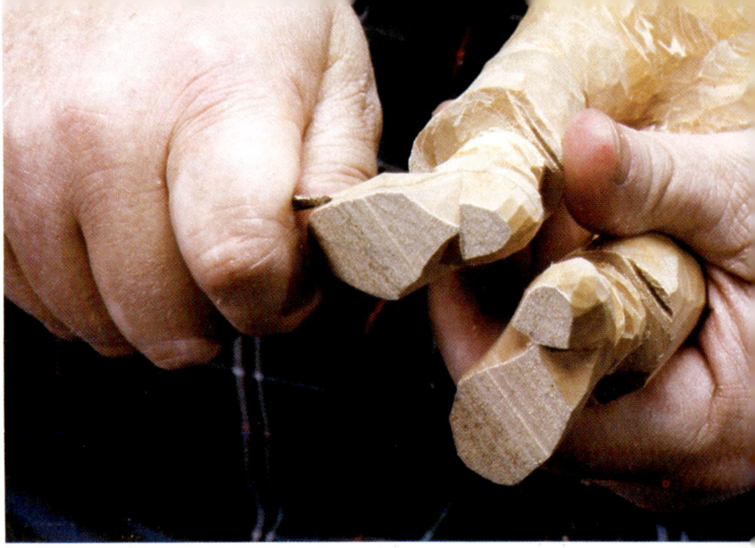

Cut a stop all around the boot.

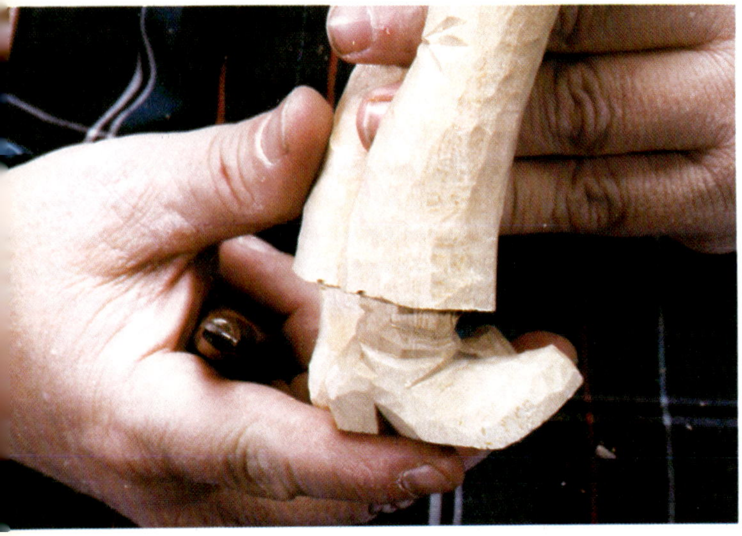

The grooves give the broken down look of a good pair of cowboy boots.

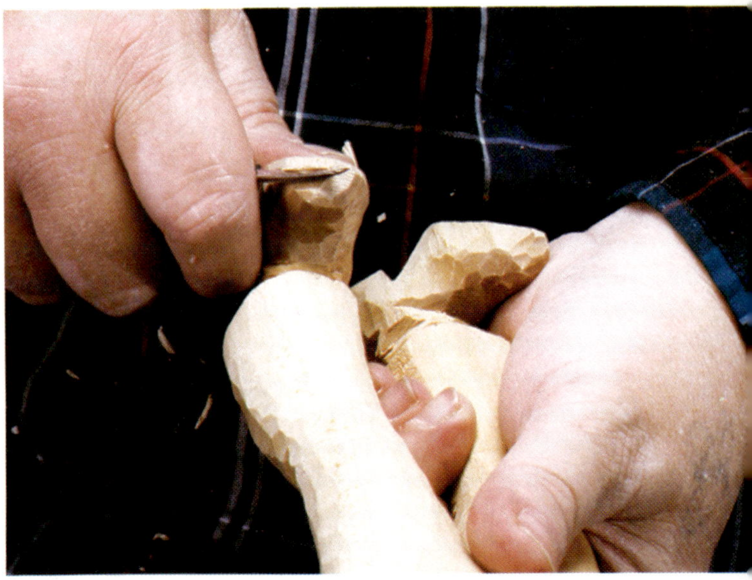

Trim back to it from the top of the boot.

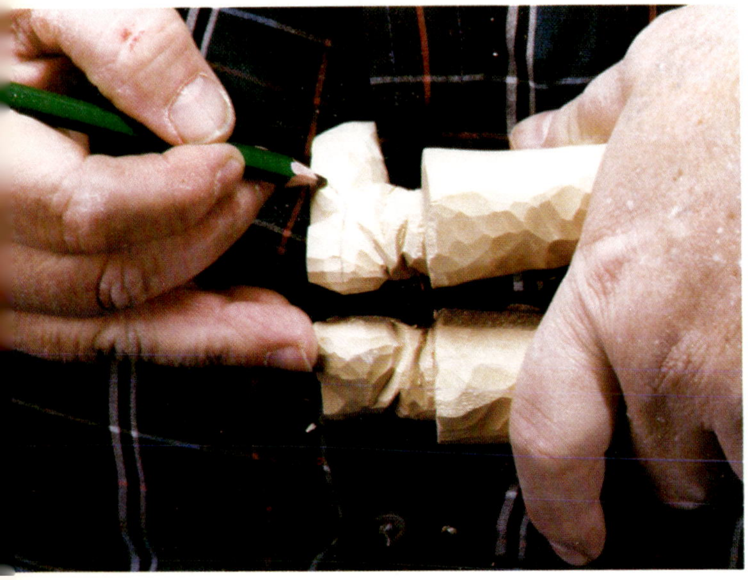

Draw a line around the sole and heel.

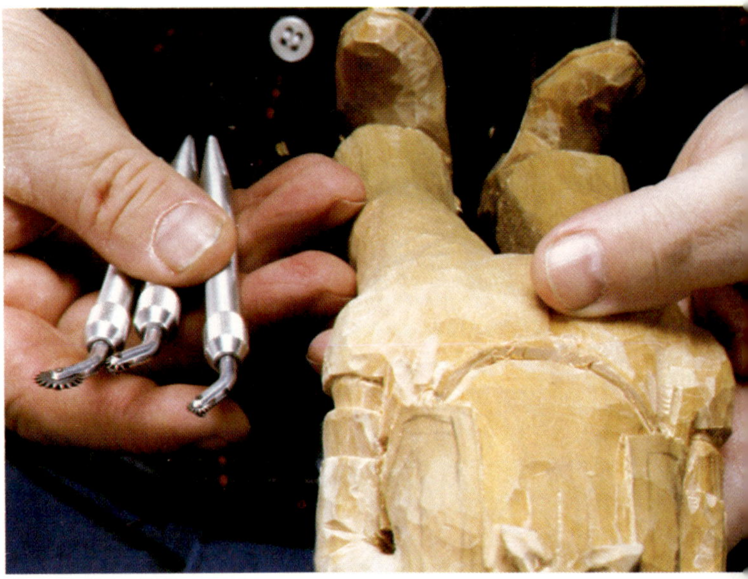

To make stitch marks I use a pattern wheel. They come in three sizes.

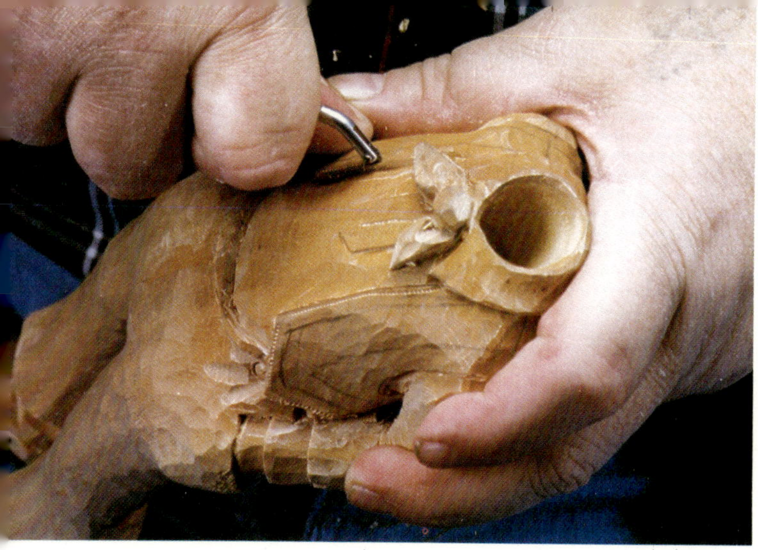

In this case I will use the finest one around the vest. Go all around the outline of the vest and across the shoulders.

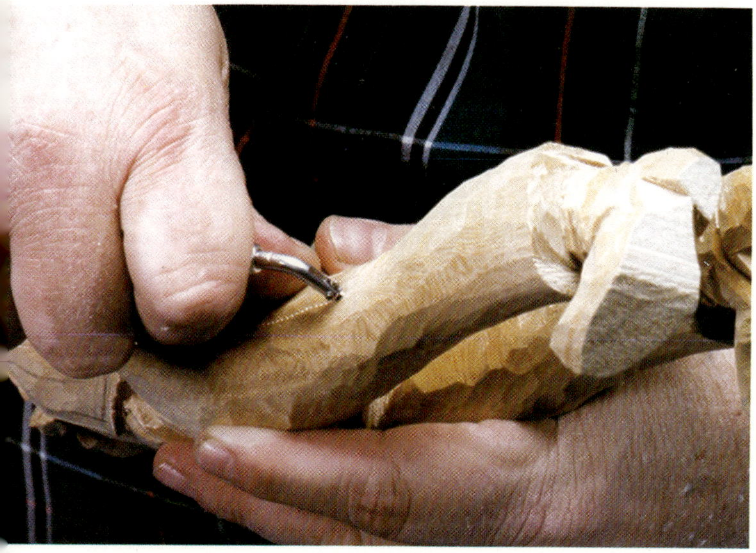

On the pants I will use a small wheel with fewer teeth to make bigger stitches. Go down the sides of the legs, down the middle of the seat, on the fly, and around the pockets. Also go around the gusset of the shirt.

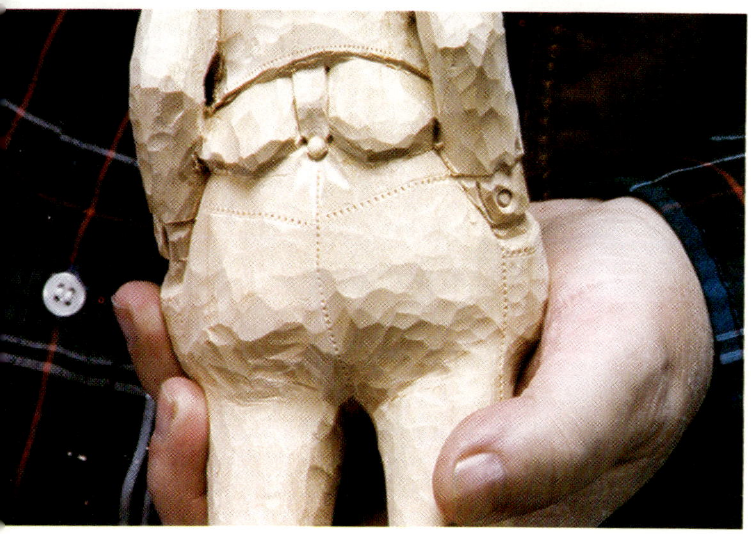

Include a yoke stitch going into the center of the seat.

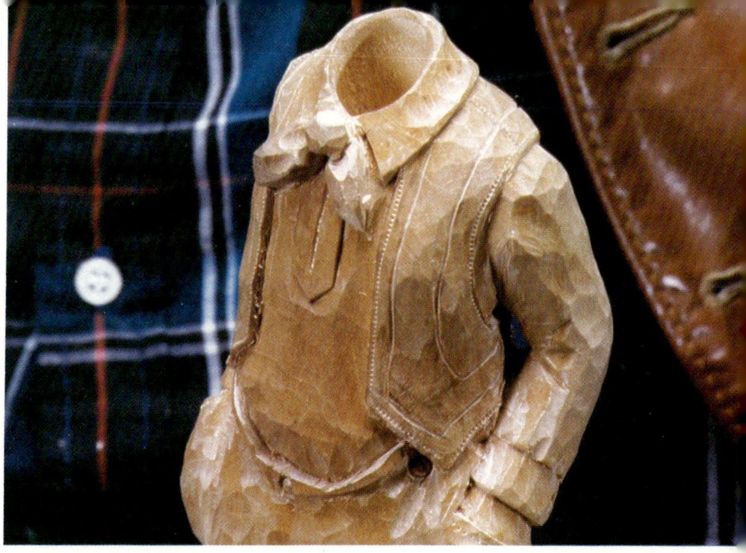

There are a couple of options for the decorative part of the vest. I could simply cut in stop lines and do the decoration with paint, simulating fabric or beadwork. Or I could use a wood burner and simulate tooling of the leather. I think I'll carve a pattern with a v-gouge and paint it.

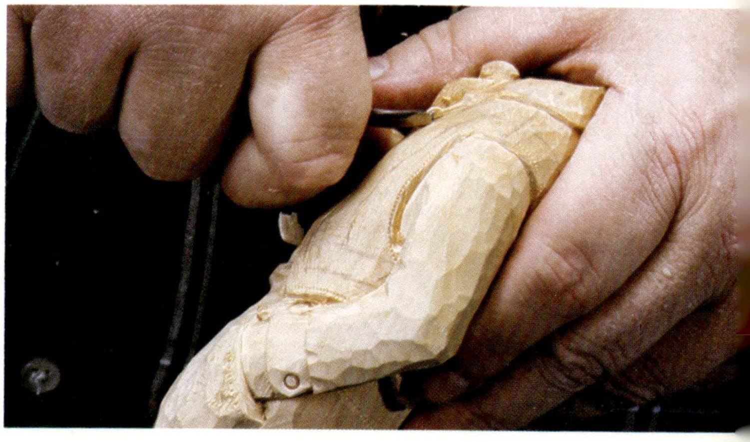

Run the v-tool over the lines...

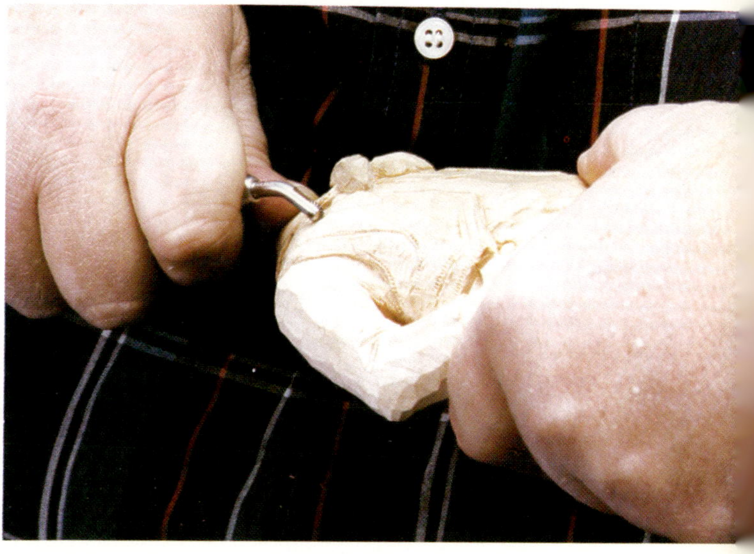

in the inner panel of the vest use the pattern wheel to make stitches so it looks as though the panel has been added on.

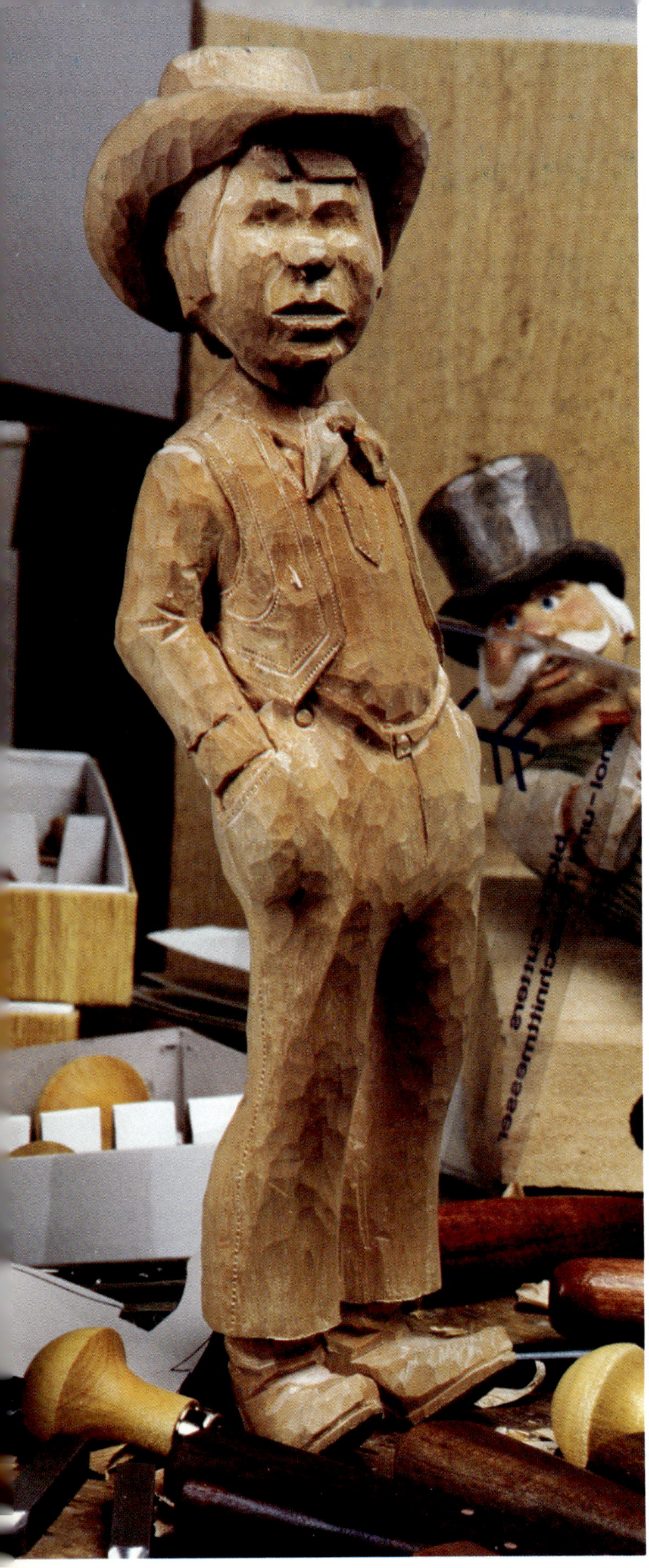

The body of the cowboy is finished. Here he is with his head attached. There is still some detail to finish on the head before they are permanently joined.

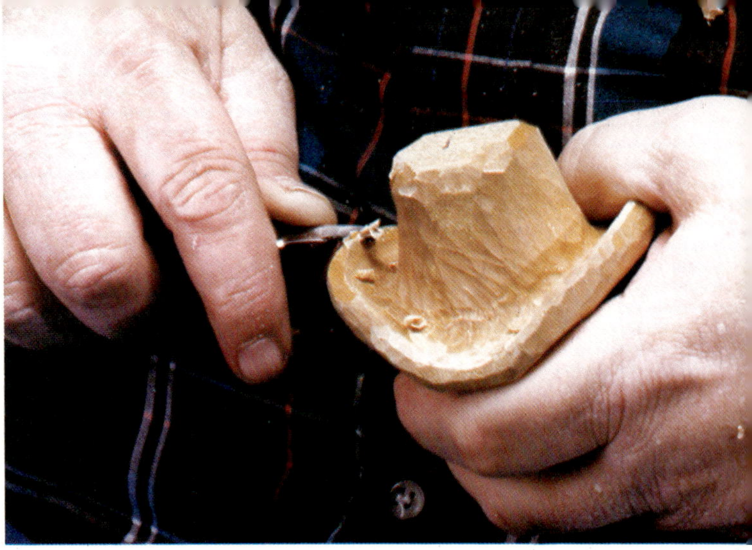

Begin by cleaning up the knife marks from the head.

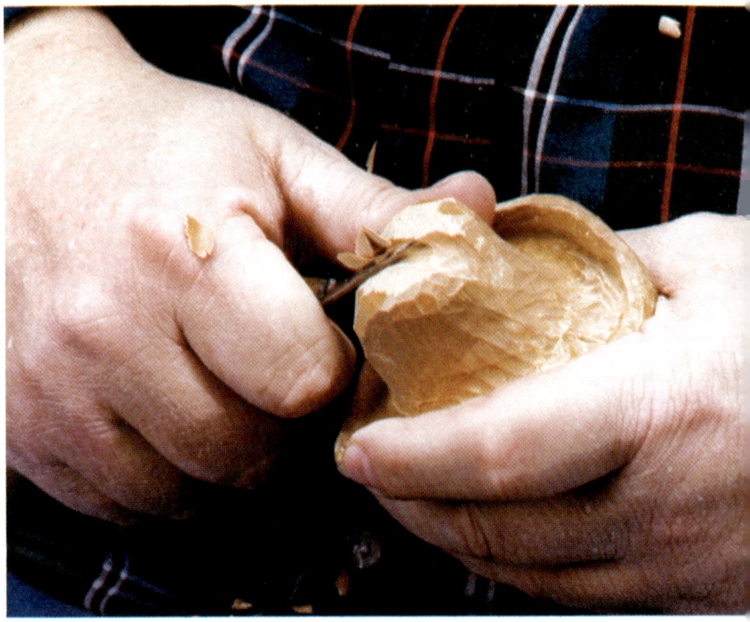

Put a crease down the middle of the crown.

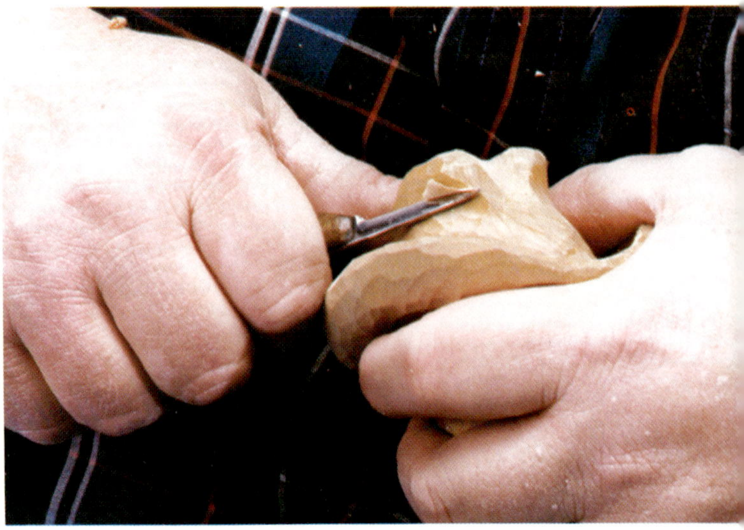

Then add indentations on either side of the front of the crown.

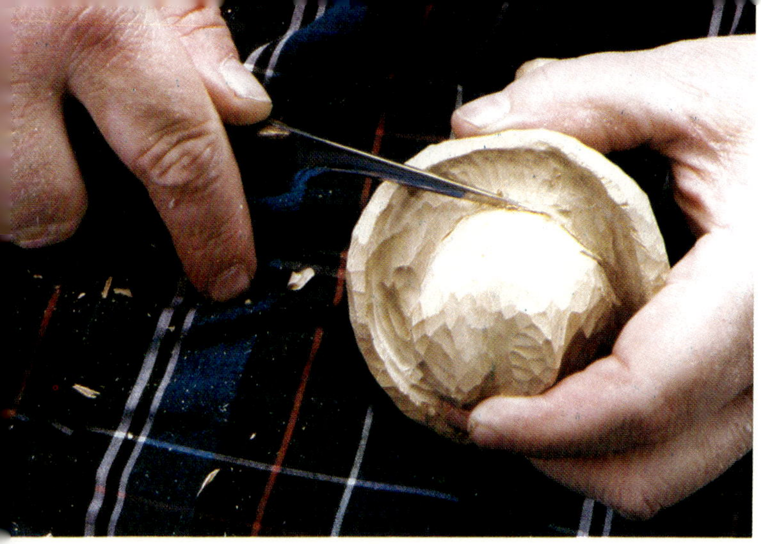

Cut a groove around the crown to mark the bottom of the hat band.

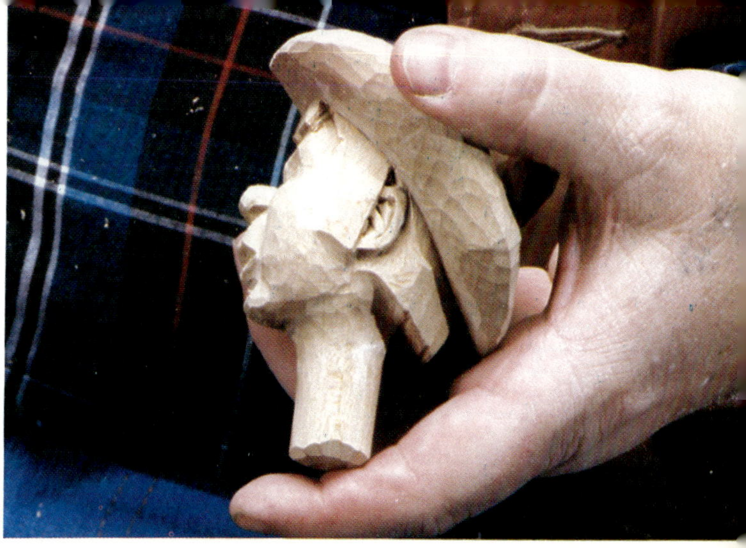

Cut another at the bottom of the ear pointed the opposite direction. Then cut a slice that follows the curve of the ear. This gives the basic shape to the ear.

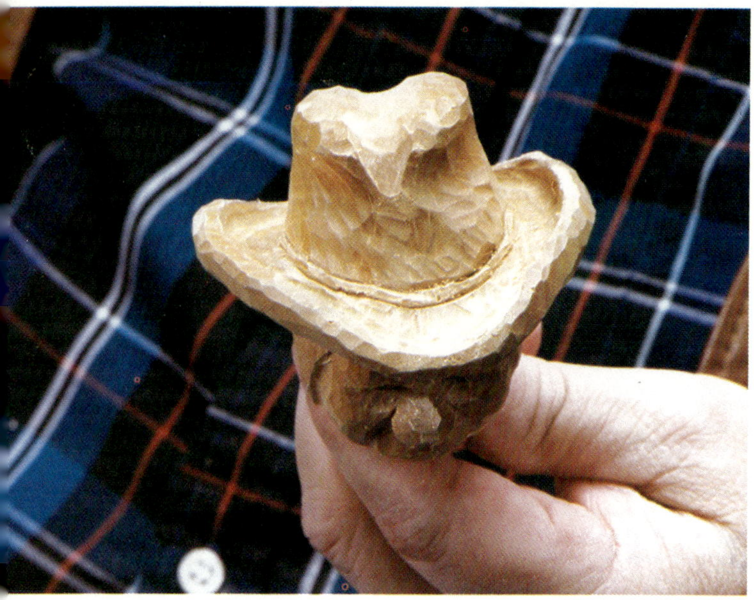

In the same way, cut around the top of the band to give this result.

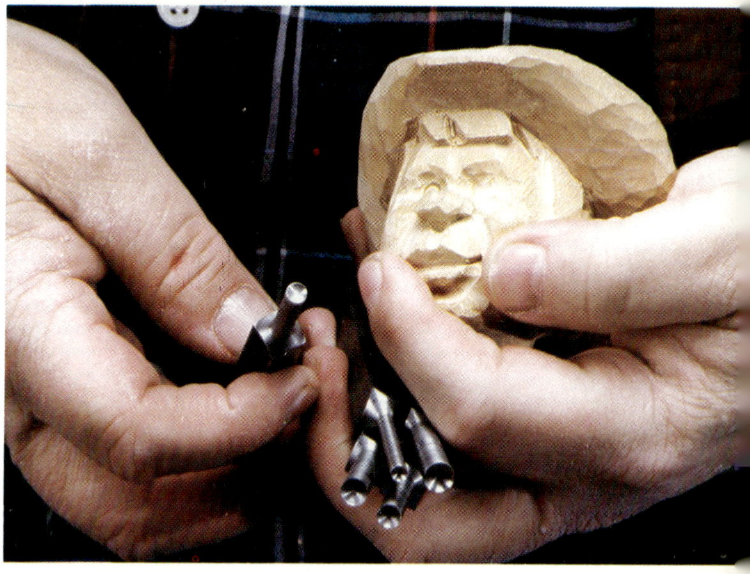

Use an eyepunch to form the iris. The punches come in different sizes.

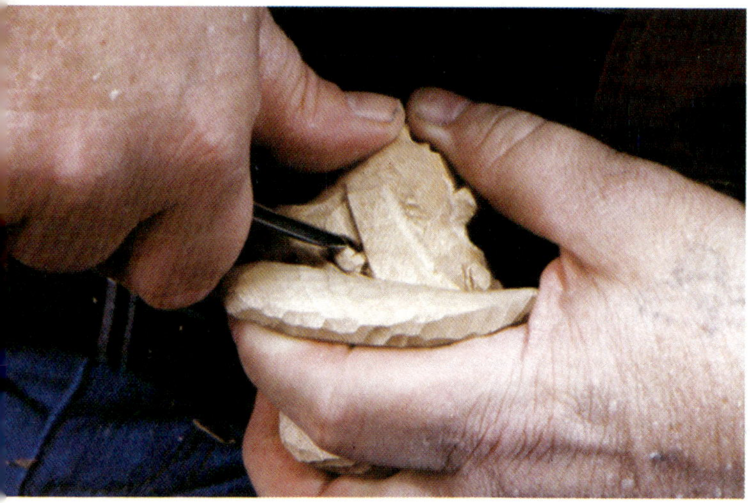

Cut a small three-cut triangle at the top of the inside of the ear with the point coming toward the sideburn.

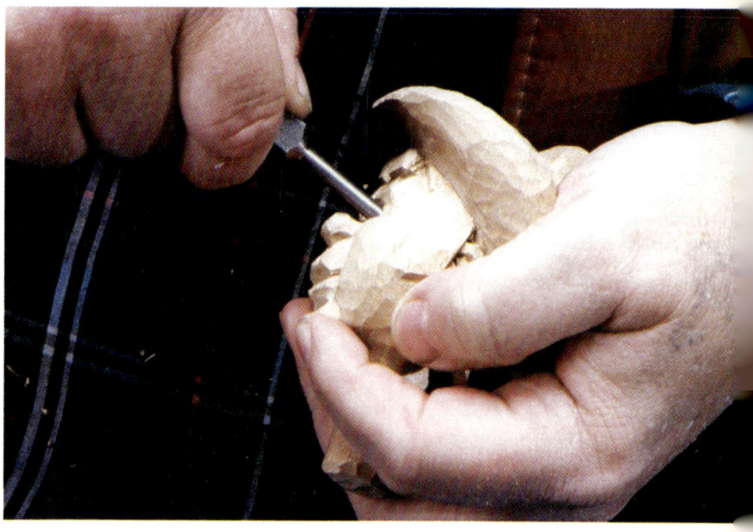

Pick the size that looks best and push it in place and turn.

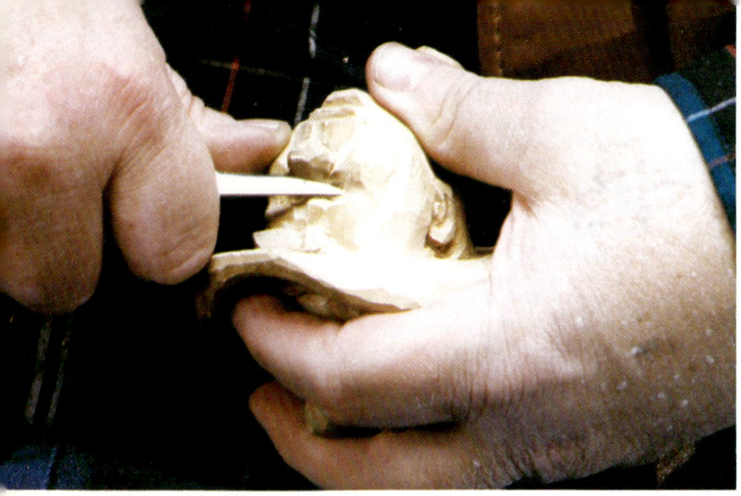

To form the corners of the eyes come straight in at an angle over the iris.

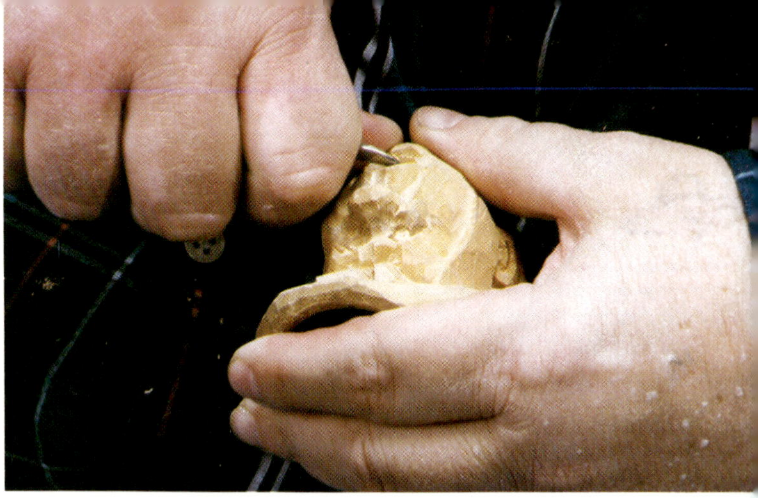

Refine the face as you go, smoothing, removing saw marks, reducing things that are obviously too big, and add details.

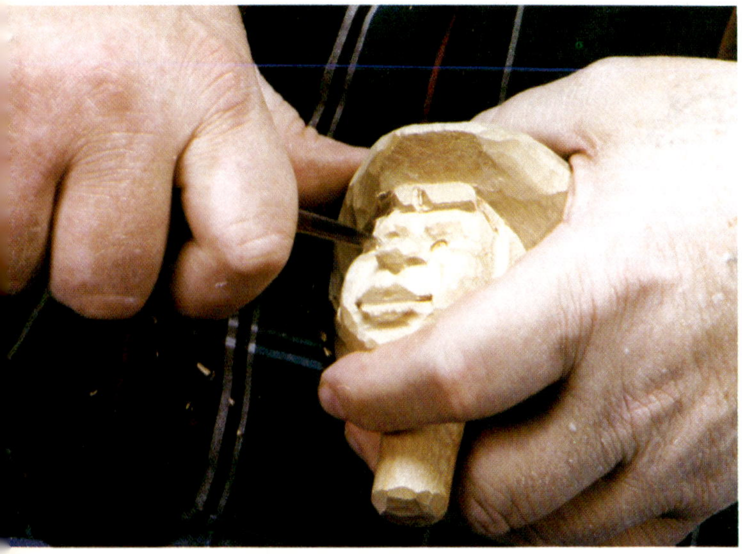

Come back to this cut with two others from the corner of the eye to form a triangle. The same is done on the inside of the eye, though the triangle will be smaller. When the triangles are formed go over the iris with the punch again to redefine the lines.

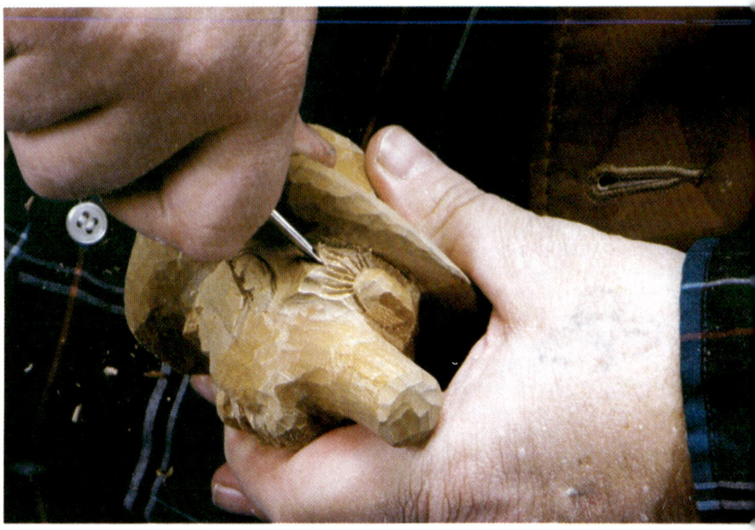

Carve a little knot in the back of the hair. This traditional form was used by sailors and cowboys, and was often covered with tar. It was called a "jacktar." Begin to add hair lines with the veiner.

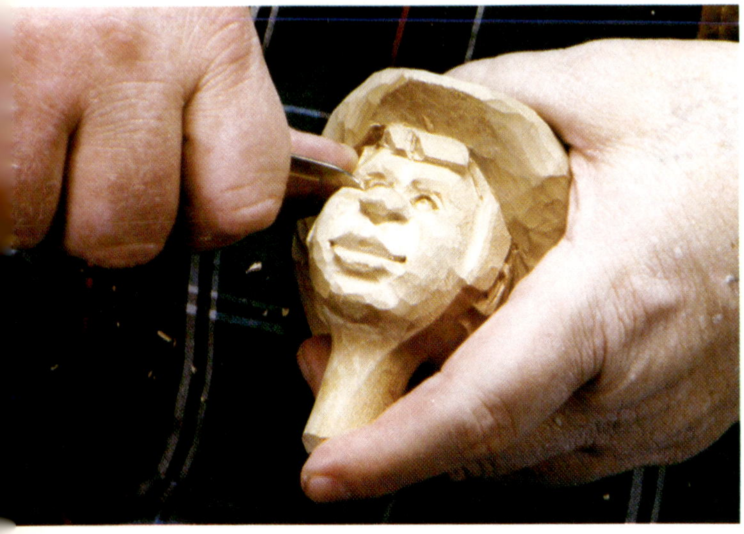

Make a small incised cut over the eye to form the lid.

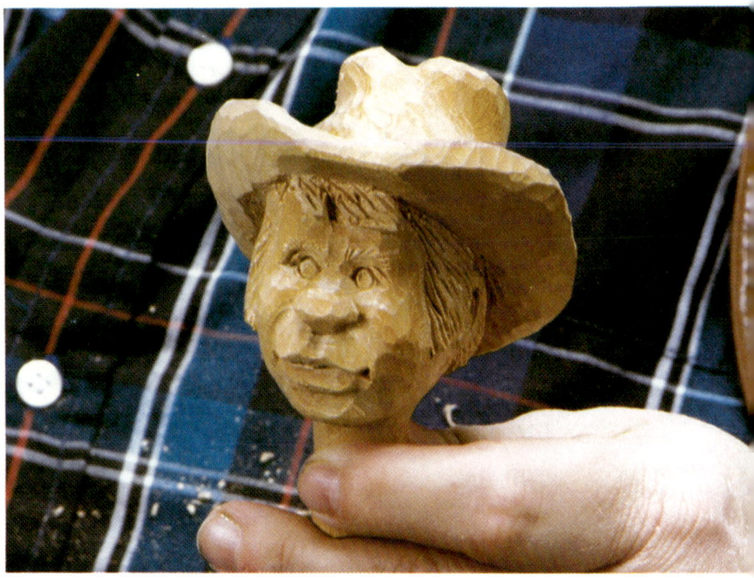

The hair and eyebrows completed.

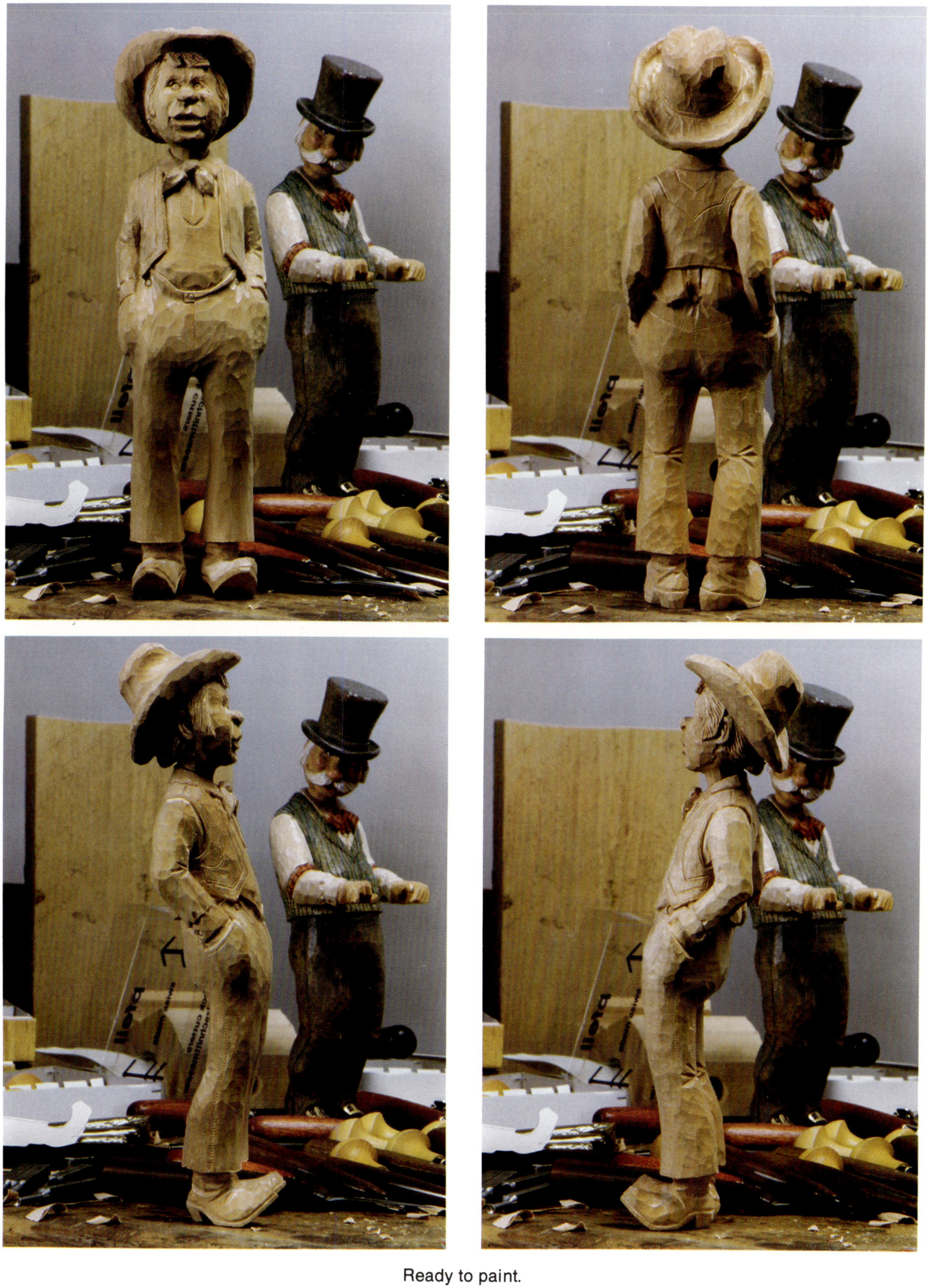

Ready to paint.

Painting the Cowboy

For wood carving I use Winsor and Newton Alkyd tube paints. These are thinned with turpentine to a consistency that works with the carving. I mix my paints in glass juice bottles, putting a bit of paint and adding turpentine. I don't use exact measurements. Instead I use trial and error, adding a bit of paint or a bit of turpentine until I get the thickness I want.

What I look for is a watery mixture, almost like a wash. In this way the turpentine will carry the pigment into the wood, giving the stained look I like. It has always been my theory that if you are going to cover the wood, why use wood in the first place. It should be noted that with white the concentration of pigment needs to be a little stronger.

The juice bottles are handy for holding your paints. They are reclosable, easy to shake, and have the added advantage of leaving a concentrated amount of color on the inside of the lid and the sides of the bottle which can be used when more intense color is needed.

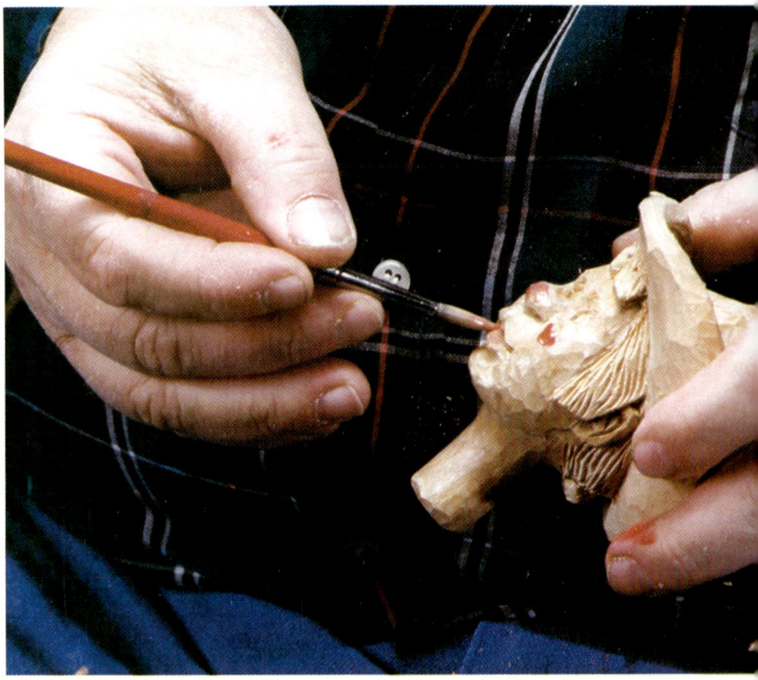

Add a little red to the nose, cheeks, and lips. Spread and blend with a dry brush.

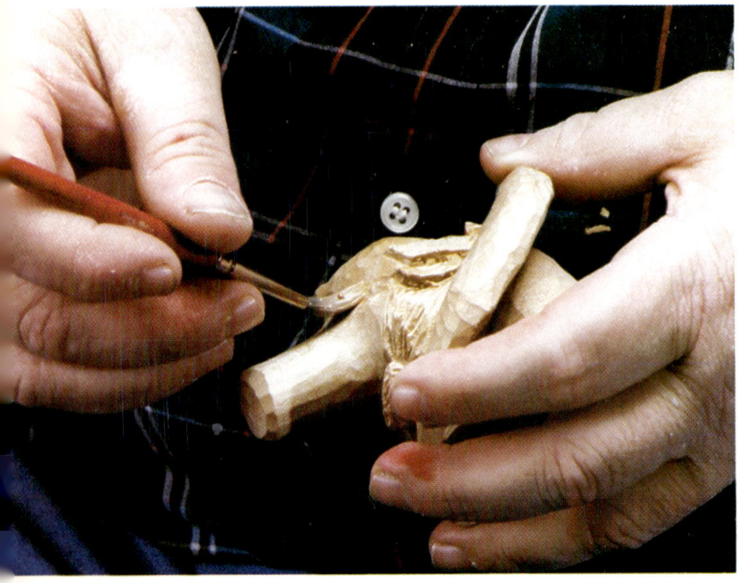

Begin with the flesh tones on the face and where the hand shows above the pocket. For skin I use a tube flesh color with raw sienna added. This takes away some of the pink.

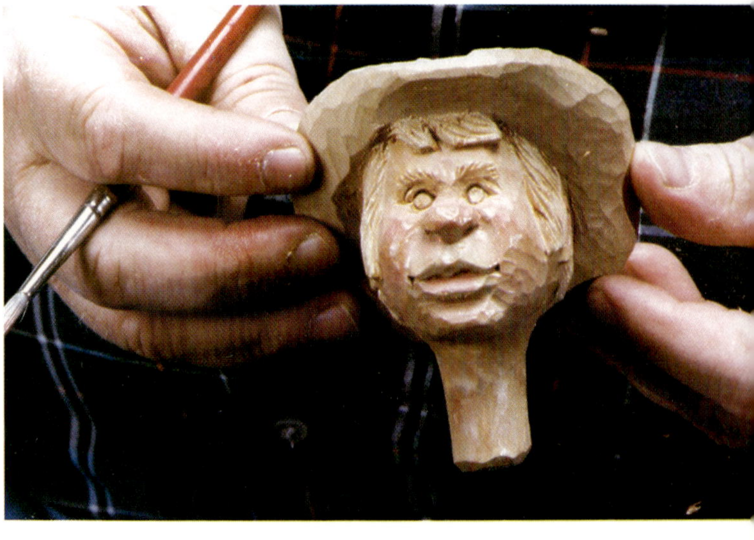

This gives him an outdoorsy look. You can also put a bit of red on the top of his ears and the back of his neck.

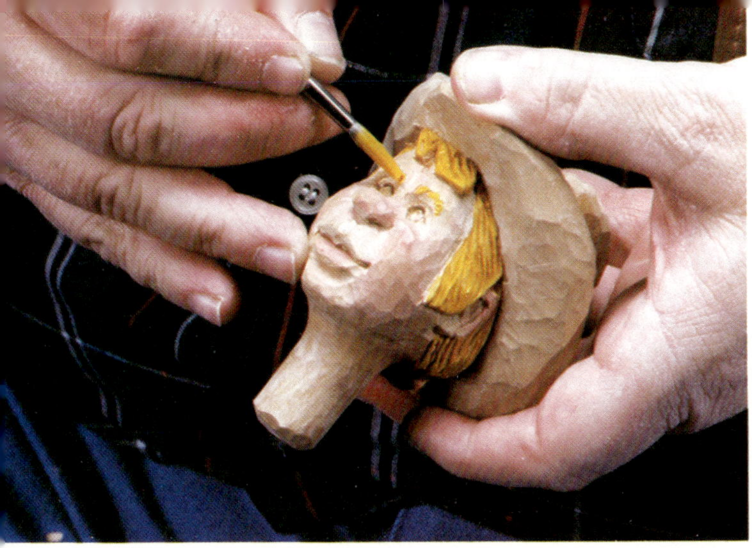

Our cowboy will have red hair, which is yellow paint with just a little red mixed with it.

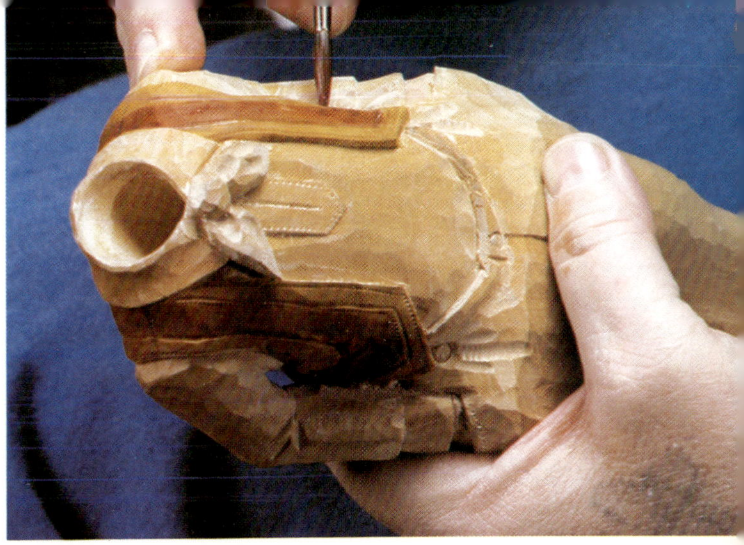

On the body continue with the burnt sienna on the boots. Apply raw sienna to the whole vest before painting the inside decorative panels with burnt sienna.

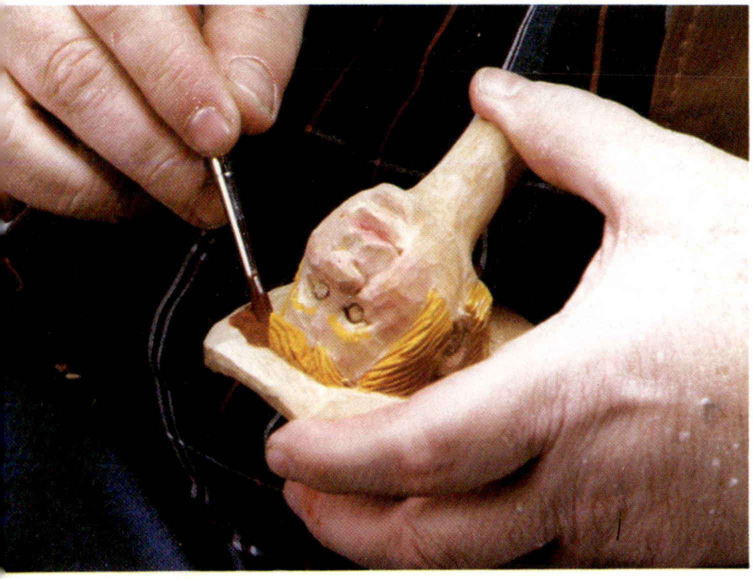

The hat is burnt sienna. Start under the brim so if it soaks through it will be toward the top of the hat where it will do no harm. Paint the hat band burnt umber.

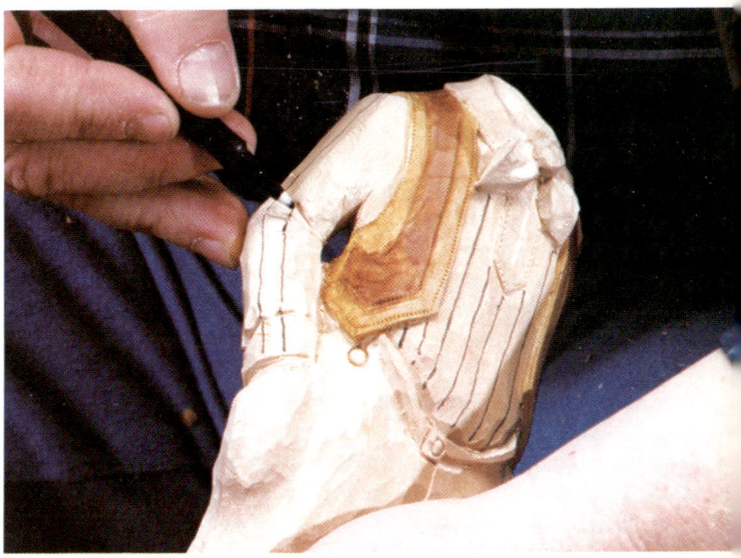

To make patterns I use a Flair™ pen. Since it is a water soluble ink, it is important to go over it quickly with the turpentine based paint. This seals it. I'm going to make the shirt striped.

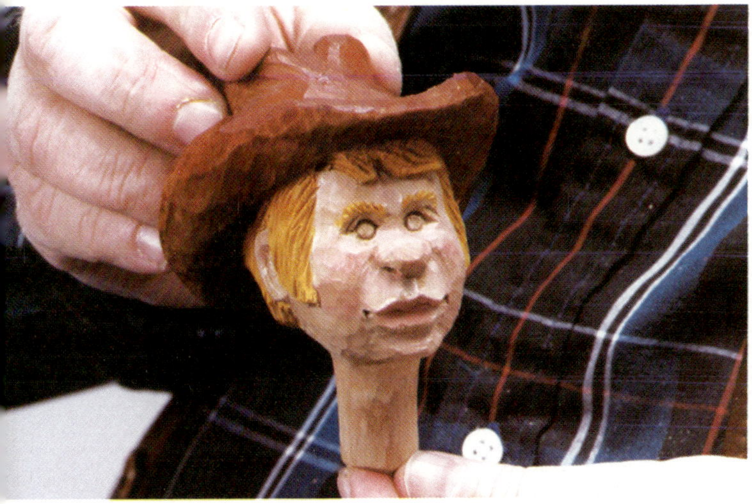

The painted head and hat. The eyes will be the last thing to be painted.

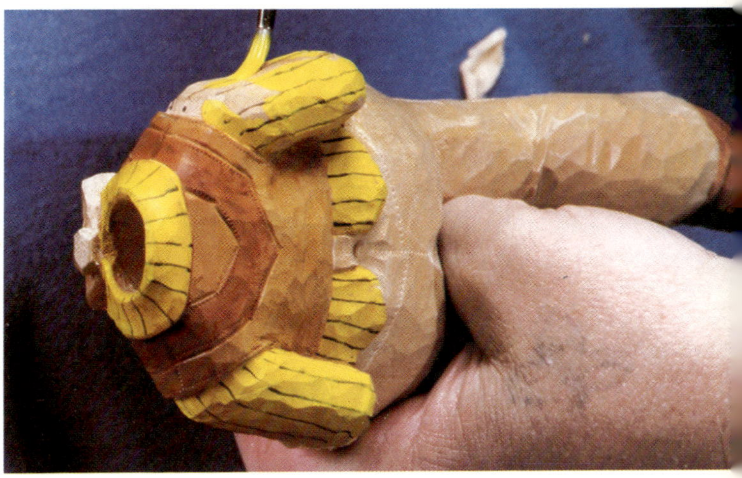

After striping the shirt, I've decided to paint it yellow. Paint the buttons of the shirt and the pants burnt sienna.

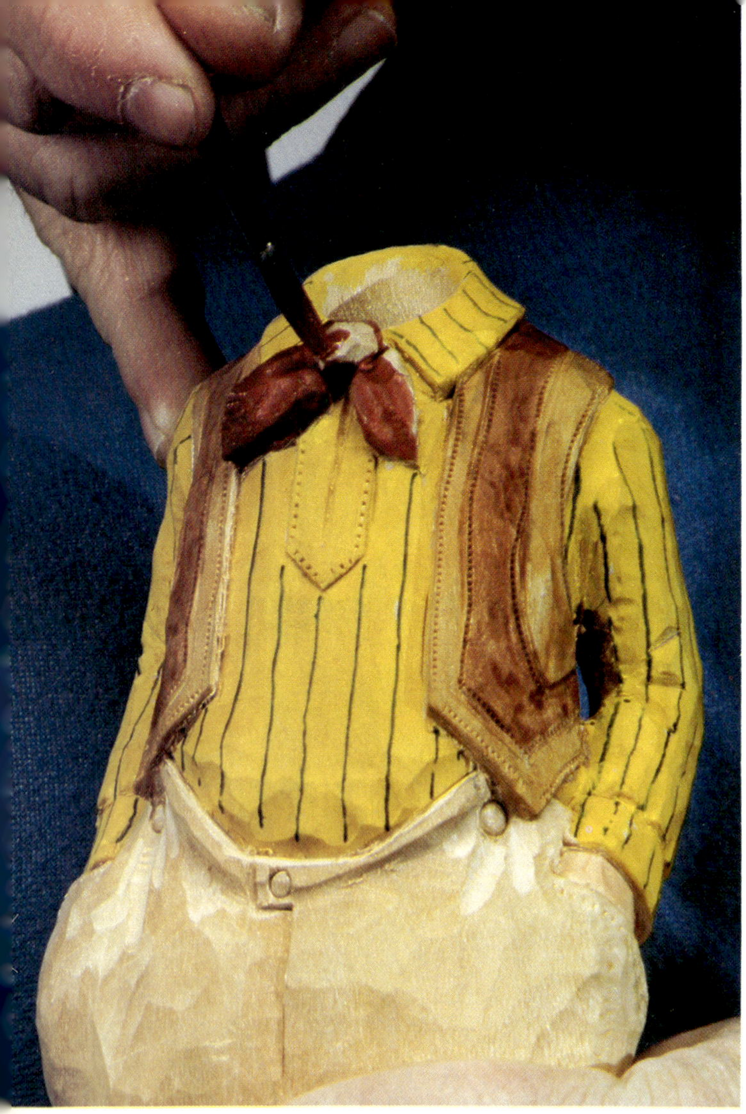

For the neckerchief and the back of the suspenders I will be using Alizarin crimson.

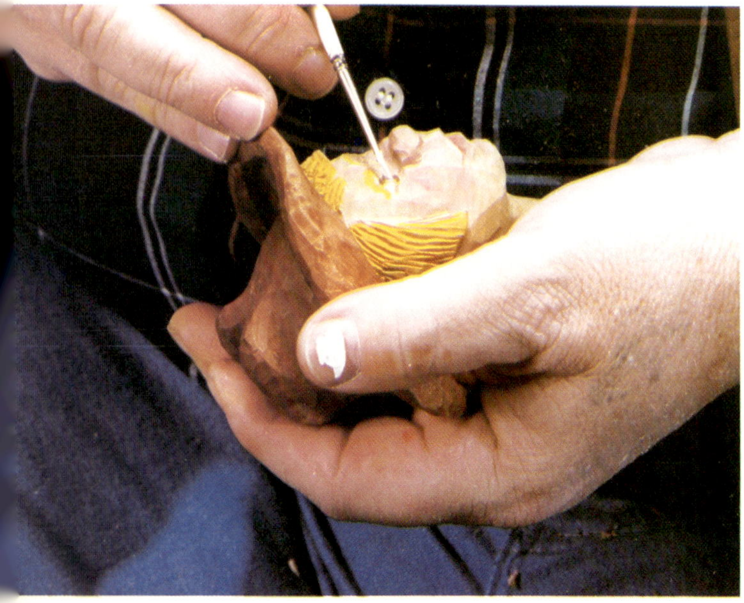

Using your thumb as a palette and a small brush apply white to the eyes.

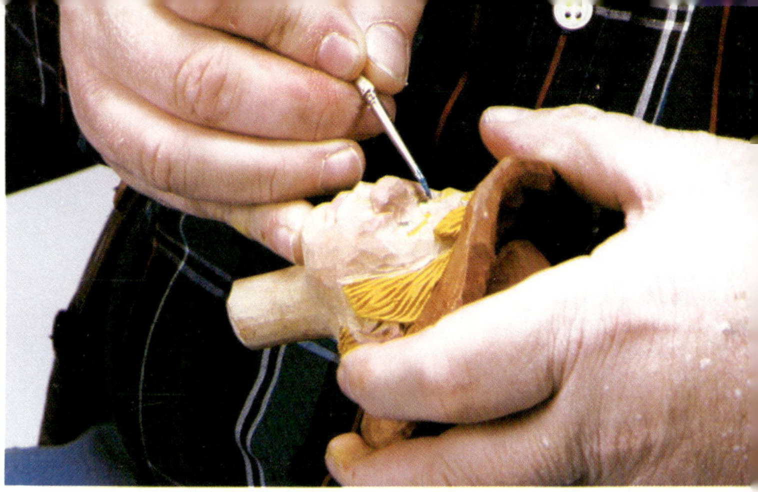

Take blue from the top of the paint bottle, where it is concentrated, and apply it to the irises.

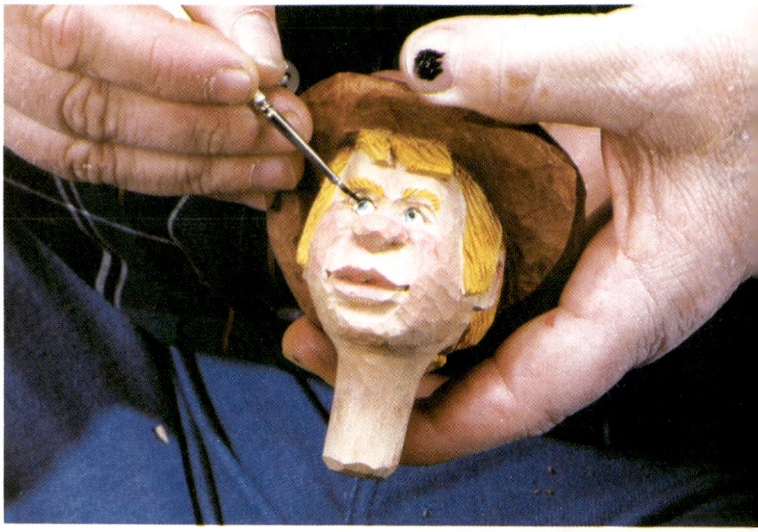

Use black from the bottle cap and paint the pupils. Again use your thumb for a palette and a very small brush with just a dab of paint.

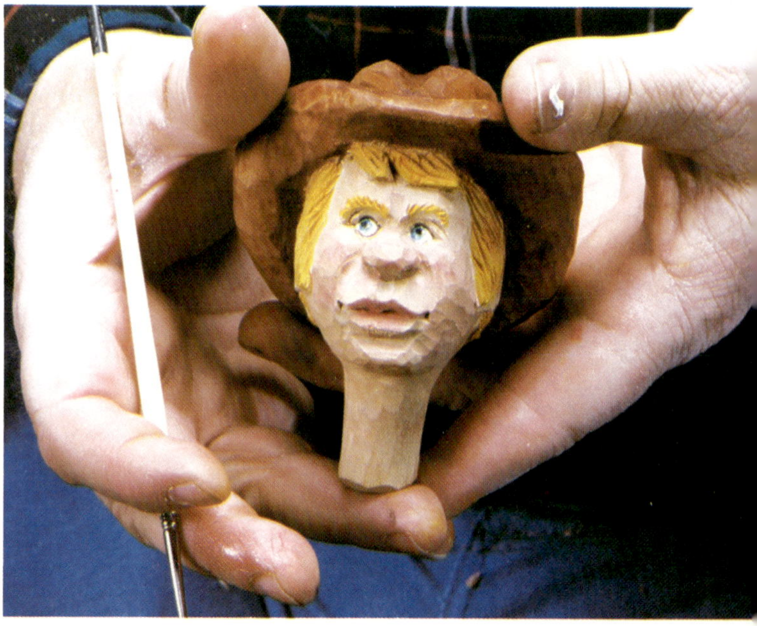

Finally add a glint of white paint to bring the eyes to life.

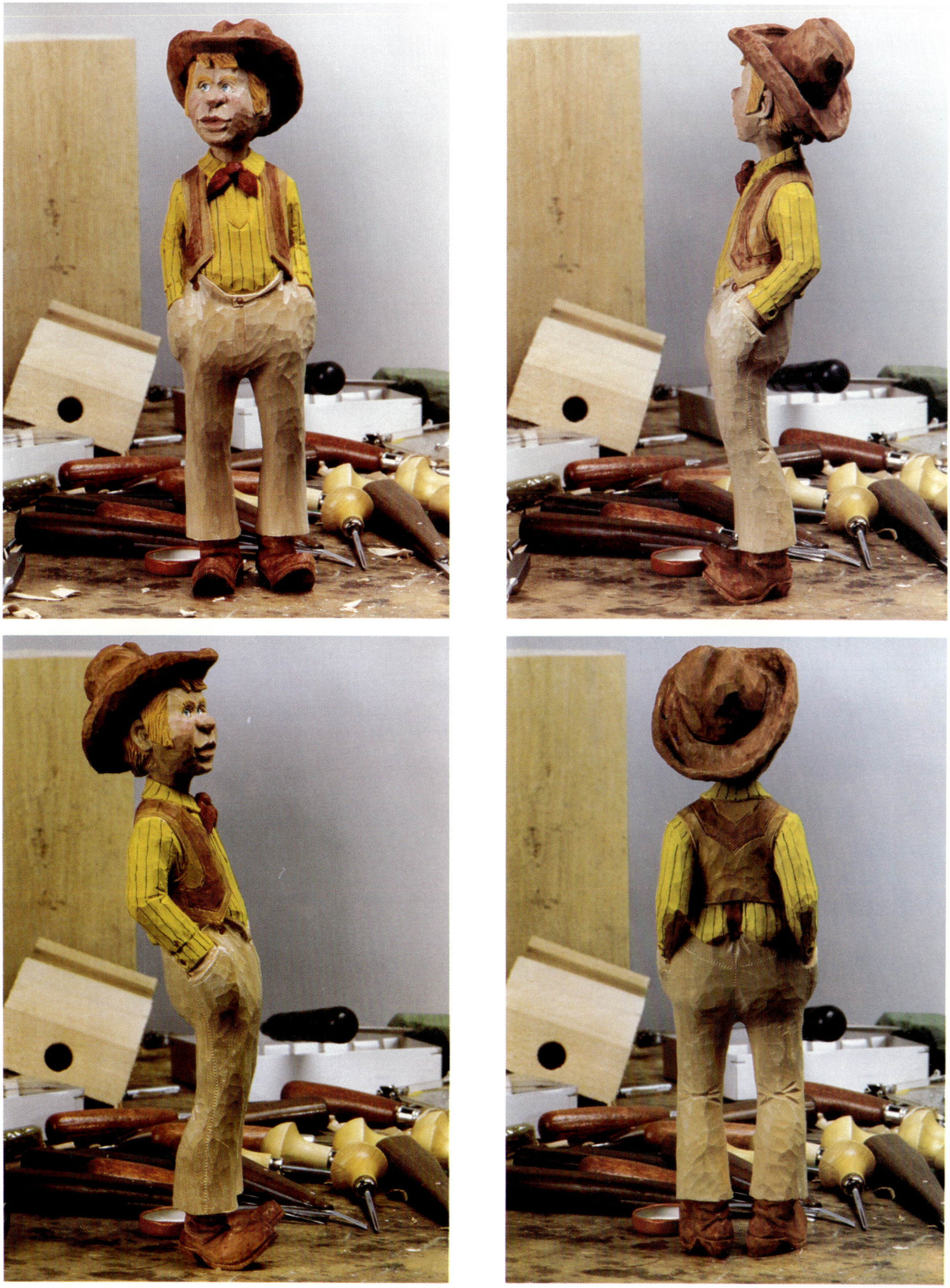

After you have the head set the way you want it, glue it in place. Here is the finished cowboy.

Gallery of the Saloon

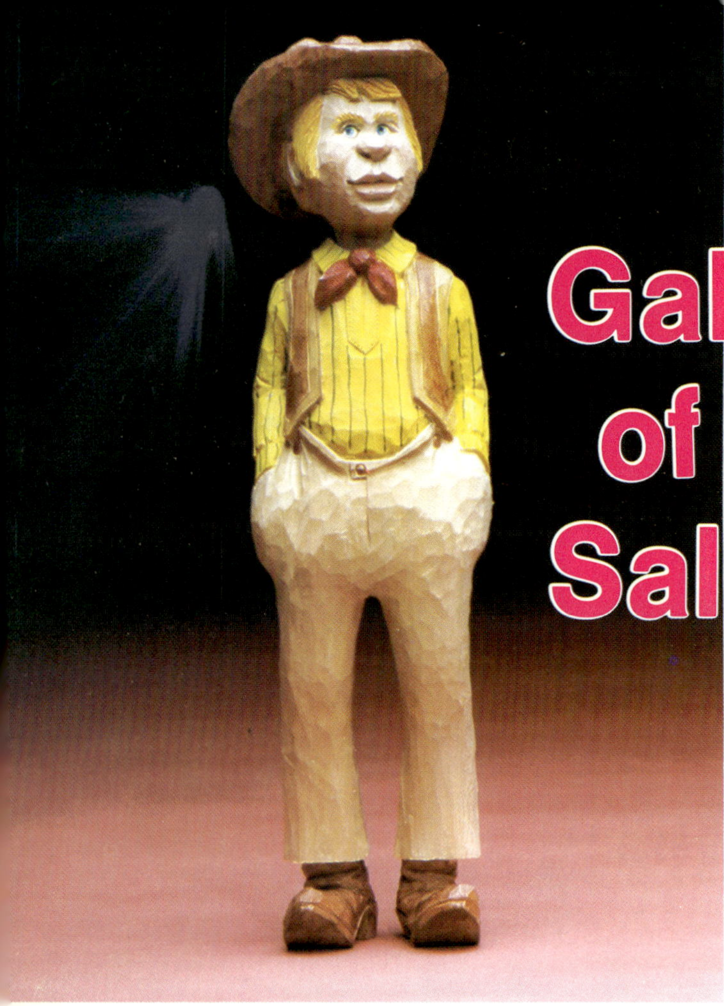

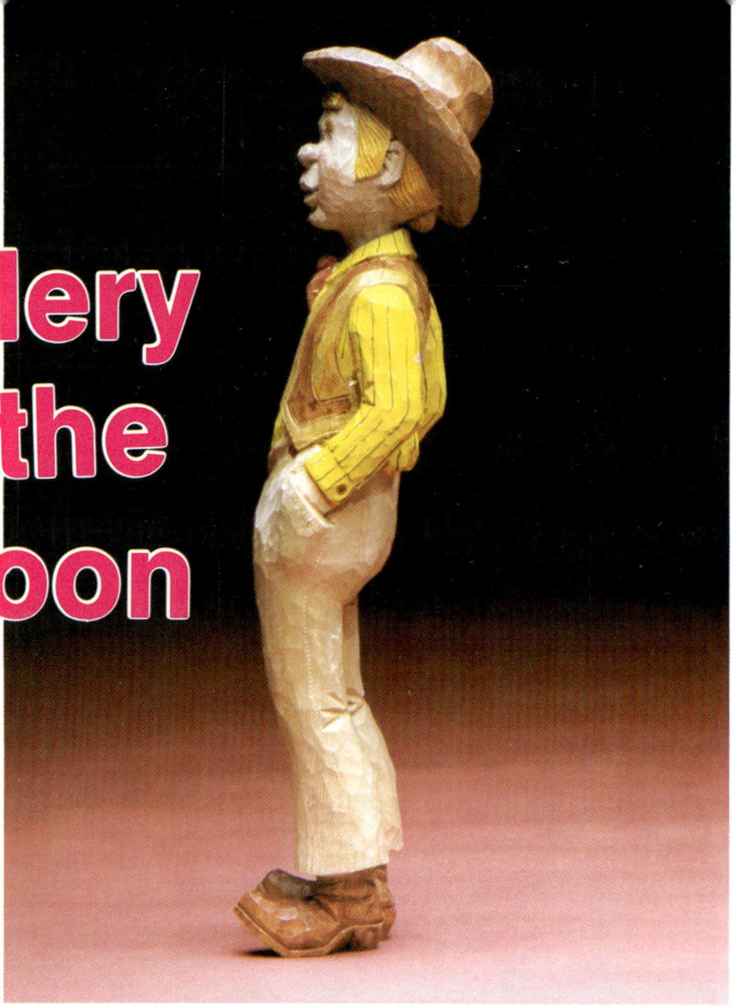

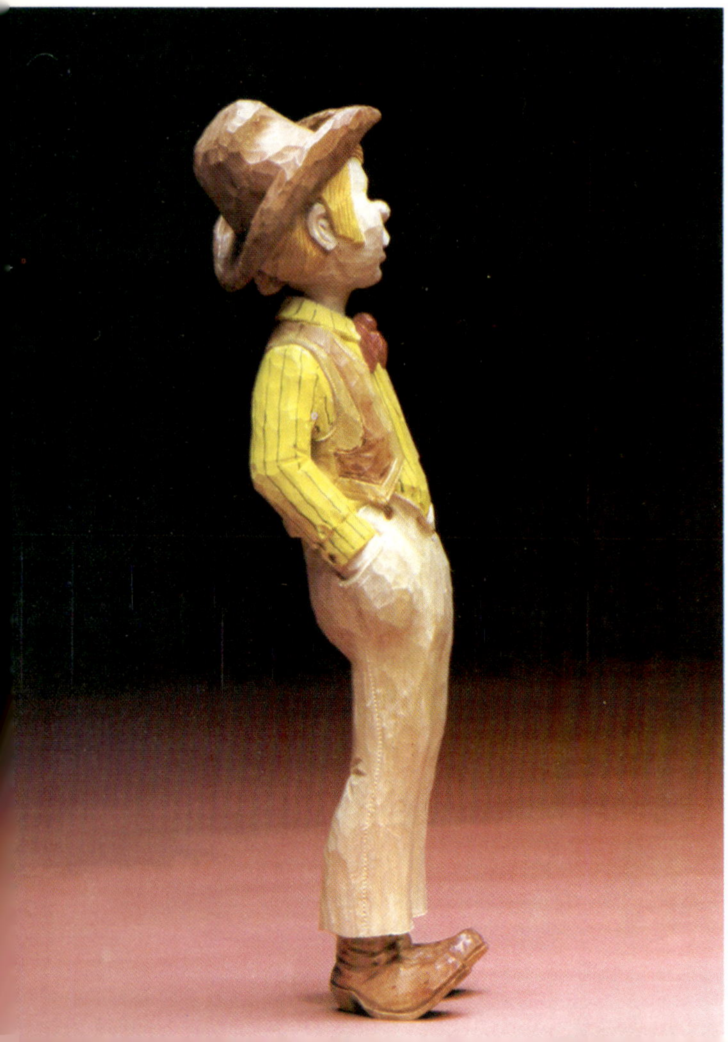

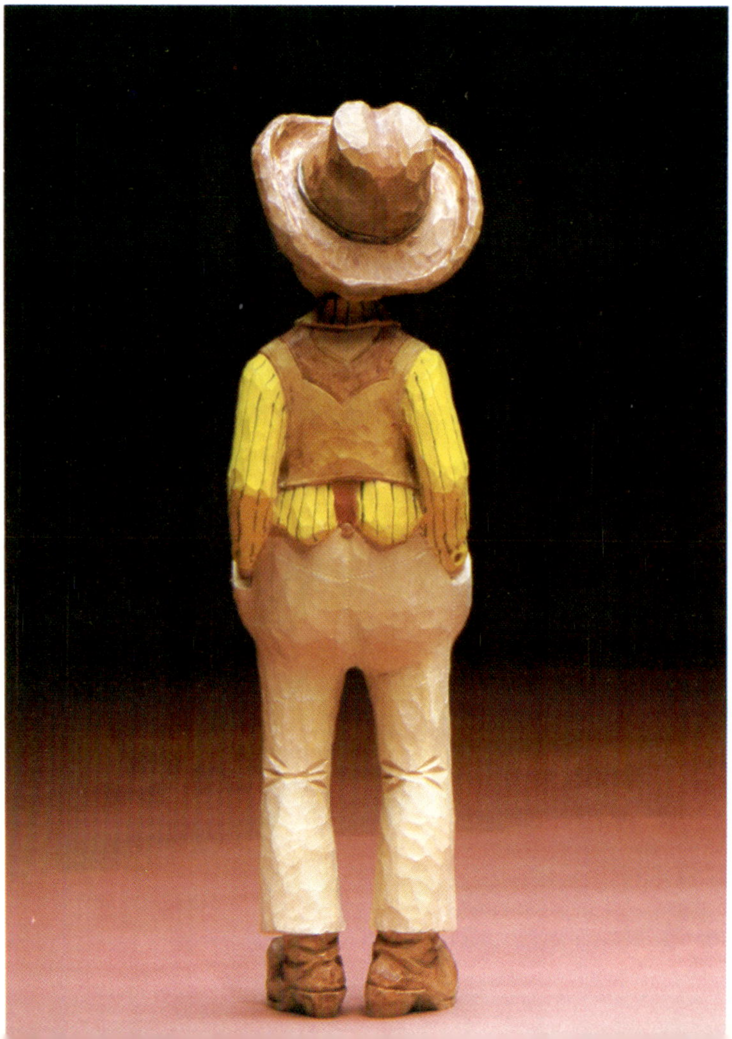

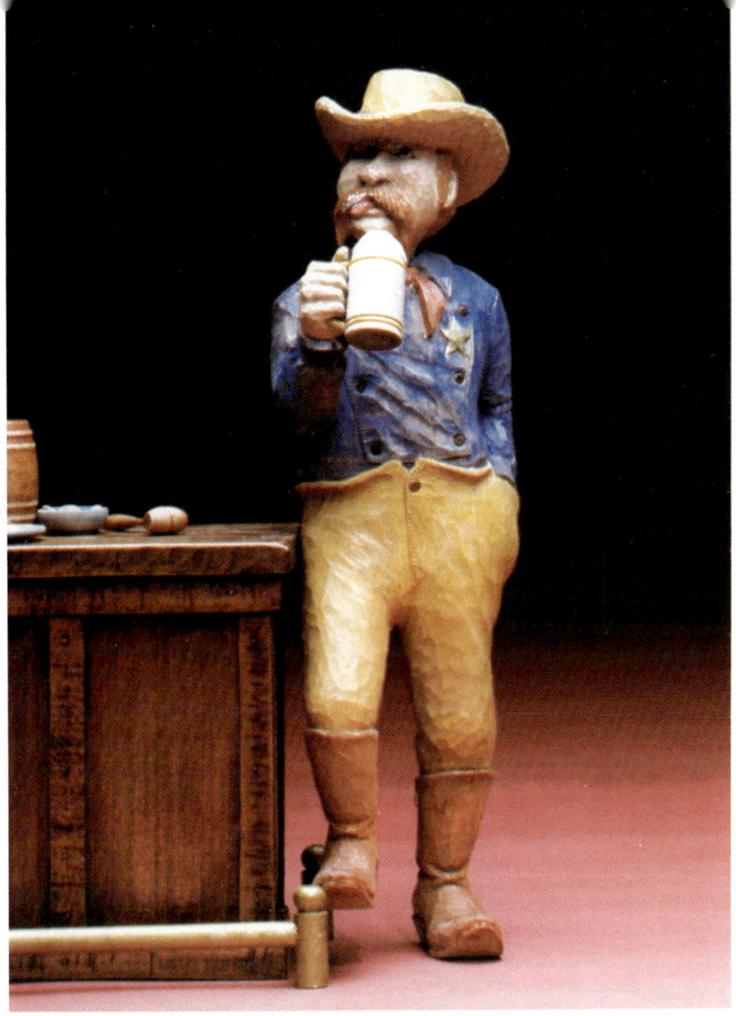
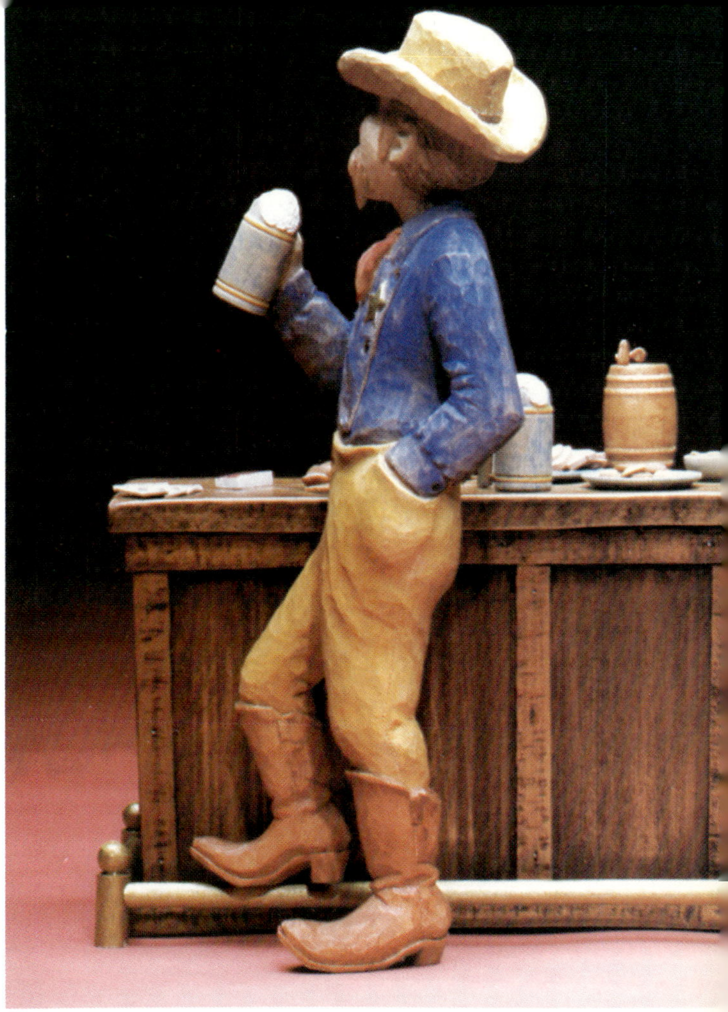
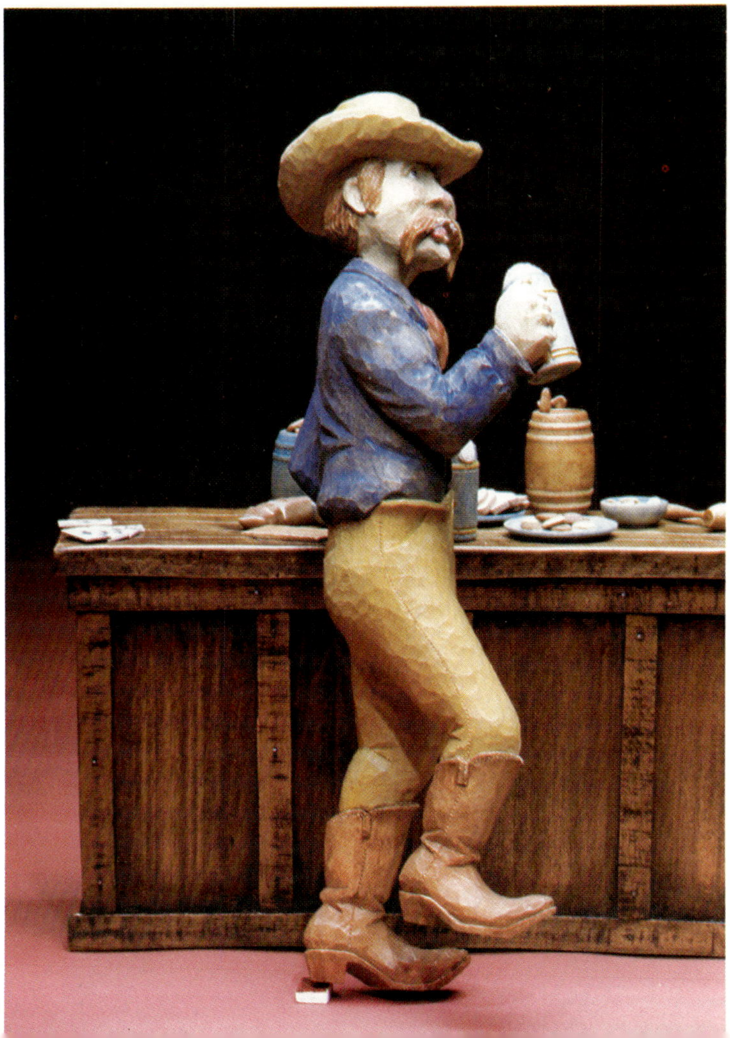
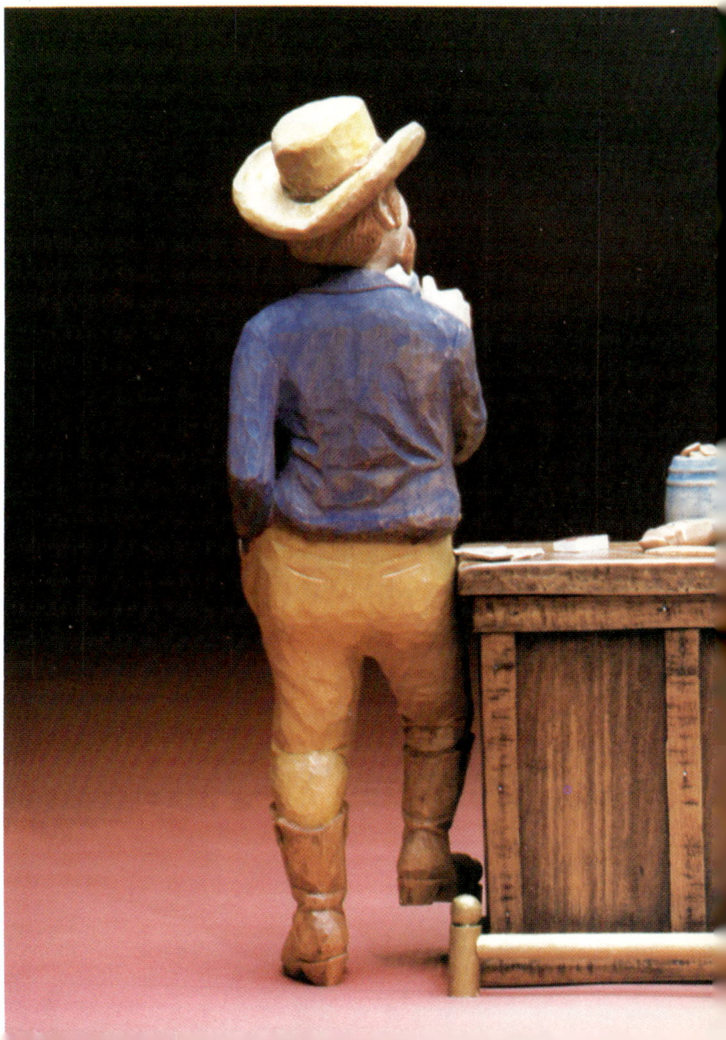

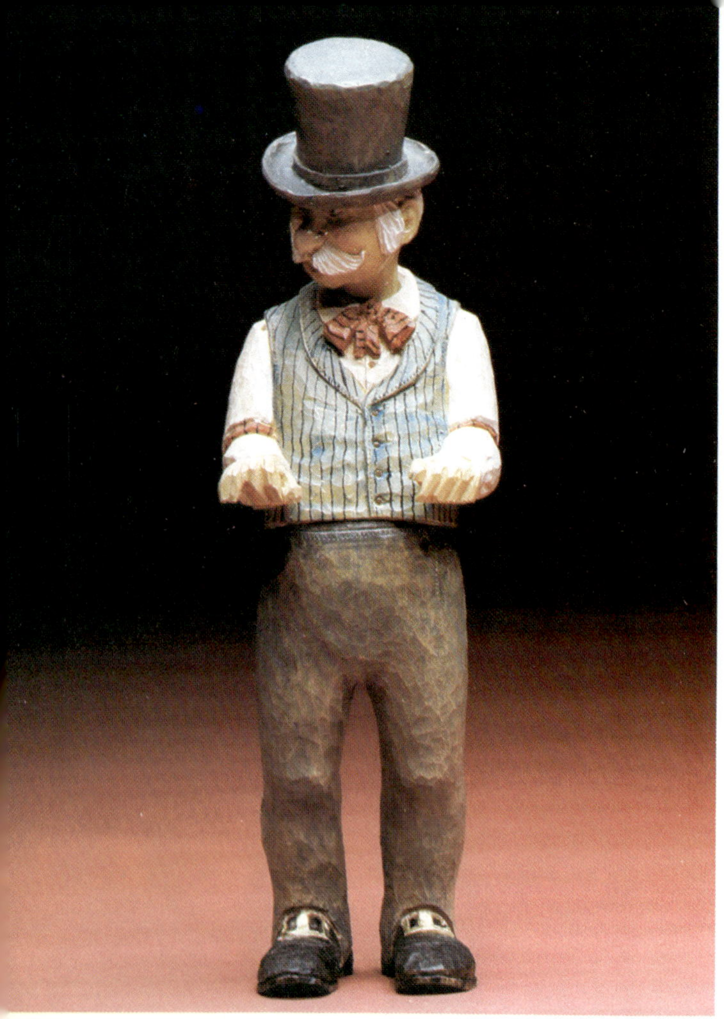
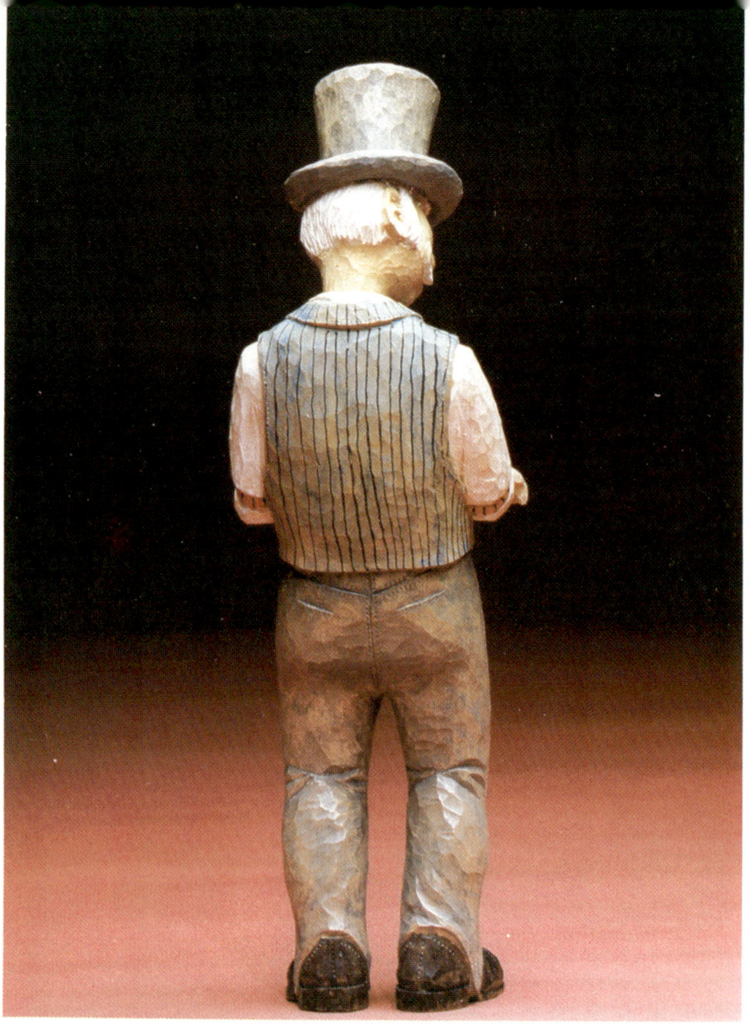
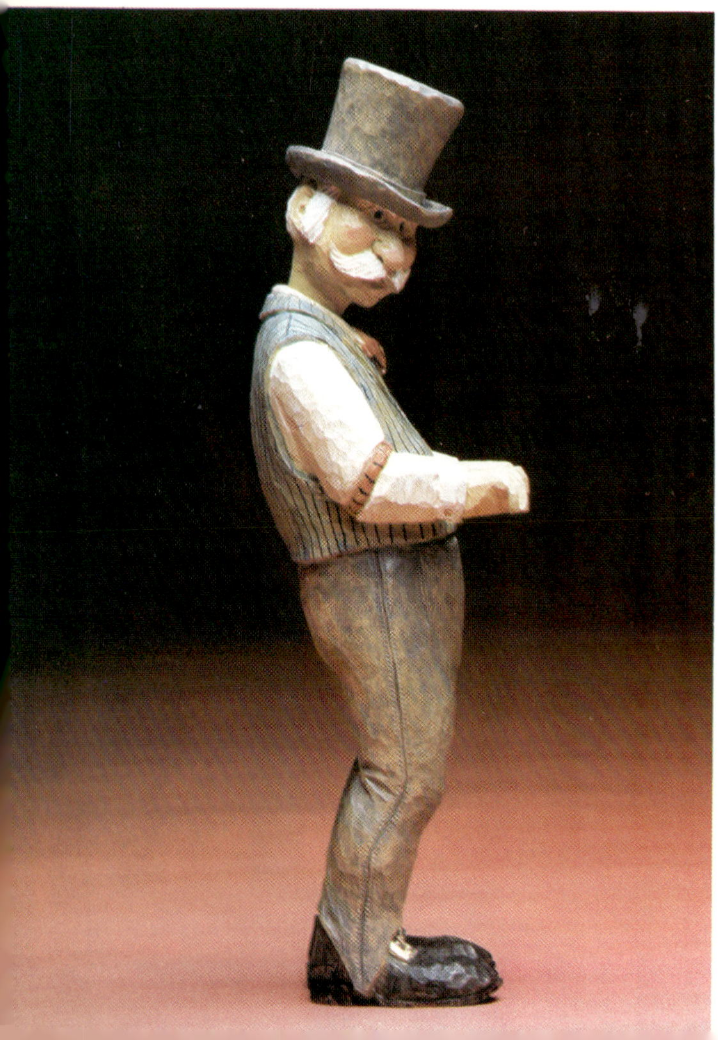
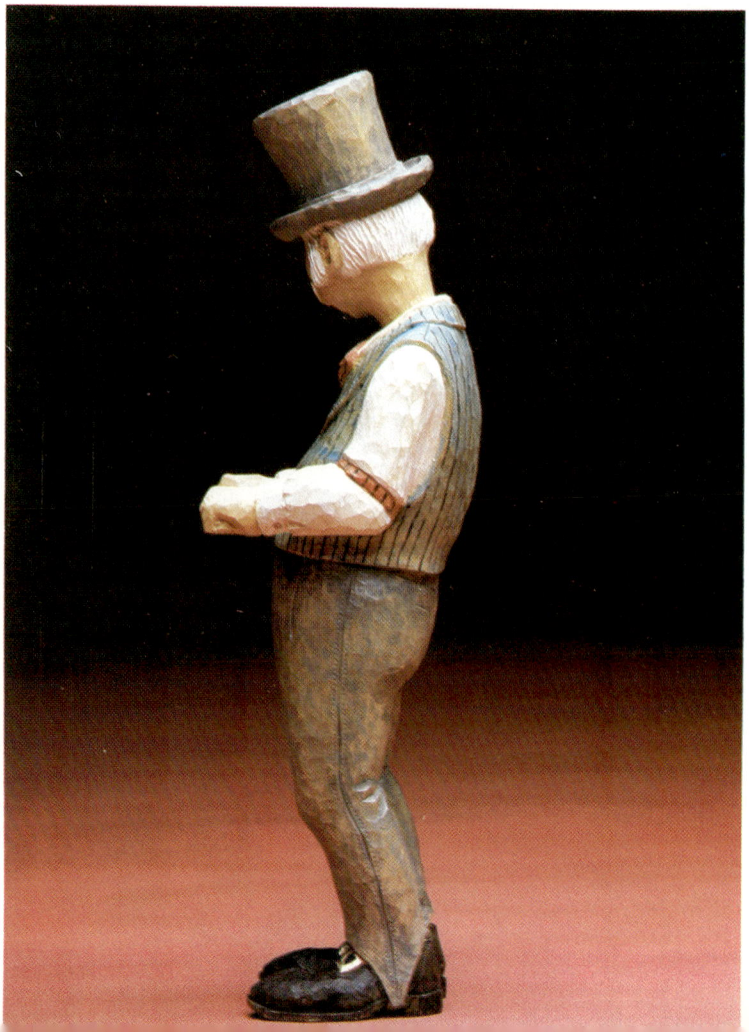

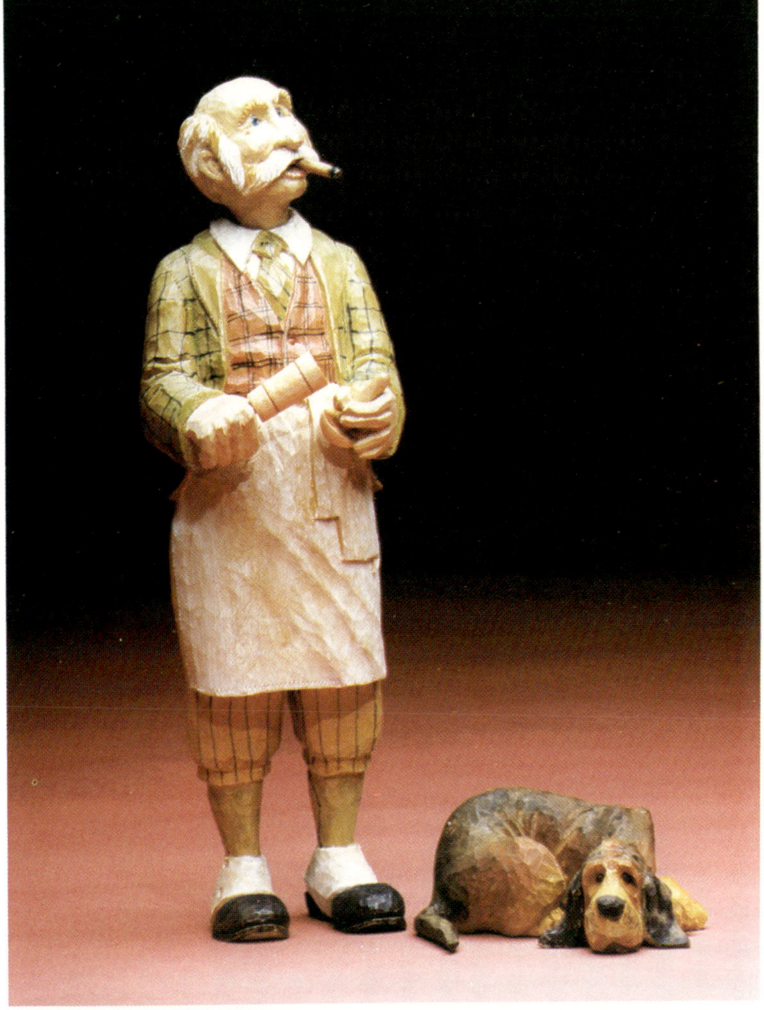
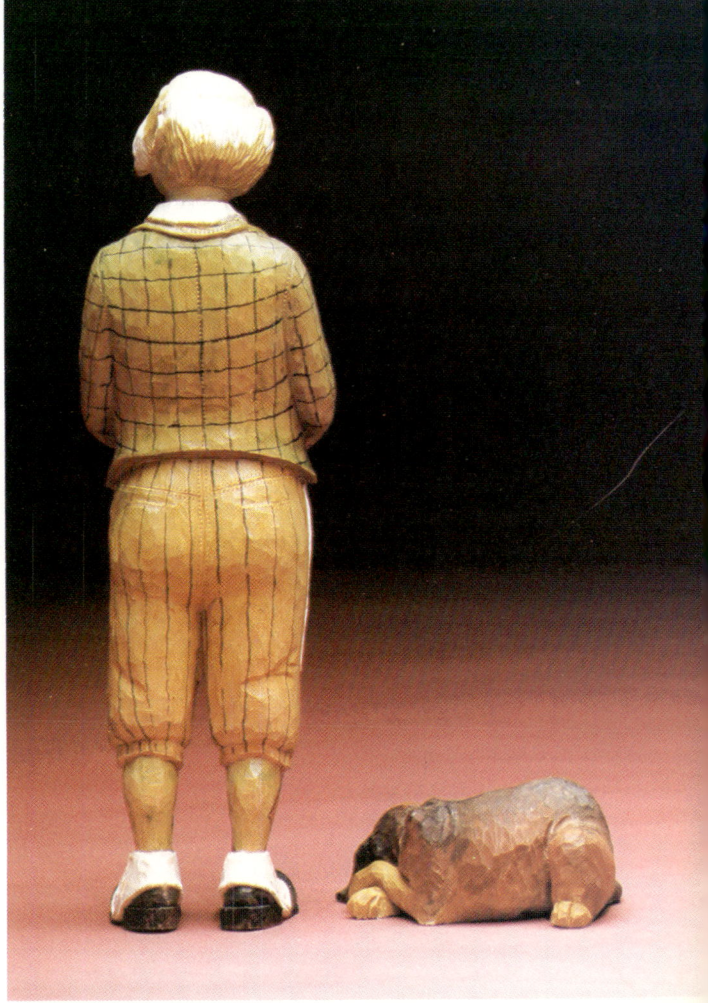
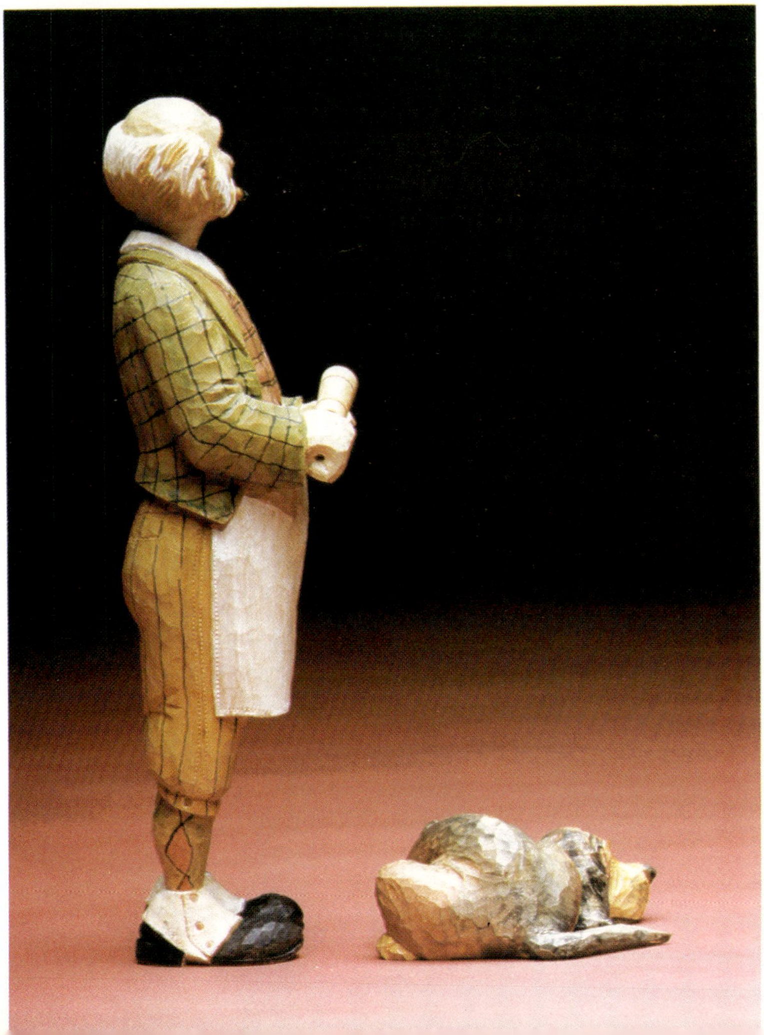
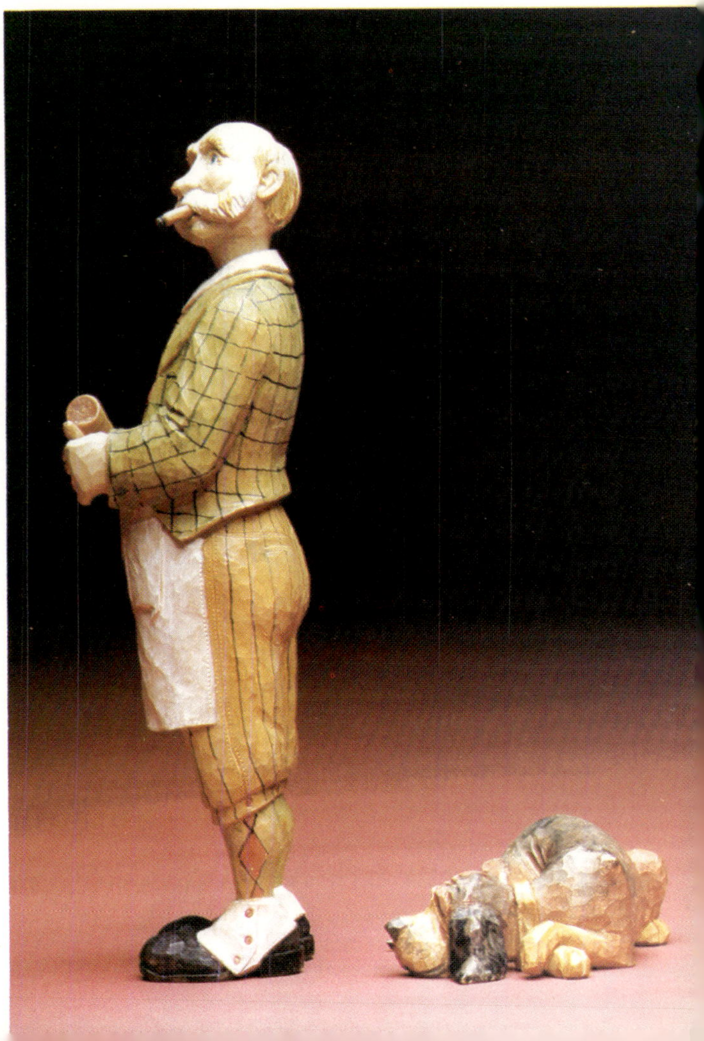

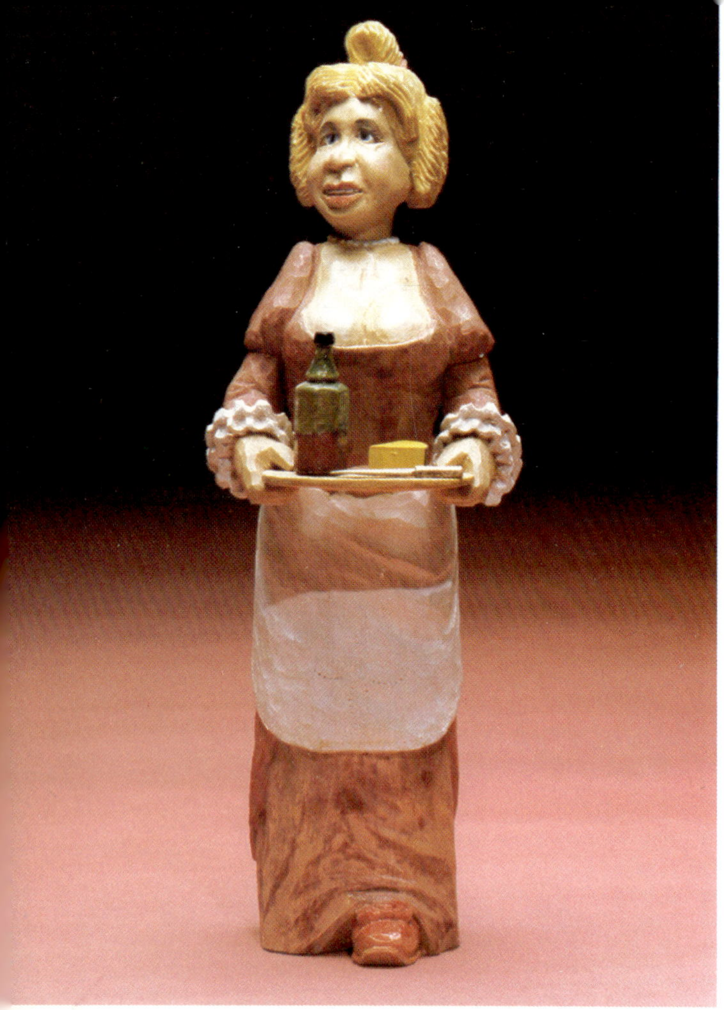
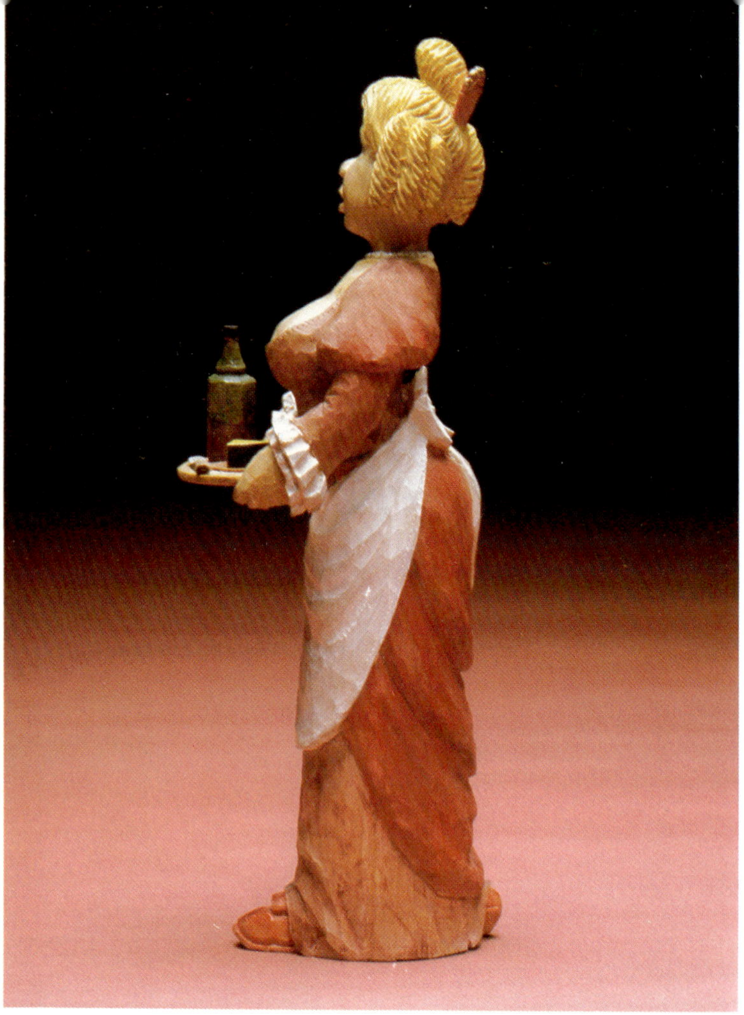
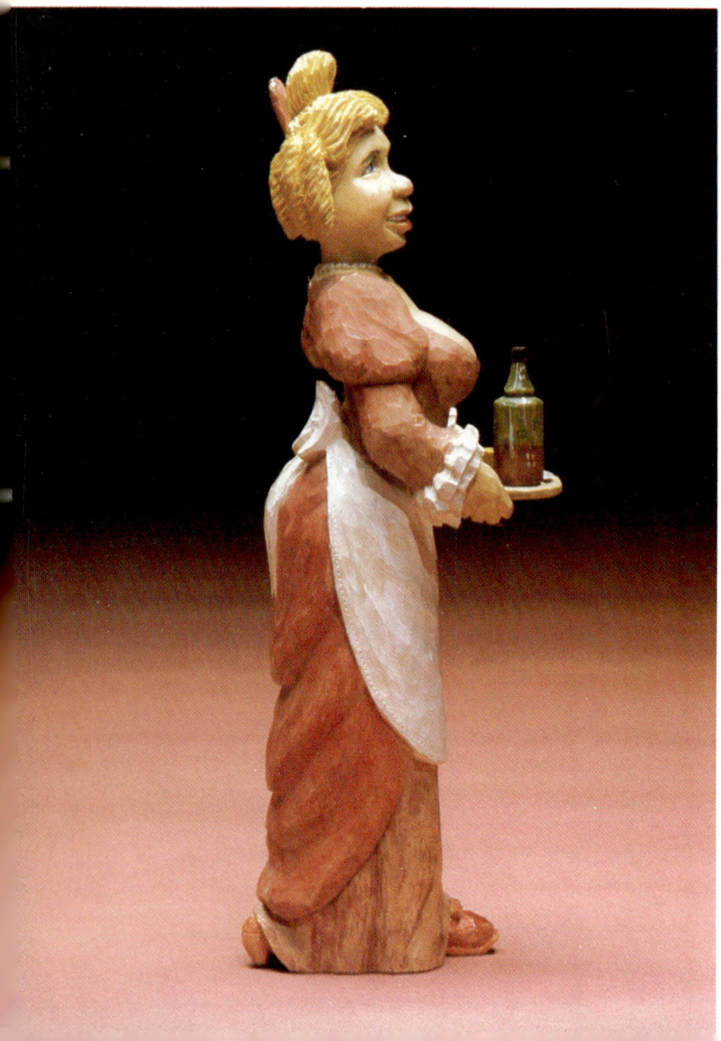
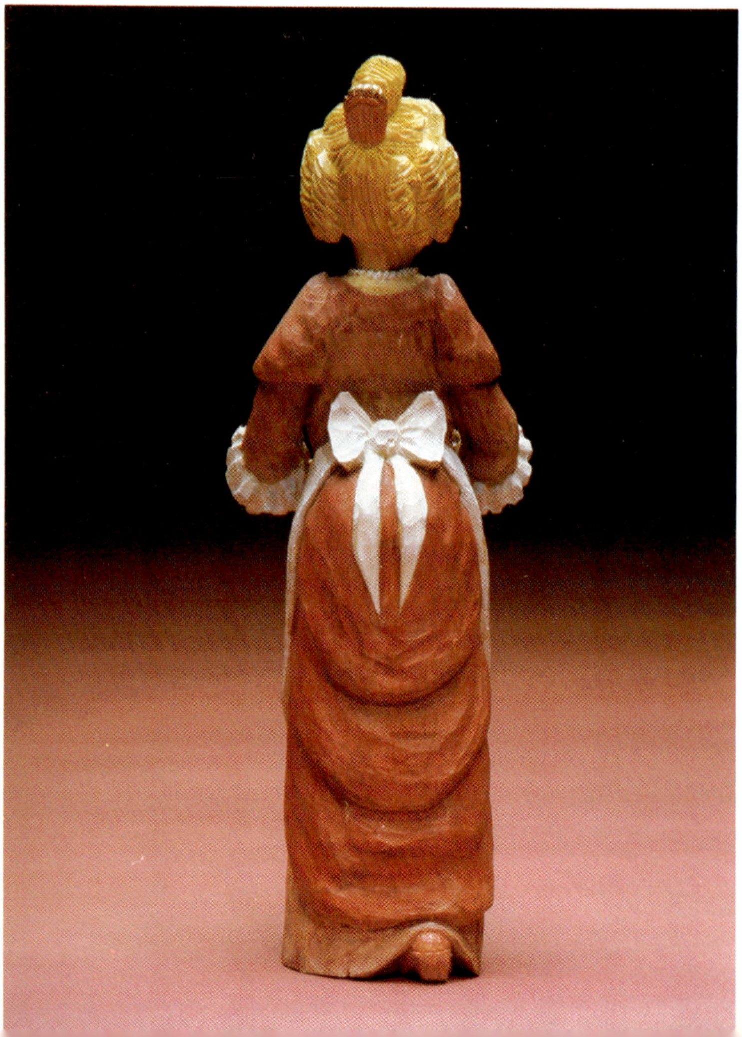